VIR TRILINGUIS

A Study in the Biblical Exegesis of
Saint Jerome

VIR TRILINGUIS

A Study in the Biblical Exegesis of
Saint Jerome

Dennis Brown

Kok Pharos Publishing House
Kampen – The Netherlands

CIP-GEGEVENS KONINKLIJKE BIBLIOTHEEK, DEN HAAG

Brown, Dennis

Vir Trilinguis: a study in the biblical exegesis of Saint Jerome/Dennis Brown. –
Kampen: Kok Pharos
Met lit. opg.
ISBN 90-390-0031-X
NUGI 632
Trefw.: Hieronymus Sophronius Eusebius/exegese.

© 1992, Kok Pharos Publishing House,
POB 130, 8260 AC Kampen, The Netherlands
Cover by Rob Lucas
Typesetting: Elgraphic bv, Schiedam

ISBN 90 390 0031 X
NUGI 632

All rights reserved. No part of this book may be reproduced in any form by
print, photoprint, microfilm or any other means without written permission
from the publisher.
Niets uit deze uitgave mag worden verveelvoudigd en/of openbaar gemaakt door
middel van druk, fotokopie, microfilm, of op welke andere wijze ook zonder
voorafgaande schriftelijke toestemming van de uitgever.

Contents

Acknowledgements 7
Abbreviations 9
Introduction 11
Chapter 1: Jerome – The Exegetical Background 13
Chapter 2: Jerome – Bibliophile and Textual Critic 21
Chapter 3: Jerome and the *Hebraica Veritas* 55
Chapter 4: Jerome as a Translator 87
Chapter 5: Jerome and the Literal Sense 121
Chapter 6: Jerome and the Spiritual Sense 139
Chapter 7: Jerome, Jews and Judaism 167
Conclusions 195
Bibliography 203
Index of Biblical references 223

Acknowledgements

It is a pleasure to thank all those who have helped in the production of this book. Various scholars have spent many hours correcting errors and suggesting improvements, including Professor J. Barr and Dr. I.A. Moir, who read sections of the work at an earlier stage. It is also a pleasant task to thank two busy colleagues, Dr. R.A. Lock and Mr. P.R. Ponder, who graciously offered their expertise on various aspects of the book.

I wish to record my appreciation of the staff of various libraries, notably the Bodleian, Pusey House, Mansfield College, the Oriental Institute (all in Oxford), and the John Rylands University Library in Manchester for their courteous help and assistance.

To my parents, who have supported and encouraged me through these many years, I can at last say that 'Jerome' is completed, and I thank them for their love and patience.

Lastly, to my wife Catherine, who has given unstintingly of her time and effort to discuss Jerome, I offer my love and heartfelt thanks.

Abbreviations

BJRL	Bulletin of the John Rylands Library
Cavallera	F. Cavallera: *Saint Jérôme: sa Vie et son Oeuvre* 2 Vols Louvain 1922
CCL	Corpus Christianorum Latinorum
CHB	Cambridge History of the Bible
CSEL	Corpus Scriptorum Ecclesiasticorum Latinorum
GCS	Die Greichischen Christlichen Schriftsteller der ersten Jahrhunderte
Grützmacher	G. Grützmacher: *Hieronymus. Eine biographische Studie* 3 Vols Berlin 1901, 1906, 1908.
HTR	Harvard Theological Review
HUCA	Hebrew Union College Annual
JBL	Journal of Biblical Literature
JJS	Journal of Jewish Studies
JQR	Jewish Quarterly Review
JSJ	Journal for the Study of Judaism
JSS	Journal of Semitic Studies
JTS	Journal of Theological Studies
Kelly	J.N.D. Kelly: *Jerome: His Life, Writings and Controversies* London 1975
LCL	Loeb Classical Library
MGWJ	Monatschrift für die Geschichte und Wissenschaft des Judentums
NT	Novum Testamentum
NTS	New Testament Studies
Penna	A. Penna: *Principi e carattere dell' esegesi di S. Gerolamo* Rome 1950
PG	J.P. Migne: *Patrologia Graeca*
PL	J.P. Migne: *Patrologia Latina*
RB	Revue Biblique
RHE	Revue d'Histoire Ecclésiastique
RQ	Revue de Qumran
RSR	Recherches de Sciences Religieuses
RBen	Revue Bénédictine
RHPR	Revue d'Histoire et de Philosophie Religieuse
SC	Sources Chrétiennes

SJT	Scottish Journal of Theology
SP	Studia Patristica
VigChr	Vigiliae Christianae
VT	Vetus Testamentum
ZATW	Zeitschrift für die alttestamentlichen Wissenschaft
ZNTW	Zeitschrift für die neutestamentlichen Wissenschaft

Note: The page references to the Migne text of Jerome's works are taken from the late nineteenth century editions listed in the bibliography. The pagination does not correspond to that of the earlier 1845-6 editions.

Introduction

Saint Jerome is the most important exegete of biblical literature in the fourth century. He is also justly recognised for his Latin prose, controversial writings, epistles and ascetic ideals. Apocryphal lives were written, extolling his sanctity, but it was because of his work as a student and translator of scripture that Jerome was acclaimed as *Doctor Maximus sacris scripturis explanandis* in the eighth century.[1]

It is surprising, therefore, given Jerome's important place in the history of exegesis, that only two full length studies of his exegesis have been made.[2] The first, made a generation ago in Italian, while providing some good information on some sections of Jerome's exegesis (for example his use of *typus* and *allegoria*), does not, in fact, offer a study of the complete range of Jerome's exegetical principles and practice. Its author, A. Penna, does not take sufficiently into account the historical and exegetical background of Jerome's life and work, and says little about Jerome's knowledge of, interest in and use of, textual criticism. The second study, by P. Jay, appeared recently and, while this offers an extremely detailed study of Jerome's *Commentary of Isaiah*, it limits itself to a small portion of his literary output. Of course, many smaller studies and articles concerning individual aspects of Jerome's exegesis have appeared, but there is still a need for a full length, comprehensive study of Jerome as an exegete, and it is this need which the present work has attempted to begin to meet. It must be said, however, that one aspect of Jerome's exegesis lies outside the scope of the present study: his indebtedness to, and use of, specific Jewish exegetical traditions. It is well known that Jerome used many hundreds of traditions which are also extant in Jewish sources,[3] and that Jerome's writings are a mine of information for our knowledge of Jewish exegesis in the fourth century. Although this is an important area of study, I have omitted it because

---

[1] The decision to make Jerome one of the four great 'Doctors of the Church' was ratified by Pope Boniface VIII on Sept. 20th, 1295. See *Corpus iuris canonici* II, 1059, and Kelly: p. 333.

[2] A. Penna: *Principe e carattere dell esegesi di S. Girolamo*, Rome 1950; P. Jay: *L'Exégèse de saint Jérôme d'après son Commentaire sur Isaie*, Paris 1985.

[3] See especially the works of L. Ginzberg listed in the bibliography.

there are very real problems concerning the dating of post-biblical Jewish literature, and the Jewish traditions are so numerous in Jerome's writings that, to do the subject justice, a full length study of this alone would be required.

This book attempts to describe and analyse the most important elements in Jerome's exegetical principles and practice. The first chapter serves to highlight the exegetical background in both Judaism and Christianity to Jerome's work.

The study of Jerome's exegesis falls into three main sections. The first of these concerns the establishment of a sound biblical text, for, without this, one could not begin to give an adequate explanation of the scriptures. Jerome was familiar with the principles of textual criticism and used these in the task of establishing the biblical text from which he worked. We also show how and why Jerome chose to use the Hebrew text of the O.T., as opposed to the LXX, and the Jewish canon of scripture, and finally in this section, the extent of Jerome's knowledge of Hebrew and his theory and practice of translation are assessed.

The second section of the book studies Jerome's debt to the Christian exegetical tradition. Jerome took over the use of both literal and spiritual or allegorical exegesis from various of his predecessors, but it will be seen, by a detailed examination of some of his technical exegetical vocabulary, that Jerome was an eclectic scholar, appropriating some portions of 'Antiochene' and 'Alexandrian' exegetical systems, but rejecting other portions.

The third section of the book examines Jerome's knowledge of, and attitude towards, Jews of his day and contemporary Judaism. The work concludes with a brief analysis of Jerome as a biblical scholar and an assessment of his contribution to the history of exegesis.

1. Jerome – The Exegetical Background

Christian exegesis of the biblical books was based to a large extent on Jewish interpretative methods. That this was so is a necessary result of the fact that Christianity appropriated the Jewish scriptures – the Law, Prophets and Writings of the O.T. Three distinct approaches to exegesis may be observed in Judaism by the end of the first century A.D. The first is the approach adopted by Rabbinic Judaism, where the interpretation of scripture was carried on largely in terms of Torah.[1] The 'written' Torah was believed to be the supreme instance of divine revelation to humans, while the 'oral' Torah was seen as complementary to the 'written' Torah. By the time of the Middle Ages, a very large and diverse collection of this oral material had been edited and written down.[2] This included two separate recensions of the Talmud[3] (the earlier and shorter Palestinian version, and the later and much more voluminous Babylonian version), the Targumim[4] (paraphrases of scripture) and the Midrashim.[5] A 'Midrash' could be a method of interpreting scripture, whether it was a single verse or a complete biblical book, or an un-

---

[1] See J. Bonsirven: *Le Judaisme Palestinien*, Vol. 1, Paris 1934, pp. 254-274; E. Schürer: *The History of the Jewish People in the Age of Jesus Christ*, Vol. II, rev. ed. by G. Vermes, F. Miller and M. Black, Edinburgh 1979, pp. 314-380; 464-497 and literature cited there.
[2] See the article 'Jewish exegesis' by R. Loewe in *A Dictionary of Biblical Interpretation*, ed. R.J. Coggins & J.L. Houlden, London 1990.
[3] The classic introduction to the Talmud is still that of H.L. Strack, ed. Stemburger: *Introduction to the Talmud and Midrash*, Edinburgh 1990, but among a vast range of studies, reference should be made to J. Neusner (ed.): *The Formation of the Babylonian Talmud*, Leiden 1970. Idem: *Invitation to Talmud* (New York 1973); A. Corre: *Understanding the Talmud*, New York 1965; and literature cited in E. Schürer: *op.cit.*, Vol. I, pp. 84-88.
[4] On the Targumim, see the literature cited in Schürer: *op.cit.*, Vol I, pp. 106-114, especially J. Bowker: *The Targums and Rabbinic Literature*, Cambridge 1969, and the works of R. le Déaut and A. Díez Macho.
[5] See, for example, R. le Déaut: 'A propos d'une définition du Midrash', in *Biblica* 50 (1969) 395-413; G. Vermes: 'Bible and Midrash: Early Old Testament Exegesis' *CHB* I, Cambridge 1970, 199-232; P.S. Alexander: 'Midrash' in *A Dictionary of Biblical Interpretation*, ed. R.J. Coggins & J.L. Houlden, London 1990, to which I am indebted for this paragraph.

defined body of traditional commentary on scripture. As such, midrash includes a system of hermeneutical rules and techniques. Midrash could also be used of the end product of the application of this hermeneutical system, that is, a midrashic text which exemplifies this method of interpretation.

This large body of literature is usually classified in two broad categories: as Haggadah or Halakhah. Haggadah ('information' or 'anecdotage') was concerned with 'the inculcation of God-awareness into mental attitudes'.[6] It is seen largely in collections of midrash between the fifth and tenth centuries and takes the form of moralising exegesis. Various techniques were used to achieve this, including the juxtaposition of discrete biblical texts; creative elaboration of the biblical narrative; and the use of parable. This method of viewing scripture could provide profound theological insights. Jerome used a great deal of haggadic material in his works, and he was the main source through which echoes of the haggadah reached some of the Western Church Fathers.[7]

Halakhah ('procedure') was concerned with the implementation of Torah into practical matters and with self-discipline regarding what was forbidden. The function of halakhic exegesis was 'so to handle biblical institutions – especially ones which changed conditions may render problematic – that the resulting decision may, in practice, be socially feasible within the given Jewish situation, ethically tolerable, and logically defensible or acceptable in defiance of logic, in that order of priority'.[8]

The second 'school' of Jewish exegesis was that of the Qumran community,[9] where it is clear that the interpretation of the Bible was of

---

[6] *Ibid.*, p. 346.

[7] See, for example, L. Ginzberg: 'Die Haggada bei den Kirchenvätern. V: Der Kommentar des Hieronymus zu Koheleth', in *Abhandlungen zur Erinnerung an Hirsch Perez Chajes*, Vienna 1933, 22-50; *Idem*: 'Die Haggada bei den Kirchenvätern. VI: Der Kommentar des Hieronymus zu Jesaja', in *Jewish Studies in Memory of George A. Kohut*, New York 1935, 279-314; H. Graetz: 'Haggadische Elemente bei den Kirchenvätern', in *MGWJ* 3 (1864) 311-319; 352-355; 381-387; 428-431; Vol. 4 (1865) 187-192.

[8] Loewe: *art.cit.*, p. 347.

[9] Among the voluminous literature on Qumran, see F.F. Bruce: *Biblical Exegesis in the Qumran Texts*, London 1959; B.J. Roberts: 'The Dead Sea Scrolls and the Old Testament Scriptures', in *BJRL* 36 (1953) 75-96; E. Slomovic: 'Towards an Understanding of the Exegesis in the Dead Sea Scrolls', in *RQ* 7 (1969) 3-15; G. Vermes: 'The Qumran Interpretation of Scripture in its Historical Setting', in *Annual of Leeds University Oriental Society* (1969) 84-97. Especially useful is the recent study of G.J. Brooke: *Exegesis at Qumran: 4Q Florilegium in*

primary importance. The Bible was used by the community members in a variety of ways: many of the non-biblical documents have direct citations of scripture which are interpreted or used as support for the particular document; allusion to biblical texts is important in many documents; there are works which expand and retell biblical narrative (1Q ap.Gen.), Targum fragments (4Q tg Lev., 11Q tg Job), texts with midrashic features (4Q PB, 4Q Flor.), a collection of Messianic texts (4Q Test.). In addition to these, there is *Pesher* exegesis, a form of commentary which applied biblical texts to the immediate situation of the sect and its struggle against the Romans.[10]

The authoritative key to the interpretation and application of the biblical texts was the 'Teacher of Righteousness',[11] who was regarded by community members as a mediator of divine revelation. Many of the Qumran texts display an eschatological emphasis,[12] so that biblical interpretation for the community had the function of reading the signs of the time and providing guidelines for living in it.

The third 'school' of Jewish exegesis was that of the Diaspora Jews, especially at Alexandria. It is exemplified by the work of Philo, who was influenced profoundly by Hellenistic allegory. Philo was familiar with halakhic and haggadic traditions, and did not want to discourage literal adherence to the Torah, but he found that the 'impossibilities', 'impieties' and 'adsurdities' produced by a literal reading of scripture could be unravelled by utilising the philosophical truths of Stoic ethics and

---

its Jewish Context, Sheffield 1985, pp. 36-44, 279-323; cf also M.P. Horgan: *Pesharim: Qumran Interpretations of Biblical Books*, Washington DC 1979, pp. 244-247; M.P. Miller: 'Targum, Midrash and the Use of the Old Testament in the New Testament', in *JSJ* 2 (1971) 49-55.

10 For this paragraph, I am indebted to G.J. Brooke: *op.cit.*, p. 36f, and M.P. Miller: *art.cit.*, p. 50. The question of whether in the Qumran writings (especially the Pesharim) we are involved with exegesis or revelation need not concern us here, as the point we are making does not rely on one particular interpretation of the documents. For a summary of the problem, see M.P. Miller: *art.cit.*, pp. 50-55.

11 See G.W. Buchanan: 'The Priestly Teacher of Righteousness', in *RQ* 6 (1976) 553-558; G. Jeremias: *Der Lehrer der Gerechtigkeit*, Göttingen 1963; J. Carmignac: 'Qui était le Docteur de Justice?', in *RQ* 10 (1980) 235-246; H. Burgman: 'Wer war der Lehrer der Gerechtigkeit?', in *RQ* 10 (1980) pp. 553-578.

12 See the conclusion of G.J. Brooke: *op.cit.*, p. 356: 'This study has shown that one cannot approach the use of the Bible at Qumran presupposing that such use was guided, for instance, by an overall eschatological perspective... Qumran eschatology can only be discussed as it is derived from the texts.'

Platonic cosmology.¹³ By searching carefully in scripture for clues such as contradictions, strange expressions, word derivations and mysterious numbers, the exegete could discover the real message which God intended to convey. Using this system, Philo was able to unfold a wealth of critical insight and imaginative allegorisation of the biblical text.

Jerome speaks approvingly of Philo, classing him as an ecclesiastical writer, on the ground that Philo praises Christians at Alexandria, and mentions that Christianity is present in other provinces. Jerome also mentions a legend that Philo travelled to Rome to visit Peter during the reign of Claudius.¹⁴

The allegorical interpretation of biblical texts spread into Christianity through Philo, whose great influence led to the development of the catechetical school at Alexandria. The two greatest scholars of this catechetical school, Clement and Origen, were both influenced profoundly by Philo.¹⁵ For Clement, nearly all of scripture was expressed in enigmas, and it was the task of the interpreter who had received the deeper knowledge (γνῶσις) given by Christ to his apostles after his resurrection, to unlock the spiritual truth of biblical language to those capable of understanding. Following Philo, Clement allegorised the O.T. freely. His hermeneutical principle in identifying true meaning was an eclectic mixture of Hellenistic (and Gnostic) cosmology, soteriology and morality, combined with the conviction that in the Logos-Christ all foreshadowing of truth had found its goal.¹⁶ Jerome quotes approvingly a letter of Alexander, Bishop of Jerusalem, which says of Clement:

---

¹³ The bibliography on Philo is enormous. For two recent studies of his interpretative methods, see T.H. Tobin S.J.: *The Creation of Man: Philo and the History of Interpretation* (CBQMS 14), Washington DC 1983; and V. Nikiprowetzky: *Le Commentaire de l'Écriture chez Philon d'Alexandre* (ALGHJ 11), Leiden 1977; a succinct exposition of Philo's philosophical principles is found in H. Chadwick: 'Philo', in *The Cambridge History of Later Greek and Early Medieval Philosophy*, Cambridge 1967, ed. H. Armstrong, 137-157.
¹⁴ *De Vir.Illus.* 11 (*PL* 23, 658).
¹⁵ On Clement, see S. Lilla: *Clement of Alexandria; a Study in Christian Platonism and Gnosticism*, Oxford 1971; H. Chadwick: *Early Christian Thought and the Classical Tradition*, Oxford 1966; on Origen, see J. Danielou: *Origen*, London 1955; H. Crouzel: *Origène et la Philosophie*, Paris 1962; R.P.C. Hanson: *Allegory and Event*, London 1959; P. Nautin: *Origène, sa vie et son oeuvre*, Paris 1977; K.J. Torjesen: *Hermeneutical Procedure and Theological Method in Origen's Exegesis*, Berlin 1986; H. Chadwick: 'Christian Platonism in Clement and Origen', in *Origeniana Tertia*, ed. R.P.C. Hanson and H. Crouzel, Rome 1985, 217-230. See also C. Bigg's still valuable study: *The Christian Platonists of Alexandria*, Oxford 1913².
¹⁶ Clement: *Strom.* VI, 124, 5f.

'These writings, honoured brothers, I have sent to you by the blessed presbyter Clement, an illustrious and approved man, whom you also know and with whom you will now become better acquainted, a man who, when he had come here by the special providence of God, strengthened and enlarged the Church of the Lord.'[17]

Origen was probably the most influential theologian and exegete of the early Christian centuries, and much of his enormous literary output was concerned with the interpretation of the Bible. Jerome classified Origen's works in three categories: scholia (short explanatory glosses), commentaries and homilies.[18] Most of the books of the Bible are dealt with in one or more of these forms. In the treatise *De Principiis*, Origen set out to show systematically how the diversity of the world came about, and how it will eventually return to this divine unity. Fundamental to this structure is the role of scripture and its interpretation. The divinely inspired scriptures have a spiritual purpose; therefore (arguing against literalists and Marcionites) to give the scriptures a simplistic or anthropomorphic understanding was to insult the divine author of the writings. Origen argued that texts such as Prov. 22:20f suggest a threefold sense of scripture analogous to the tripartite anthropology of the philosophers: just as humans consist of body, soul and spirit, so scripture has a literal, moral and spiritual sense.[19] All biblical texts have a spiritual sense, but not all have a literal one.[20] If no spiritual significance is apparent on the surface, the interpreter must conclude that the surface meaning must be understood symbolically. Allegory is the method which provides the key to unlock the hidden, symbolic meaning of a text and it was Origen, more than any other scholar, whose influence made allegory the dominant method of biblical interpretation down to the Middle Ages. His influence may be seen in fourth century exegetes like Didymus the Blind and Athanasius. Of Didymus, Jerome speaks often, calling him *magister*, praising his learning, and testifying to his influence on the divines of his time in the

---

17 *De Vir.Illus.* 38 (*PL* 23, 687): Haec vobis, domini ac fratres, scripta transmisi per Clementem beatum presbyterum, virum illustrem et probatum, quem vos quoque scitis, et nunc plenius recognoscetis, qui cum huc venisset juxta providentiam et visitationem Dei, confirmavit et auxit Domini Ecclesiam. Cf *Transl. Hom.Orig.in Jerem.* 1 (*PL* 25, 585-6).
18 Cf *Ep.* 33, 3 (*CSEL* 54, 255); *C.Matt.*: Praef. (*CCL* 77, 4); M.F. Wiles: 'Origen as an Exegete', in *CHB* I, 464.
19 *De Princ.* IV, II, 4. It should be said, however, that in practice, Origen rarely used this tripartite division. Cf. M.F. Wiles: *art.cit.*, p. 467f.
20 *De Princ.* III, IV-V.

West as well as in the East.[21] According to Jerome, Didymus wrote commentaries on Psalms, Job, Isaiah, Hosea and Zachariah, Matthew, John, Acts, 1 and 2 Corinthians, Galatians and Ephesians.[22] Of these, only fragments and excerpts are now extant.[23]

Not all Christian scholars were convinced, however, that allegorical interpretation was the best method of discovering the truth of scripture. The 'school' of Antioch developed in reaction against the allegorising tendencies of Alexandria. The school's early history is associated with the name of Lucian, the teacher of Arius, but the most influential Antiochenes were Diodore of Tarsus, Theodore of Mopsuestia and John Chrysostom. It is Diodore who first expresses clearly the exegetical principle of the Antiochene school:

> 'We do not forbid the higher interpretation and θεωρία, for the ἱστορία does not exclude it, but is, on the contrary, the basis and substructure of θεωρία ... We must, however, be on our guard against letting the θεωρία do away with the ἱστορία, for the result would be, not θεωρία, but ἀλληγορία.'[24]

In reaction against Alexandrian exegesis, the Antiochenes wished to exclude allegory, to maintain θεωρία, and to insist upon the historical basis of the text of scripture. This insistence on the historical foundation of interpretation is seen clearly in Lucian's emphasis on the details of the text of scripture. He knew Hebrew,[25] and corrected the LXX from the original. This recension of the O.T. was widely disseminated throughout Asia Minor and became the ancestor of the earliest printed versions of the LXX.[26] Jerome praised this recension,[27] extensive fragments of which are extant in the works of John Chrysostom and Theodoret.[28]

---

[21] eg. *Ep.* 50, 1; 84, 3 (*CSEL* 54, 389; 55, 123); *Comm.Osee*: Prol.; *Comm. Ephes.*:Prol. (*CCL* 76, 5; *PL* 26, 469).

[22] *De Vir.Illus.* 109 (*PL* 23, 743); *Ep.* 112, 20 (*CSEL* 55, 390); *Comm.Matt.*: Praef. (*CCL* 77, 5); *Comm.Isa.*:Prol. (*CCL* 73, 3).

[23] For details of these, see J. Quasten: *Patrology* III, pp. 90-92.

[24] Diodore: *Praef. in Pss.* (ed. L. Mariès: *RSR* 1919) p. 88.

[25] Philostorgius: *Vita Luciani* 4. On the reconstruction of this text, see J. Bidez: *GCS* 21 (1913) pp. CXLVII-CLI; 184-201. On Lucian, see G. Bardy: *Recherches sur saint Lucien d'Antioche et son École*, Paris 1936.

[26] See H. Dorries: 'Zur Geschichte der Septuaginta im Jahrhundert Konstantins', in *ZNTW* 39 (1940) 57-110; Bardy: *op.cit.*, pp. 164-182; B.H. Streeter: *The Four Gospels: A Study of Origins*, London 1924, 39ff; 112-121.

[27] *Praef. in Paral.*; *Apol.c.Ruf.* II, 27 (*PL* 29, 423; *CCL* 79, 64).

[28] On this, see S. Jellicoe: *The Septuagint and Modern Study*, Oxford 1968, pp. 157-171; B.M. Metzger: 'The Lucianic Recension of the Greek Bible' in *Chapters in the History of New Testament Textual Criticism*, Leiden 1963, pp. 1-41.

For the Antiochenes, the historical sense, that is, the sense which the writers of the text intended, was of fundamental importance. By the exercise of insight (θεωρία), the exegete could determine whether the writer was referring to his own time or to some future event. The Antiochenes did not, however, deny the validity of prophecy, saying that, if a writer referred to future events, then that is the historical meaning of the text, and the role of the interpreter is to decide what period of history the prophecy is applicable to.[29]

One problematic text for the Antiochenes in their rejection of Alexandrian allegory was Gal. 4:24, where Paul uses the term ἀλληγορούμενα in connection with the story of Sarah and Hagar. Theodore of Mopsuestia discusses the passage in detail in his *Commentary on Galatians* 4, 24, where he argues that, when Paul says 'allegory', he meant what the Antiochenes meant by θεωρία. Paul knew the Hellenistic term but not the Hellenistic application which would treat the texts like dreams in the night; he gave history priority over all other considerations. Paul's method, states Theodore, was to use the actual events behind the historical narrative and to apply them rhetorically to his own situation. For this purpose, he (Paul) could even add features of his own invention, such as the persecution of Isaac by Ishmael. But Paul's method, states Theodore, was based on a comparison which could not point out similarities if the events compared were not real.[30]

In the Latin-speaking Western Empire, a different tradition of exegesis had developed separately from that at Alexandria and Antioch. In fact, the debate sparked off by Origen in the third century was echoed in the West only a century later, and that was due in large measure to the translation work of Jerome and Rufinus. Tertullian was a trained rhetorician, but he hesitated to apply the rules of rhetorical figuration to the analysis of biblical texts. Even the prophets, he warned, said many things without allegory or figure; not everything in the Bible comes as image, shadow or parable.[31] Tertullian, like Irenaeus, used allegory to illuminate the typical sense of the O.T., but only very carefully and spar-

---

[29] On this, see A. Vaccari: 'La *Theoria* nella scuola esegetica di Antiocha', in *Biblica* 1 (1920) 3ff.
[30] Theodore: *Commentary on Epistles of St. Paul. Latin Version with Greek Fragments*, Vol. I, ed. H.B. Swete, Cambridge 1880; also U. Wickert: *Studien zu den Pauluskommentaren Theodors von Mopsuestia*, Berlin 1962, especially pp. 45-61.
[31] *De Resurr.* 19-21. This treatise was written, according to T. Barnes (*Tertullian*, Oxford 1971, p. 38), in 203, and thus when Tertullian's ideas are 'tinged' with Montanism (Barnes: p. 45). On Tertullian's exegesis, see T.P. O'Malley: *Tertullian and the Bible*, Utrecht 1971.

ingly. The biblical text had primarily a natural meaning, with (usually) some moral message. It was heresy to find allegories, parables and enigmas everywhere. Proper interpretation resulted in strict adherence to the Rule of Faith.[32] In N. Africa, the *Testimonia* tradition, exemplified by Cyprian, was prevalent, this being the result of pastoral and catechetical concerns.[33]

This is the general background of exegesis in Judaism and Christianity into which Jerome entered, and it is against this background that we should attempt to study his exegetical method, and the influences on his exegesis.

---

[32] *Scorpiace* 11, 4. Tertullian was writing against a background of struggle with Jews, Marcionites and Gnostics.
[33] On Cyprian's use of the Bible, see J.J. Fahey: *Cyprian and the Bible*, Tübingen 1971.

2. Jerome – Bibliophile and Textual Critic

Before Jerome could begin to exercise his skills of exegesis of scripture, he had to be certain of the precise text on which he was to comment. For this, he had to be aware of the principles of textual criticism. In fact, Jerome, more than any other Church Father of the first five centuries, including Origen, was very well versed in the principles and techniques of the art of textual criticism, and it is due to his intense labours in this area that modern scholars can learn much about the texts and textual readings in the O.T., LXX, Hexapla and N.T. in the fourth century.

In this chapter, we shall study what Jerome himself says about his interest in books and manuscripts, his use of *notarii* and *librarii*, the faults of copyists, including the reasons why manuscripts become corrupted, and the techniques of external and internal criticism. We shall also discuss several examples of Jerome's explicit references to manuscripts of the O.T. and N.T., in order to assess Jerome's performance as a textual critic.

Jerome's interest in manuscripts and books

Jerome seems to have acquired his interest in manuscripts and books in his early adult life. Even before he had left Rome at the end of his schooling, he had made manuscript copies of classical authors.[1] During his sojourn at Trier, he laboriously copied out Hilary's commentaries on Psalms and the *De Synodis*.[2] Jerome began his study of Hebrew in the Syrian desert under the tutelage of a converted Jew, and it is likely that this Jew owned some scrolls which Jerome may have copied out, both as practice in learning the language, and to begin his collection of biblical

---

[1] This seems to be the logical deduction from the phrase *quam mihi Romae summo studio ac labore confeceram* in *Ep.* 22, 30 (*CSEL* 54, 189).
[2] *Ep.* 5, 2 (*CSEL* 54, 22): Interpretationem quoque psalmorum Dauiticorum et prolixum ualde de synodis librum sancti Hilarii, quae ei apud Treueris manu mea ipse descripseram.

manuscripts.³ Jerome also mentions that a Nazoraean group at Beroea in Syria allowed him to copy a book used by them which he describes as the original Hebrew text of Matthew's Gospel.⁴ It is likely, however, that Jerome's stay in the Syrian desert was of too short a duration for him to have acquired many manuscripts or books.⁵

By the time Jerome wrote from Rome in 384, he appears to have had at his disposal the text of most of the Hebrew Bible. At the time of writing, he was comparing Aquila's version with scrolls of the Hebrew text in order to discover whether the Jews had altered the text, because of their hatred of Christianity. He had already collated the Prophets, Solomon, the Psalter, and the books of Kings, and was currently working through Exodus and hoping to go on to Leviticus. Jerome had concluded from this labour that there were many things which – far from justifying his fears – had confirmed the faith.⁶

Among his travels, one of the most advantageous from the point of view of acquiring manuscripts was his visit to the famous library at Caesarea. This collection of books and manuscripts had been undertaken by the priest and martyr Pamphilus, friend of Eusebius of Caesarea. Jerome relates that he (Pamphilus) was so 'impassioned with sacred literature that he transcribed the greater part of the works of Origen, and these are still preserved today in the library of Caesarea'. Jerome says that he himself owns twenty-five volumes of Origen's commentaries, 'which I hug and guard with such joy that I consider myself to have Croesus' wealth'.⁷

---

3 *Ep.* 125, 12 (*CSEL* 56, 131): Dum essem iuuenis et solitudinis me deserta uallarent, incentiua uitiorum ardoremque naturae ferre non poteram; quae cum crebris ieiuniis frangerem, mens tamen cogitationibus aestuabat. ad quam edomandam cuidam fratri, qui ex Hebraeis crediderat, me in disciplinam dedi.

4 *De Vir.Illus.* 3 (*PL* 23, 643): Ipsum Hebraicum habetur usque hodie in Caesariensi bibliotheca. quam Pamphilus martyr studiosissime confecit. Mihi quoque a Nazaraeis, qui in Beroea urbe Syriae hoc uolumine utuntur, describendi facultas fuit.

5 According to Cavallera, (I, ii, p. 154), Jerome was in the desert of Chalcis from 375-377.

6 *Ep.* 32, 1 (*CSEL* 54, 252).

7 *De Vir.Illus.* 75 (*PL* 23, 722A): Pamphilus presbyter, Eusebii Caesariensis episcopi necessarius, tanto Bibliothecae divinae amore flagravit, ut maximam partem Origenis voluminum sua manu descripserit, quae usque hodie in Caesariensi bibliotheca habentur. According to Jerome, Euzoius, a later Bishop of Caesarea, tried to restore the library of Pamphilus and Origen (*De Vir.Illus.* 113 [*PL* 23, 746B]. Other references to this famous library include *De Vir.Illus.* 81 (*PL* 23, 726); *Apol.* II, 21 (*CCL* 79, 57).

Jerome became so attached to the manuscripts he had collected that he could not bear to be parted from them. So when he moved from one place to another, he took his ever-expanding library with him.[8] In a letter to Paul of Concordia, Jerome suggests a deal which they can make with each other: Jerome will send to Paul a copy of his newly composed treatise, the *Life of Paul the Hermit*, if, in return, Paul - who is the owner of a considerable library himself - will give Jerome copies of several books, including the 'commentaries of Fortunatian, the History of Aurelius Victor and the letters of Novatian', so that Jerome may increase his personal collection. Unfortunately, we do not know whether or not the deal was closed and the books exchanged.[9]

Much as Jerome enjoyed collecting manuscripts and books, he did not collect them because they were finely bound, but because of their content. Given the choice between a book which had an elaborate binding but contained erroneous material, and a cheaper but correct edition, Jerome would always, he says, choose the latter book:

> 'Let whosoever wishes have their old books, either in purple coverings written in gold and silver and in uncials, as the people say, written burdens rather than codices, provided I and my friends may have our poor leaves and not so much beautiful codices, as correct ones.'[10]

Later in life, Jerome complains that he is no longer able to read his Hebrew scrolls, due to his failing sight. He says:

> 'By artificial light, we simply cannot re-read the Hebrew scrolls, for the smallness of the characters makes it difficult for us to decipher them even in broad daylight.'[11]

There were those in the monastery at Bethlehem who could help by reading the works of the Greek commentators, but no-one who could assist him in the same way for the Hebrew text of the Bible. His two friends, Paula and her daugher Blesilla, knew some Hebrew, thanks to Jerome's

---

8 *Ep.* 22, 30 (*CSEL* 54, 189): ...bibliotheca, quam mihi Romae summo studio ac labore confeceram, carere non poteram.
9 *Ep.* 10, 3 (*CSEL* 54, 38).
10 *In Iob*: Praef. (*PL* 28, 1142A-B): Habeant qui volunt veteres libros, vel in membranis purpureis auro argentoque descriptos, vel uncialibus, ut vulgo aiunt, litteris, onera magis exarata, quam codices, dummodo mihi meisque permittant pauperes habere schedulas, et non tam pulchros codices, quam emendatos.
11 *Comm.Ezek.*: Praef.lib. 7 (*CCL* 75, 277-8): Accedit ... quod caligantibus oculis senectute et aliquid sustinentibus beati Isaac, ad nocturnum lumen nequaquam ualemus Hebraeorum uolumina relegere, quae etiam ad solis dieique fulgorem, litterarum nobis paruitate caecantur. Composed in 411-414.

instruction, and could sing the Psalms in Hebrew,[12] but they were not sufficiently proficient in the language to read other books aloud, for the reason that Jerome's scrolls were unpointed. Jerome specifically relates this fact several times. For example:

> 'The word which we have translated "death" has in Hebrew three letters, Daleth, Beth, Resh, without any vowel. If they are read *Dabar*, they mean "word"; if *"Deber"*, "pestilence".'[13]

The question of whether Jerome's library was in roll or codex form is an interesting one, although his terminology is somewhat inconsistent and confusing. Traditionally in the Greco-Roman world, literary works were written on scrolls or rolls and these were referred to as *volumina* (a *volumen* being something rolled up). However, from the second century A.D., the emergent Christian Church began to use the codex format, for various reasons, including convenience of use, relative cheapness and differentiation from the Jews who used scrolls.[14] Wax covered tablets were also used.

Jerome frequently uses *volumen* to refer to biblical manuscripts.[15] However, we also find him using *codex* and *liber* of O.T. books.[16] Jerome says that, in his youth, Hilarion had copied a *codex* of the Gospels himself. He had valued this book highly, but offered it to a ship's captain in payment for his passage and that of a certain Gazanus.[17] Of course, this incident shows that, because of their relative scarcity, books were of considerable value, but it does not help very much with the question of the exact meaning of the term.

---

[12] *Ep.*, 108, 26; *Ep.* 39, 1 (*CSEL* 55, 344-5; 54, 294).

[13] *Comm.Hab.* 3, 5 (*CCL* 76A, 626): Pro eo quod nos transtulimus mortem, in Hebraeo tres litterae positae sunt, daleth, beth, res, absque ulla uocali, quae si legantur dabar, uerbum significant, si deber, pestem ... See also *Comm.Hier.* 10, 22 (*CCL* 74, 109); *Comm.Isa.* 9, 7ff (*CCL* 73, 129). On the question of pointing in Jerome's texts, see J. Barr: 'St. Jerome and the sounds of Hebrew' in *JSS* XII (1967) 1-36); *Idem*: 'Vocalization and the Analysis of Hebrew among the Ancient Translators' in *Baumgartner Festschrift* VTS XVI (1967) 1-11; E.F. Sutcliffe: 'Jerome's pronounciation of Hebrew', in *Biblica* XXIX 1948 112-125.

[14] On this, see B.M. Metzger: *The Text of the N.T.*, Oxford 1963, pp 5-7; P. Katz: 'The Early Christians' use of codices instead of rolls', in *JTS* XLIV (1945) 63-5; C.H. Roberts & T.C. Skeat: *The Birth of the Codex*, Oxford 1983 pp. 56ff; C.H. Roberts: *Manuscript, Society and Belief in Early Christian Egypt*, London 1979, pp. 26-48; T.C. Skeat: 'Early Christian Book Production: Papyri and Manuscripts', in *CHB* 2 Cambridge 1969, 72f.

[15] E.g. *Comm.Matt.* 1, 12 (*CCL* 77, 9); *Comm.Isa.* 8, 1-4 (*CCL* 73, 111); *Ep.* 54, 16; 65, 1; 73, 5 (*CSEL* 54, 483; 617; 55, 18).

[16] E.g. *Ep.* 107, 12 (*CSEL* 55, 302); *Comm.Osee* 7, 13 (*CCL* 76, 79).

[17] *Vita Hilar.* 35 (*PL* 23, 48C).

Jerome referred to the *antiqui codices* when he talked of the ancient translations made by the Greeks,[18] but also mentioned several times that pagan literature, namely Greek philosophy and history, were transmitted in *volumina*.[19] Jerome referred more than once to his own works as *volumina*. He applied this term to his epistles[20] as well as to his commentaries.[21] The writings of others were called *volumina*.[22] Sometimes Jerome used *volumen* to describe the small books of the O.T., as, for example, the books of Ruth and Esther.[23] However, he also referred to the book of Job at least ten times as a *volumen*, and Isaiah merited the title of *grande volumen*.[24]

Occasionally, Jerome used the phrase *nostri codices* to refer to books which had been accepted by the Latin Church,[25] and in one epistle he even says that the readings contained in these books or *codices* derive from the LXX text.[26]

From the evidence presented above of Jerome's use of the terms *volumen* and *codex*, it is evident that he did not make a clear distinction between them, and because of this fact, it is impossible to ascertain the form which his manuscripts took. The vagueness of his terminology means that we are unable to answer the question of whether Jerome's manuscripts were in 'roll' or 'book' form. It could be the case that he used both *volumina* and *codices*, although the balance of the external evidence may indicate that he was more likely to have used the *codex* form. We know that the *codex* took over from the *volumen* as the most popular form of book during the 4th century, but that before then the *codex* was in use almost exclusively for Christian texts.[27]

---

18 *Ep.* 106, 63 (*CSEL* 55, 278).
19 *Comm.Matt.* 21, 21 (*CCL* 77, 191); *Ep.* 57, 12 (*CSEL* 54, 526); *Comm.Dan.*: Prol.lib. I (*CCL* 75A, 771).
20 E.g. *Ep.* 108, 33 (*CSEL* 55, 350).
21 *Comm.Isa.*: Prol. (*CCL* 73, 3); ibid., XVIII: Praef. (*CCL* 73A, 742).
22 E.g. Paulinus' works [*Ep.* 58, 9 *CSEL* 54, 539]; Origen's works (*Comm.-Mich. lib. II*, Praef. [*CCL* 76, 473]; *Ep.* 127, 10 (*CSEL* 56, 153); also other ecclesiastical writers e.g. Tertullian and Cyprian (*Ep.* 130, 19 [*CSEL* 56, 200]); *De Vir.Illus.* 40 (*PL* 23, 690).
23 *Ep.* 65, 1 (*CSEL* 54, 617).
24 *Comm.Isa.* 8, 1-4 (*CCL* 73, 111).
25 E.g. *Ep.* 29, 1 (*CSEL* 54, 233); cf *HQG* I, 2; XLIII, 11; XLV, 9 (*CCL* 72, 1; 48; 49).
26 *Ep.* 29, 4 (*CSEL* 54, 238); cf *Ep.* 29, 6 (*CSEL* 54, 240).
27 In the 2nd century, for instance, of 871 pagan items, only 14 are in the *codex* form, whereas all the surviving Christian biblical papyri (eleven in number) are in *codex* form. Further, of 172 biblical mss or fragments of mss up to the turn of the 5th century, approximately 158 are *codices*, and only 14 are rolls. The *codex* is also preferred for non-biblical Christian literature during the same period (83 out of 118 texts). Cf Roberts and Skeat: *op.cit.*, pp. 38-44, for these statistics.

Jerome makes a few comments concerning the use of papyrus and parchment for writing. Parchment was used only rarely for letter writing in Classical times.[28] It may be that a passage in Jerome is the first reference to the use of parchment for letter writing. He writes to three friends, Chromatius, Jovinus and Eusebius:

> 'Why is it that, when we are separated by so great a distance of land and sea, you have sent me such a short letter? Is it that I have not deserved any better treatment, since I did not write to you first? I cannot believe that papyrus can have failed you while Egypt continues to supply its wares. Even if a Ptolemy had closed the seas, King Attalus would still have sent you the parchments from Pergamum, and so by his skins you could have made up for the lack of papyrus. The very name parchment is derived to this day from an historical incident of the kind which happened generations ago.'[29]

It seems a reasonable inference from this passage that Jerome regarded papyrus as the normal material on which letters were written. Parchment is here suggested as a suitable alternative, especially if there was a good reason, such as a shortage of papyrus.

Jerome makes other statements which confirm this inference. In reply to Sunnia and Fretela's questions on the text of the Psalter, Jerome says that he will discuss the readings *iuxta digestionem schedulae uestrae*.[30] The point to note here is that Jerome uses the word *schedula* as equivalent to *epistola*,[31] and shows that, because letters were customarily written on papyrus, the term by which such sheets were designated could be used for the letter itself. Also, he speaks of the letters of the Church as *chartae ecclesiasticae* and *ecclesiasticae epistolae*.[32]

A third medium for writing was the wax covered tablet. Although he

---

28 See K.K. Hulley: 'Light cast by Jerome on certain palaeographical points' in *Harvard Studies in Classical Philology* LIV (1943) 82-93.

29 *Ep.* 7, 2 (*CSEL* 54, 27): Quibus hoc primum queror, cur tot interiacentibus spatiis maris atque terrarum tam paruam epistulam miseritis, nisi quod ita merui, qui uobis, ut scribitis, ante non scripsi. chartam defuisse non puto Aegypto ministrante commercia. et si aliqui Ptolemaeus maria clausisset, tamen rex Attalus membranas e Pergamo miserat, ut penuria chartae pellibus pensaretur; unde pergamenarum nomen ad hanc usque diem tradente sibi inuicem posteritate seruatum est. For the historical allusions in this passage, see Pliny: *Hist.Nat.* XIII, 21; 70.

30 *Ep.* 106, 2 (*CSEL* 55, 248).

31 For other examples of this usage, see *Epp.* 11, 1; 62, 1; 106, 86 (*CSEL* 54, 39; 583; 55, 289). See Aug.: *Ep.* 125, 5.

32 *Ep.* 123, 9 (*CSEL* 56, 82); *Apol.* II, 20; III, 42 (*CCL* 79, 56; 113).

does not mention this often, it is worth looking briefly at a few of the statements he does make. In two passages he shows that wax tablets are used by both young and old, for he advises that young girls should first practise writing on wax tablets,[33] and, in another epistle, he congratulates his old friend Paul of Concordia, that, although he is now 100 years old, he can still write in straight and even lines on his wax tablets.[34] More important, perhaps, are his comments concerning *notarii* using wax tablets. The most important passage is:

> 'Inasmuch as a manifold explanation continues even to the end of the chapter, and we have now filled the wax tablets that receive our words, let it be sufficient to have dictated this much.'[35]

Here, the word *cerae* is clear proof that wax tablets were being used, and the fact of dictation is indicated by the verb *dictare*.

As to the instruments used for writing, Jerome says little. In *Ep.* 65, he says that the *stilus* is suited to writing on wax tablets, while the *calamus* is for use on papyrus, parchment and any other writing material.[36] His only other remark is interesting as it suggests either that the supply of pens was inadequate or that some pens were better than others.[37] In his preface to the Four Gospels,[38] Jerome mentions the use of red ink. In his original, Jerome has written numbers in red ink under numbers in black ink in order to distinguish between parts of the work. He urges that this be exactly reproduced in copies of the work. Jerome did not wish copyists to exercise their personal tastes in the use of red ink, for, in another preface, he is scornful of the use of red ink for decoration.[39]

The mechanics of book production

Jerome was a prolific author and made use frequently of the chief agents of transcription, the *notarius* and the *librarius*, i.e. the stenogra-

---

33 *Ep.* 107, 4 (*CSEL* 55, 294).
34 *Ep.* 10, 2 (*CSEL* 54, 37).
35 *Ep.* 18A, 16 (*CSEL* 54, 96): Et Quoniam usque ad finem capituli explanatio multiplex sequitur et excipientes iam inpleuimus ceras, hucusque dictasse sufficiat. See also *Ep.* 64, 21 (*CSEL* 54, 613).
36 *Ep.* 65, 7 (*CSEL* 54, 623-4); cf also *Adv.Pelag.* 1, 3 (*CCL* 80, 8).
37 *Tract. in Ps.* 119 (*Anec.Mar.* III, ii, p. 231): Dimisimus possessionem, dimisimus patriam, dimisimus saeculum et propter calamum rixam facimus in monasterio.
38 *Praef. to Quat.Evang.* (*PL* 29, 560).
39 *Chron.Eus.*: Praef. (*PL* 27, 226). See the words: Unde praemonendum puto, ut prout quaeque scripta sunt, etiam colorum diversitates serventur, ne quis irrationabili aestimet voluptate oculis tantum rem esse quaesitam...

pher and the copyist. The *notarius* was more commonly used by the early Church Fathers than the *librarius*. The task of the *notarius* was to write in shorthand from dictation, or to make a record of a public speech. That so many of the sermons of the Fathers of the early Church are extant today is very largely due to the work of the *notarii*.[40]

That the early Church Fathers made use of the *notarii* is well attested. Eusebius, for example, quotes a remark of Origen that, at 60 years of age, he gave permission for his discourses to be taken down by stenographers, 'a thing which he had never before allowed'.[41] In the same way, Cyril of Jerusalem's catechetical sermons were preached without a prepared text[42] and taken down by interested people as they were being delivered.[43] Also, it seems that *notarii* were present at the 'Farewell Sermon' of Gregory of Nazianzus, because he says:

>'Farewell, you lovers of my discourses, in your eagerness and assembly, you pencils seen and unseen, and you railing, pressed upon by those who thrust themselves forward to hear the word.'[44]

The 'pencils seen and unseen' can only refer to *notarii* who were present to take down Gregory's words.

The works of Jerome often bear witness to the fact that he frequently employed *notarii*. Sometimes, however, it seems that he could not afford the clerical services of a *notarius*. In his preface to the translation of the books of Solomon, written to Bishops Chromatius and Heliodorus, he says:

---

[40] See R.J. Deferrari: 'St. Augustine's method of composing and delivering sermons', in *American Journal of Philology* 43 (1922) 97-123, esp. pp. 106-110: p. 107: 'The preservation of the homilies of the great preachers of the church, whose sermons bear such marks of spontaneity, can be satisfactorily explained only by the use of a shorthand system by men skilled in the same and present in the church for the express purpose of recording the spoken word.' Also, see Jerome: *Epp.* 34, 6; 65, 7; 117, 12; 118, 1; 124, 1 (*CSEL* 54, 264; 624; 55, 434; 435; 56, 96).

[41] *HE* VI, 36 (Loeb Eus. Vol. 2, p. 90).

[42] The first sermon has the heading: 'To those who are to be enlightened, delivered extempore at Jerusalem, as an introductory lecture to those who had come forward for baptism' (*PG* 33, 369).

[43] At the end of Lecture 18, the following phrase is found in the older Munich manuscripts: 'Many other lectures were delivered year by year, both before baptism and after the neophytes had been baptised. But these alone were taken down when spoken and written by some of the earnest students in the year 352 of the advent of our Lord and Saviour Jesus Christ.' See R.J. Deferrari: *art.cit.*, p. 107f. Whether or not Cyril can have preached his sermons at this date is a totally separate question and does not detract from the point being made here. See art. 'Cyrillus von Jerusalem' in *TRE* 8 (Berlin 1981) and literature cited there.

[44] *Oratio* 42 (*PG* 36, 492).

'You send help in the matter of expenses, and you support our stenographers and copyists, that our talent may exert itself as much as possible for you.'[45]

Again, when Pammachius urges Jerome to write a commentary on Ezekiel after he has completed that on Isaiah, Jerome says that he is worn out with age and sickness, and that he has no stenographer to assist him.[46]

In the prologue to book five of the *Comm.Isa.*, Jerome quotes part of a letter to Bishop Amabilis, and here he mentions the employment of a *notarius*.[47] Further, at the beginning of the *C.Lucif.*, Jerome says that a *notarius* was called upon to take down what each party said to ensure that an accurate record of the debate was kept.[48] Elsewhere, Jerome complains that he has been forced to dictate to a *notarius* because of the swiftness with which he has had to compose, and this is especially unfortunate since he has been ill for three months.[49] Yet again, Jerome rather boastfully says that he employed a *notarius* to write down what he was dictating in Latin, while another (Jewish) man was dictating to him (Jerome) in Chaldaean (i.e. Aramaic), a language, he says, similar to Hebrew, with which he was familiar.[50]

During the bitter controversy with Rufinus over Origen, Rufinus warns Jerome not to attempt to bribe his *notarius* with a large sum of money in order to obtain information. Jerome laughs at the ridiculous notion that he could afford to bribe anyone, and asks sarcastically if Rufinus thinks that he can compete with the legendary wealth of Croesus and Darius.[51] Earlier, Rufinus had said that Jerome had paid his *notarii* higher fees for transcribing the *Dialogues* of Cicero than was usual for other (i.e. ecclesiastical) works.[52] The implication here was that Jerome could certainly afford the assistance of *notarii*, and would not hesitate to do so.

At least twice, Jerome mentions that he dictates to a *notarius* very rapidly; but occasionally he goes too slow for a stenographer, and when this happens, the stenographer is likely to show his impatience by a gesture rather than orally.[53]

---

45 *Lib.Sal.*: Praef. (*PL* 28, 1307A): Mittitis solatia sumptuum: notarios nostros et librarios sustentatis, ut vobis potissimum nostrum desudet ingenium.
46 *Comm.Isa.* X.: Prol. (*CCL* 73, 396f).
47 *Comm.Isa.* V.: Prol. (*CCL* 73, 160).
48 *C.Lucif.* 1 (*PL* 23, 163B).
49 *Comm.Matt.*: Prol. (*CCL* 77, 5).
50 *Vulg. in Lib.Tob.*: Praef. (*PL* 29, 25-6A). For a further discussion of this passage, see below, p. 82f.
51 *Apol.* III, 4 (*CCL* 79, 76).
52 Rufinus: *Apol.c.Hier.* II, 11 (*CCL* 20, 92).
53 *Comm.Gal.* IV: Prol. (*PL* 26, 427B-C); *In Lib. II Chron.Eus.*: Praef. (*PL* 27, 226-7).

The other main agents of transcription are the *librarii*, known sometimes as *scriptores*[54] or even *scribae*.[55] It would seem that the term *antiquarius*, used many times in this sense by Tacitus, is used only very rarely by Jerome.[56] The *librarii*, who were mostly slaves or freedmen, played an important part in the transmission of written material. Jerome's use of the term *librarius* shows that he thought of the *librarii* as copyists, and distinguished them from the *notarii*. The basic difference in function between them was that the *notarius* wrote down in shorthand what was spoken, while the *librarius* was responsible for copying out in longhand what the *notarius* had written in shorthand.

Jerome's use of *librarius* was clearly shown by the study of A. Wikenhauser.[57] Wikenhauser showed, on the basis of a study of eight passages where Jerome uses the word, that the sense is always 'copyist' (Bücherabschreiber). The ideas of *notarii* and *librarii* are generally separate, but the two functions are often carried out by the same person.[58]

In his letter to Niceas, Jerome gives the supposed etymology of the word *librarius* as:

et scriptores a libris arborum librarios vocavere,[59]

which, as the bark of the tree served as the raw material from which the *librarius* was able to effect his occupation, is an ingenious etymology!

In connection with the way in which *notarii* and *librarii* wrote words down, it is worth mentioning here that Jerome often refers to two critical symbols – the *obelus* and the *asteriscus* – which he also calls *veru* or *virgula* and *stella* respectively.[60] Jerome never actually states that these sigla were developed in Classical times, although, in a letter to the two Gothic clergy Sunnia and Fretela, he makes the following statement:

'Whenever there occurs in Greek an omission, which the Hebrew has, Origen added the omitted works from Theodotion's transla-

---

[54] E.g. *Vulg. in Lib.Jos.*: Praef. (*PL* 28, 505); *Comm.Isa.* 15, 9 (*CCL* 73, 179); *Comm.Ezek.* 40, 14 (*CCL* 75, 556); *Comm.Matt.* 13, 35 (*CCL* 77, 111).
[55] E.g. *Comm.Isa.* 36, 1 (*CCL* 73, 430).
[56] *Ep.* 5, 2 (*CSEL* 54, 22) written from the desert of Chalcis.
[57] A. Wikenhauser: 'Der heilige Hieronymus und die Kurzschrift', in *Theol. Quartalschrift* XCII (1910) 50-87.
[58] Wikenhauser: *art.cit.*, p. 84-5. See the following list, which is not exhaustive: *Epp.* 5, 2; 8, 1; 61, 4; 65, 11; 71, 5; 106, 30; 126, 2 (*CSEL* 54, 22-3; 31-2; 580; 628; 55, 5; 261; 56, 144); *Apol.* II, 17 (*CCL* 79, 51); *De Vir.Illus.* 61 (*PL* 23, 707); *Vulg.Ezra*: Praef (*PL* 28, 1472); *Vulg.Sal.*: Prol. (*PL* 28, 1241A).
[59] *Ep.* 8, 1 (*CSEL* 54, 32).
[60] E.g. *Ep.* 106, 7 (*CSEL* 55, 252); *Vulg. in Lib.Psalm.*: Praef. (*PL* 29, 123).

tion, putting an asterisk, that is, a star, in order that it should light up and make clear that which previously was unclear. On the other hand, whenever something is found in the Greek texts which is not in the Hebrew, he placed an obelus in front of it, that is, a horizontal line, which we may call in Latin a dart, to indicate that what is not found in the authentic texts should be slaughtered and transfixed. These signs are also found in Greek and Latin poetry.'[61]

The last sentence of this passage appears to make acknowledgement that these two signs originated in the criticism of secular texts, although Jerome gives no hint of the knowledge that they were first used at Alexandria.[62] Jerome correctly attributes the introduction of these critical sigla into biblical texts to Origen, who used the *obelus* (-, ⨪, ÷) to indicate spurious passages in the LXX, and the *asteriscus* (※) to indicate passages which, although not found in the LXX, were read by Theodotion and supported by the Hebrew text.[63] Jerome does not, however, mention the third critical sign used by Origen in the Hexapla, the *metobelus* (/., ˙/., ⵟ) which showed the end of the passage added or omitted. Instead, Jerome introduced a new sign, consisting of two dots (:) by which he marked the end of passages affected either by the *obelus* or the *asteriscus*.[64] Jerome seems to have taken over the *obelus* and *asteriscus* from Origen and gave to them the same significance as that scholar had done.[65]

When he composed a work, Jerome usually had to have a copy made immediately. This was so that, if the original never reached its destination, Jerome would have a copy of it, or so that, if any of Jerome's correspondents quibbled about some point of detail, then Jerome could easily look it up and give his answer.[66]

---

61 *Ep.* 106, 7 (*CSEL* 55, 252): Ubi quid minus habetur in Graeco ab Hebraica ueritate, Origenes de translatione Theodotionis addidit et signum posuit asterisci, id est stellam, quae, quod prius absconditum uidebatur, inluminet et in medium proferat; ubi autem, quod in Hebraeo non est, in Graecis codicibus inuenitur, obelon, id est iacentem, praeposuit, quam nos Latine 'ueru' possumus dicere, quo ostenditur iugulandum esse et confodiendum, quod in authenticis libris non inuenitur. Quae signa et in Graecorum Latinorumque poematibus inueniuntur.
62 Cf A. Güdeman: 'Kritische Zeichen', in *RE* 11 (1922) 1920-1923.
63 See *Apol.* 2, 27 (*CCL* 79, 64f); *Praef. in Pentateuch* (*PL* 28, 179).
64 *Praef. in Lib.Psalm.* (*PL* 28, 1183ff).
65 *Praef. in Pentateuch* (*PL* 28, 179).
66 See, for instance, the exchange of letters between Jerome and Augustine, where both scholars are forced to refer to the copies of letters and other writings which had failed to reach their destination. *Epp.* 101-5; 110; 112; 115-6.

Early in his career, Jerome had failed to keep copies of all his correspondence. He admits to Pope Damasus that he does not now possess copies of the letters Damasus sent to him in the desert.[67] Later in life, however, he was able to transcribe long extracts from letters and work written much earlier, showing that he must have had access to copies of these.[68]

In connection with the keeping of records, either private or public, Jerome uses several terms. The most frequently used term in this context is *scrinium*. Jerome relates that soon after a pronouncement by the Arian Bishop Valens, in which he condemned everyone who denied that Christ was the Son of God, he was given an ovation by the Bishops and congregation, which consisted of a measured stamping (*tripudium*). If anyone thinks he is making this up, Jerome says, let him go and examine the public archives (*scrinia*), and the ecclesiastical archives (*arcae*).[69] This example may give the impression that, for Jerome, the *scrinium* was similar to the *bibliotheca*, the library. However, E.P. Arns makes a distinction between the two.[70] The *bibliotheca* was a collection of books or the place where these books were kept,[71] as it is today. On the other hand, the word *scrinium* signified simply a case or box in which documents were kept. The public had no access to these, and they were administered by the *notarii*, who were not employed by the public libraries.

The rare word *scriniolum* is used by Jerome to denote the box in which books or records were kept. He opines that heretical books, like those of the Pelagians, ought to be locked in these boxes, so that the public will not be led astray by them.[72] Similarly, Jerome says that his own commentary on Obadiah, composed when he was very young, ought to rest hidden in a locked case.[73] Fabiola, having asked questions on the Gospels and Psalms, was keeping Jerome's answers in the *scriniolum* of her heart.[74] The terms *scrinium* and *scriniolum*, therefore, denote either the receptacle of public or private documents, and are to be distinguished from the *bibliotheca*, the public library.

---

67 *Ep.* 35, 1 (*CSEL* 54, 265).
68 For examples of this, see *Apol.* II, 25 (*CCL* 79, 61); *Comm.Isa.* 6, 1 (*CCL* 73, 84).
69 *C.Lucif.* 18 (*PL* 23, 180C): In hoc vero cuncti episcopi, et tota simul Ecclesia plausu quodam et tripudio Valentis vocem exceperunt. Quod si quis a nobis fictum putat, scrinia publica scrutetur. Plenae sunt certe Ecclesiarum arcae, et recens adhuc rei memoria est. See also *Apol.* III, 3 (*CCL* 79, 75); *Apol.* II, 19 (*CCL* 79, 55f); article 'Scrinium', in *PW* 2nd ser. II, 1, 893-904.
70 E.P. Arns: *La Technique du Livre d'après Saint Jérôme*, Paris 1952, p. 188.
71 See *Ep.* 22, 30 (*CSEL* 54, 189); *De Vir.Illus.* 13 (*PL* 23, 662).
72 *Adv.Pelag.* I, 24 (*PL* 23, 541C) (= I, 25 in *CCL* 80, 33).
73 *Comm.Abd.*: Prol. (*CCL* 76, 349).
74 *Ep.* 77, 7 (*CSEL* 55, 44).

In one passage, Jerome refers to the archives of the Roman Church, and uses the word *chartarium*.[75] This is the only occurrence of this term in the whole of Latin literature. Jerome challenges Rufinus to ask for the original of a letter which is held in the *chartarium* of the Roman Church, if he thinks that Jerome has forged it.

Among other terms used occasionally by Jerome are *arca*, which had already been used by Tertullian as a synonym for 'case',[76] and *armarium*, 'cupboard' or 'bookcase'. Jerome says St. Paul is designated as a 'cupboard of the holy scriptures',[77] because he had received scripture and kept it safe.

At various places, Jerome mentions several facets of the process of researching when writing a book. He knows of the *index*: he says, for instance, that to list all the works of Didymus the Blind would require an *index* to itself.[78] He does not mention all the works of Origen because it was not his purpose to make a catalogue (*index*) of all his writings.[79] He actually made this list of the major works of Origen in *Ep.* 33.[80]

Jerome knew that manuscripts deteriorated very rapidly and easily. Bishop Euzoius had been forced to replace many of the volumes in the famous library at Caesarea, even though they were not very ancient.[81] He also knew some of the causes of the deterioration of books: water and humidity render books black and rotten.[82] Again, while this was lamentable with old manuscripts, it was partly because the materials could not resist the action of time.

Jerome speaks several times of *exemplaria*. For him, these are the most important manuscripts, calling them *veriora exemplaria*.[83] He cites the 'ancient manuscripts' in connection with a passage found in Lk. 14: 27; '...whoever does not bear his cross daily and come after me cannot

---

[75] *Apol.* III, 20 (*CCL* 79, 91).

[76] *Comm.Matt.* 23, 5 (*CCL* 77, 212); Tert.: *De Pud.* 7 (*CCL* 2, 1292).

[77] *Ep.* 53, 3 (*CSEL* 54, 448-9): sanctarum scripturarum armarium. See also *Ep.* 22, 32 (*CSEL* 54, 193); *Ep.* 48, 4 (*CSEL* 54, 349); *Comm.Matt.* 23, 5 (*CCL* 77, 212).

[78] *De Vir.Illus.* 109 (*PL* 23, 743B): et infinita alia quae digerere proprii indicis est.

[79] *Ep.* 84, 8 (*CSEL* 55, 131): ne videar operum eius indicem texere.

[80] *Ep.* 33, 2-4 (*CSEL* 54, 254-9); cf *De Vir.Illus.* 54 (*PL* 23, 699); E. Klostermann: 'Die Schriften des Origenes in Hieronymus' Brief an Paula' in *Sitzungsberichte der kon. preuss. Akad. der Wiss. zu Berlin* 2 (1891) 855-870.

[81] *De Vir.Illus.* 113 (*PL* 23, 746B).

[82] *Comm.Isa.* 18, 1 (*CCL* 73, 275).

[83] *Comm.Osee* 1, 10 (*CCL* 76, 17). See also Aug.: *Ep. ad. Hier.*; Jer.: *Ep.* 110, 1 (*CSEL* 55, 357): mittere exemplaria veriora; *Comm.Isa.* 58, 11 (*CCL* 73A, 671): emendatis et ueris exemplaribus.

be my disciple'.[84] The more ancient a manuscript witness, the more faithful will be that witness.

Jerome also makes several rather vague references to *exemplaria*. Phrases such as *quaedam exemplaria*,[85] *plura exemplaria*,[86] *pleraque exemplaria*,[87] *multa exemplaria*,[88] thinking it unnecessary to be more specific about his sources, and demurring from making a minute collation, may be seen at several places throughout Jerome's works. Arns[89] suggests that, even at Jerusalem and Rome, the libraries of books did not allow a sufficiently exhaustive classification to arrive at an 'archetypal' exemplar or even an exact genealogy, and that this explains all of Jerome's imprecise terminology.

Jerome and manuscripts

Textual criticism is fundamentally concerned with variant readings in texts. Jerome certainly realised this, and asked where these variant readings came from, and what their causes were. He announces his text critical intentions in the preface to his translation of the Four Gospels:

> 'We must confess that, as we have it in our language, (the N.T.) is marked by discrepancies, and now that the stream is distributed into different channels, we must go back to the fountainhead.'[90]

We shall be studying Jerome's attitude to the basic text critical questions below, but it is interesting to note briefly that he postulates three different text types. Jerome attributes variations in text to their place of origin. In the preface to the translation of Chronicles from Hebrew, he says:

> *Cum pro varietate regionum diversa ferantur exemplaria.*[91]

Speaking of the LXX, Jerome says:

> 'Alexandria and Egypt recommend Hesychius for their authority, from Constantinople as far as Antioch, in their version of the LXX the martyr Lucian is accepted; for the provinces situated be-

---

84 *Ep.* 127, 6 (*CSEL* 56, 150).
85 *Comm.Ezek.* 16, 23 (*CCL* 75, 189); *Ep.* 119, 2 (*CSEL* 55, 447).
86 *Ep.* 106, 78 (*CSEL* 55, 287).
87 *Comm.Matt.* 22, 3 (*CCL* 77, 200).
88 *Ep.* 106, 20 (*CSEL* 55, 257).
89 Arns: *op.cit.*, p. 78.
90 *Pref. to Four Gospels* (*PL* 29, 559): Hoc certe cum in nostro sermone discordat, et diversos rivulorum tramites ducit; uno de fonto quaerendum est.
91 *Pref. to Vulg.Paral.* (*PL* 28, 1391A); cf also *Apol.* II, 27 (*CCL* 79, 64).

tween these two, the Palestinian manuscripts, elaborated by Origen and popularised by Eusebius and Pamphilus. And the whole world disputes over this tripartite division.'⁹²

Each of these three text-types rests on a different authority and holds a preferential position only in that area.

For Jerome, the critic's task is to remove the errors which have arisen in the text and to establish a trustworthy text.⁹³ Texts could be corrupted in many ways, of course, and it is our purpose now to show how aware Jerome was of the principles of textual criticism.⁹⁴

Many faults were produced by errors made – either accidentally or intentionally – by careless or incompetent copyists.⁹⁵ Jerome observes that these emendations attempted by copyists, resulted, not in a better text, but only in added confusion of the text.⁹⁶ Some copyists do not pay attention to their work and even go to sleep over it,⁹⁷ or they carelessly change the reading of a text, writing not what they see in front of them, but what they understand. So, at *Comm.Matt.* 13, 35, the copyist wrote Isaiah instead of Asaph, because the former name was more familiar, and he believed the previous copyist to have been mistaken in writing Asaph.⁹⁸ Jerome was of course aware that errors thus made were likely to be transmitted in subsequent copies.⁹⁹ The corruption of the biblical text made justifiable his new translation from the Greek and Hebrew.¹⁰⁰

---

92 *Ibid.* (*PL* 28, 1392-3A): Alexandria et Aegyptus in Septuaginta suis Hesychium laudat auctorem; Constantinopolis usque Antiochiam, Luciani martyris exemplaria probat. Mediae inter has provinciae Palaestinos codices legunt: quos ab Origene elaboratos Eusebius et Pamphilus vulgaverunt: totusque orbis hac inter se trifaria varietate compugnat.

93 *Ep.* 27, 1 (*CSEL* 54, 224).

94 For other treatments of this, see E.P. Arns: *op.cit.*, pp. 68-9; K.K. Hulley: 'Principles of textual criticism known to St. Jerome', in *Harvard Studies in Classical Philology* LV (1944) 87-109.

95 *Ep.* 71, 5 (*CSEL* 55, 5-6).

96 *Ep.* 71, 5 (*CSEL* 55, 5-6); *Praef. in Quat.Evang.* (*PL* 29, 560); *Tract. in Ps.* 77 (*Anec.Mar.* III, 2, p. 60).

97 *Praef. in Quat.Evang.* (*PL* 29, 559); *Ep.* 106, 30 (*CSEL* 55, 261-2).

98 *Comm.Matt.* 13, 35 (*CCL* 77, 111): Et primum scriptorem non intellexisse Asaph et putasse scriptoris uitium atque emendasse nomen Esaiae, cuius uocabulum manifestius erat. *Ep.* 71, 5 (*CSEL* 55, 6); *Comm.Ephes.* 2, 1 (*PL* 26, 495). Jerome made several pleas that the copying of manuscripts should be done exactly; see *Ep.* 80, 3 (*CSEL* 55, 105); *De Vir.Illus.* 35 (*PL* 23, 683A); *Praef. in Esther* (*PL* 28, 1505).

99 *Praef. in lib.Paral.iuxta LXX* (*PL* 29, 423-4); *Comm.Ezek.* 40, 5 (*CCL* 75, 558-9).

100 *Praef. in Vulg. Iob* (*PL* 28, 1141): Aut certe scriptorum vitio depravata.

Copyists had found the proper transcription of proper names a particular stumbling block: the 'forest of names' became inextricable, and the errors severe.[101] Taking just two examples of this, he says that 'Jechonias' becomes 'Joiacim',[102] and that 'Dimon' is transcribed as 'Dibon'.[103]

Errors in manuscripts could be produced by one of two causes – accidental or intentional. Accidental errors could be attributed almost always to mistakes made by copyists when transcribing manuscripts, although, because the *exemplar* from which they worked was not always corrected, it was unavoidable that errors became compounded.[104] Because of this, the most ancient books lose their authority in transmission due to the caprice of copyists (*scriptores*) and their proof readers (*lectores*), who, remarks Jerome, are greedy to correct them.[105]

In addition to making these rather general statements about accidental errors in manuscripts, Jerome frequently mentions detailed causes of corruption.[106] Punctuation, for instance, is very important for the correct understanding of a passage, and faulty punctuation may be a cause of error.[107] The confusion of number symbols was another cause of error. Jerome makes the interesting comment that the reason why Mark appears to disagree with Matthew and John about the exact time of Jesus' crucifixion was due to a copyists' error. The copyist, Jerome says, confused the number symbols S' and Y' and therefore caused an error in the text.[108] Similarly, Jerome recognises that copyists could easily confuse similar letters. Most of Jerome's references to this, however, re-

---

101 *Praef. in Vulg.Paral.* (*PL* 28, 1394); cf *Comm.Hier.*: Prol. (*CCL* 74, 1).
102 *Comm.Matt.* 1, 12 (*CCL* 77, 9).
103 *Comm.Isa.* 15, 9 (*CCL* 73, 258-9).
104 *Comm.Ezek.* 40, 5 (*CCL* 75, 559).
105 *Comm.Ezek.* 5, 12 (*CCL* 75, 60).
106 For this paragraph, I am indebted to K.K. Hulley's article, cited above.
107 *HQG* 3, 8 (*CCL* 72, 5); *Ep.* 140, 6 (*CSEL* 56, 274); *Tract. in Ps.* 89 (*Anec. Mar.* III, 2, p. 107). See also Rufinus' warning about correct punctuation (quoted in *Ep.* 80 of Jerome's correspondence): 'I advise and require everyone reading or copying these books of mine... let him compare his transcript with the copies from which it is made, let him correct it to the letter and let him punctuate it correctly. He must reject every manuscript that is not properly corrected and punctuated; for otherwise the difficulties in the text arising from lack of punctuation will make obscure arguments still more obscure to those who read them' (Jerome: *Ep.* 80, 3 [*CSEL* 55, 105]).
108 *Tract. in Ps.* 77 (*Anec.Mar.* III, 11, p. 60): Error scriptorum fuit: et in Marco hora sexta scriptum fuit, sed multi pro ἐπισήμῳ Graeco putaverunt esse gamma. See K.K. Hulley: *art.cit.*, p. 96.

late to the confusion of Hebrew letters by the translators of the LXX, especially the letters *resh* and *daleth*, distinguished only by a small stroke,[109] and the letters *yod* and *vau*, which differ, he says, only in size.[110] He does occasionally refer to a confusion of Greek letters, as, for example, when he criticises copyists for writing Δ instead of A, and Ω instead of O.[111] Also noticed by Jerome are occasional occurrences of dittography and haplography,[112] metathesis of letters,[113] assimilation,[114] omission of words,[115] and transposition.[116]

Intentional corruption of manuscripts shows a lack of scruple in copyists, which, Jerome implies, is sustained by a wild fanaticism which knows no boundaries.[117] It is very noticable that almost all of Jerome's comments on the intentional corruption of manuscripts were made during the years of the Origenist controversy and were directed against his erstwhile friend, Rufinus. Rufinus had complained that Origen's writings had been tampered with and that any 'unorthodox' views now to be found in Origen's writings were the result of malicious interpolations by a person or persons unknown. This novel theory is derided by Jerome and Rufinus is subjected to some of Jerome's most vitriolic criticism.

---

[109] E.g. *Comm.Isa.* 44, 24ff (*CCL* 73A, 503).
[110] E.g. *HQG* 41, 2 (*CCL* 72, 47).
[111] *Comm.Hier.* 29, 14ff (*CCL* 74, 282); *Tract. in Ps.* 131 (*Anec.Mar.* III, 2, p. 244); cf *Comm.In Ps.* 131 (*Anec.Mar.* III, 1, p. 90); *Comm.Gal.* 5, 6 (*PL* 26, 425).
[112] Copyists, for instance, read *Iudaeae* instead of *Iudae* (*Comm.Matt.* 2, 5 [*CCL* 77, 13]); and *Bariona* for *Bar Ioanna* (*Comm.Matt.* 16, 17 [*CCL* 77, 140f]); cf *Comm.Ezek.* 40, 5ff (*CCL* 75, 563).
[113] *C. Zach.* 12, 9f (*CCL* 76A, 868): Si enim legatur dacaru, ἐξεκέντησαν, id est compunxerunt siue confixerunt accipitur; sin autem contrario ordine, litteris commutatis, racadu, ὠρχήσαντο id est saltauerunt intellegitur. Et ob similitudinem litterarum error est natus.
[114] Part of the preceding line may be copied again (*Ep.* 106, 27 [*CSEL* 55, 260]: ...sed hoc male et de superiore versiculo additum est...), or it may be substituted for what should have come next (*Ep.* 106, 43 [*CSEL* 55, 267]: In eodem: Donec adnuntiem brachium tuum. Et dicitis in Graeco vos repperisse: mirabilia tua, quod de superiori versiculo est...)
[115] Copyists may pass over everything between the first occurrence of a word and the second; e.g. *Ep.* 121, 2 (*CSEL* 56, 10); cf *Comm.Isa.* 40, 6-8 (*CCL* 73, 456).
[116] Errors caused by disturbance in the order of words, phrase or larger units are criticised sharply by Jerome because they make the thought of the passage more obscure, cf *Praef. in lib.Sal.* (*PL* 29, 427); *Comm.Ezek.* 7, 1f (*CCL* 75, 71); *Ep.* 18A, 15 (*CSEL* 54, 94): '...pro qua prophetia, licet in plerisque codicibus ordo peruersus sit...'.
[117] *Apol.* III, 37 (*CCL* 79, 105); cf *Apol.* III, 26 (*CCL* 79, 98); *Apol.* II, 17 (*CCL* 79, 50f).

An interesting passage is where Jerome complains that an unknown copyist had incorporated into the text of a passage on the Psalter a marginal note which Jerome had written for the benefit of the reader. He says:
> 'I wonder why some rash person has thought that the note: "the correct form is not καταπαύσωμεν, as some think, but κατακαύσομεν, that is, *incendamus*," which was placed by me in the margin for the guidance of the reader, should be put into the body of the text... Whenever anything has been added in the margin for the sake of note-taking, this should not be put into the body of the text, in order not to corrupt the original translation according to the whim of the copyists.'[118]

As well as discussing detailed points of textual criticism, Jerome also engaged in what is now called literary criticism. He was primarily concerned with questions relating to the authorship of the biblical books and the authenticity of sections of those books. Although he does not use the terms, Jerome's criteria for judging the authenticity of a book can be grouped under two headings – 1) external evidence, and 2) internal evidence.

1) External evidence
One method of assuring the authenticity of a writing is the *subscriptio*. The apostle Paul, Jerome reports, had used his signature, along with a few words, to lift from false teachers the opportunity of tampering with his own doctrines.[119] A practical example for Jerome of this criterion is found in *Ep.* 102,[120] written to Augustine. This is Jerome's reply to Augustine's *Ep.* 67 (= *Ep.* 101 in Jerome's correspondence) in which he (Augustine) denied having written a treatise which criticised Jerome's interpretation of Gal. 2:11-14. Jerome refused to discuss this treatise until he had assured himself of its authenticity. He says that it lacks Augustine's autograph subscription and could therefore have been written by someone else.[121]

---

118 *Ep.* 106, 46 (*CSEL* 55, 269f): et miror, quomodo e latere adnotationem nostram nescio quis temerarius scribendam in corpore putauerit, quam nos pro eruditione legentis scripsimus hoc modo: non habet καταπαύσωμεν, ut quidam putant, sed κατακαύσωμεν, id est incendamus ... Unde, si quid pro studio e latere additum est, non debet poni in corpore, ne priorem translationem pro scribentium uoluntate conturbet.
119 *Comm.Gal.* 6, 11 (*PL* 26, 463C-D).
120 *CSEL* 55, 234-236; = *Ep.* 78 in Augustine's corpus. Kelly dates this letter to 402/3 – cf Kelly: p. 265f.
121 Kelly (p. 265f) believes that this was merely procrastination on Jerome's part because he had been stung by the criticisms of the treatise in question. He would surely have known that Augustine was its author – Jerome admitted that its style

In any case, the subscription was not a very good criterion by which to judge a book's authenticity. The signature could be forged or imitated. Another criterion was the *anulus signatorius*, or seal, which one put on letters or other works. Jerome's close friend and correspondent, Marcella, possessed a seal-ring.[122] Jerome is familiar with the use of the seal; this is shown in his comment on the phrase, *et date anulum in manu illius* (Lk. 15:22) in *Ep.* 21. It is the seal which imprints on us the resemblance of Christ.[123] Jerome's use of the term *signaculum* to mean 'a trace' indicates that he was familiar with the ancient habit of using a seal to sign one's name,[124] although Jerome also know of the ornamental use of the *anulus*.[125]

2) Internal evidence

One method of verifying the authenticity of a book is to judge whether its contents are consistent with those of its supposed author. So, for instance, with a book by the Pythagorean author and philosopher Sixtus, whom Rufinus equates with the Christian martyr Sixtus, Jerome applies this criterion and establishes that in this entire volume there is no mention of Christ or the apostles. How then, could it have been written by a Christian martyr?[126]

From the point of view of judging the authenticity and authorship of biblical books, this criterion is of great value for Jerome. It is interesting to see his comments on the authorship of the Epistle to the Hebrews. He notices striking resemblances in style between Hebrews and the letter of Clement of Rome to the Corinthians:

> 'which seems to me to agree in character with the epistle to the Hebrews which passes under the name of Paul, but it uses many things from this same epistle, not only in many of its ideas, but even in the word order; its likeness in either of these respects is very great.'[127]

---

and method of argumentation were Augustine's, and it was taken for granted at Bethlehem that Augustine was the author. By stalling in this way, Jerome was probably indicating that he wished to drop the subject altogether.

122 *Ep.* 127, 3 (*CSEL* 56, 147): aurum usque ad anuli signaculum repudians...
123 *Ep.* 21, 24 (*CSEL* 54, 127).
124 On this, see Arns: *op.cit.*, p. 176.
125 *Ep.* 147, 8 (*CSEL* 56, 324): ...digitos anulis oneras...
126 *Comm.Ezek.* 18, 5-8 (*CCL* 75, 236).
127 *De Vir.Illus.* 15 (*PL* 23, 663C): ...quae mihi videtur characteri Epistolae, quae sub Pauli nomine ad Hebraeos fertur, convenire, sed et multis de eadem Epistola, non solum sensibus, sed juxta verborum quoque ordinem abutitur. Omnino grandis in utraque similitudo est.

For Jerome, Clement could have been the editor of Hebrews. In *De Vir. Illus.* 5, he puts forward various views on the authorship of Hebrews:

'The epistle which is called Hebrews is not considered his [Paul's] on account of the differences of style and language, but it is reckoned, either according to Tertullian to be the work of Barnabas, or, according to the others, to be by Luke the evangelist or Clement, later Bishop of the Church at Rome, who, they say, an associate of Paul himself, arranged and adorned the ideas of Paul in his [Clement's] own language.'[128]

It is interesting to note that in both these comments, Jerome applies the criterion of internal evidence. He himself is uncertain as to the authorship of the epistle to the Hebrews, but he judges some suggestions to be more or less likely than others on the basis of internal evidence. It is probably incorrect to say, as Hulley does,[129] that Jerome's 'references to the opinions of various persons... seems to indicate that he was aware of the subjective element in judgements of this sort'. In citing various authorities, Jerome was merely following his normal practice in commenting, and Hulley is here attempting to read too much into Jerome's words.

When different writers have the same name, there can sometimes be an uncertainty about authorship. Jerome points this out in his account of the writings of the apostle John. John was the author of the fourth Gospel and of one epistle (i.e. 1 John). Some people, he says, believe that he wrote two more letters, but these were written by another John, called the Elder or Presbyter.[130] Jerome later refers to a catalogue Papias had made, which distinguished between the two Johns, and states clearly that John the Elder was the author of these two epistles (i.e. 2 & 3 John).[131]

When Jerome discusses the suspicions concerning the authenticity of the Letter to Philemon, he again uses the criterion of internal evidence. Certain critics held that it was not a genuine letter of Paul on account of its brevity, its seemingly inferior subject matter, and its mundane tone. Jerome, however, argues forcefully that if this letter is rejected because

---

128 *De Vir.Illus.* 5 (*PL* 23, 647C-650A): Epistola autem quae fertur ad Hebraeos, non ejus creditur, propter styli sermonisque dissonantiam, sed vel Barnabae, juxta Tertullianum, vel Lucae evangelistae, juxta quosdam vel Clementis Romanae postea Ecclesiae episcopi, quem aiunt ipsi adjunctum sententias Pauli proprio ordinasse et ornasse sermone. Cf Tertullian: *De Pud.* 20.
129 *Art. cit.*, p. 108.
130 *De Vir.Illus.* 9 (*PL* 23, 654-5).
131 *De Vir.Illus.* 18 (*PL* 23, 670).

of its brevity, then other letters must also be rejected, for instance Obadiah, Nahum, Zephaniah, and the rest of the 12 Minor Prophets. He also states that brevity in a document which has in it so much of the beauty of the Gospel, is a sign of its inspiration. Further, many of the other (undisputed) epistles mention mundane, worldly matters, like the cloak left at Troas (2 Tim. 4.13). To suppose that common life is distinct and separate from God is to approach the heresy of Manichaeanism, Jerome warns. Should these powerful arguments based on internal evidence not be enough to convince some people, Jerome also uses one argument based on external evidence – he says that Marcion, who altered many of the epistles of Paul, did not touch the epistle to Philemon,[132] believing it to be genuinely by Paul. If even Marcion believed it to be authentic, Jerome says, then no orthodox Christian should have any reason to doubt it.

Jerome, himself a great stylist, was able to recognise differences of style in two works, and could use this as a method of discerning authorship. He recognised that the book *De Fato* or *Against the Mathematicians*, was obviously the work of a talented man, but it did not seem to him to correspond stylistically (*stylo*) with the *Octavius* of Minucius Felix, to whom the *De Fato* was attributed.[133] Jerome does not, however, go into further detail on these stylistic differences.

Jerome was aware, then, of various criteria of external and internal evidence for judging the authenticity and authorship of books, and availed himself of these criteria at every suitable opportunity, although he was also aware, like any good textual critic, that they must be used with restraint and caution.

Jerome's explicit references to O.T. manuscripts

At this point in our study, we may profitably explore one avenue of Jerome's knowledge and use of textual criticism. It is proposed that all the passages where Jerome explicitly mentions variant readings in manuscripts of his day will be noted and discussed, in order to illuminate his acumen as a textual critic.[134]

---

132 *Comm.Philem.*: Praef. (*PL* 26, 635-8).
133 *De Vir.Illus.* 58 (*PL* 23, 706).
134 On a very few occasions, Jerome refers explicitly to manuscripts of the works of the Church Fathers, which provides us with evidence of textual variation within the works of the Fathers themselves. For example, in *Adv.Iovin.* I, 13 (*PL* 23, 241), Jerome discusses what Gregory of Nazianzus, whom Jerome calls

K.K. Hulley is incorrect when he states that Jerome's *Comm.Hab.* 2, 19f presents a 'perhaps unique' place where Jerome refers to a difference of reading in the Hebrew texts of the O.T.[135] We have, in fact, discovered several explicit references to O.T. manuscripts. Not all of these refer, however, to *Hebrew* manuscripts of the O.T.; some refer to Latin manuscripts, some to Greek manuscripts, and some are indeterminate as regards the language of Jerome's exemplar. In *HQG* there are four explicit references to O.T. manuscripts but none of these specifically mentions 'Hebrew' manuscripts.[136] Most of Jerome's explicit references to O.T. manuscripts are to be found in one of Jerome's most fascinating works, *Ep.* 106, written between 404 and 410[137] to Sunnia and Fretela, two Gothic clergy. These two clergy were perplexed by the many discrepancies between Jerome's Gallican Psalter (based on Origen's *Hexapla*), and the Greek (LXX) text which was current in their area. They had sent Jerome a list of 178 variant readings from 83 Psalms. Jerome's reply in

---

'my teacher' (*praeceptor meus*), says about marriage and virginity. He says: 'I now briefly beg my reader to note that in the Latin manuscripts we have the reading "there is a difference also between the virgin and the wife"...' (*Nunc illud breviter admoneo, in Latinis codicibus hunc locum ita legi: Divisa est virgo et mulier*). It is not possible to trace precisely the passage in question in the works of Gregory of Nazianzus, although it is somewhat similar to *Oration* 37, 10 (*PG* 36, 293C-D).

What is perhaps most interesting about this passage is that the corruption of Gregory's text should have taken place within 12-15 years of its composition (if it comes from the *Orations*). Gregory's *Orations* were composed between the years 379-381, and Jerome's treatise *Adv.Iovin.* was written in 383-4. While it is known that Rufinus translated some of Gregory's *Orations*, it is not known who made the translation of *Orat.* 37. See Quasten: *Patrology* III, 240.

135 K.K. Hulley: 'The Principles of textual criticism known to St. Jerome', in *Harvard Studies in Classical Philology* LV (1944) p. 92. See *Comm.Hab.* 2, 19f (*CCL* 76A, 616: Praeterea sciendum in quibusdam Hebraicis uoluminibus non esse additum, omnis, sed absolute, spiritum legi).

136 *HQG* 3, 8 (*CCL* 72, 5: In plerisque codicibus Latinorum pro eo, quod hic posuimus 'ad vesperam, post meridiem' habet); *HQG* 23, 2 (*CCL* 72, 28: Hoc, quod hic positum est 'quae est in ualle', in authenticis codicibus non habetur); *HQG* 25, 8 (*CCL* 72, 31: Illud quoque, quod nos posuimus 'in senectute bona senex et plenus', in graecis codicibus ponitur 'plenus dierum'); *HQG* 37, 36 (*CCL* 72, 45: In plerisque locis archimagiros [id est cocorum principes] pro magistris exercitus scriptura commemorat: μαγειρεύειν quippe graece interpretatur occidere).

137 On the date of this letter, see Kelly: p. 285f and B. Altaner: 'Wann schrieb Hieronymus seine *Ep.* 106 and Sunniam et Fretelam de Psalterio?' in *Vig.Chr.* 4 (1950) 246-8.

Ep. 106 is, as Kelly says, 'an exhaustive critical examination of all the points raised' and 'a thoroughgoing correction of his Gallican Psalter'.[138] All the explicit references to O.T. manuscripts will be set out below in connection with the Psalm concerned.

1. *Ps. 31:22:* *'I had said in my alarm, "I am driven far from thy sight"'.*[139]

Jerome comments on this verse as follows:

> 'In the same: *ego autem dixi in excessu mentis meae.* For what the Latin codices had: *in pauore meo*, I too translated according to the Greek: ἐν τῇ ἐκστάσει μου, that is, *in excessu mentis meae.* For the Latin cannot express ἔκστασιν except by *"mentis excessum"*. I knew that I had read in the Hebrew the differing version: *in stupore et in admiratione mea.*'[140]

In this passage, the specific reference to manuscripts is to Latin codices, which is the reading of the Gallican Psalter and the Vulgate. The O.L. had read *in pauore meo*, but Jerome admits that he had followed the LXX's reading at this point. Jerome does mention yet another reading, this time in the 'Hebrew' text, but this reading does not appear to be attested by any extant Hebrew manuscript. We might conclude that Jerome has here preserved a witness to a fourth century Hebrew reading, were it not for the fact that his Hebrew Psalter does not have the same reading, but instead: *Ego autem dixi in stupore meo*, with no mention of *et in admiratione mea.* When he cites this phrase in *Ep.* 106, he may well have been attempting to recall the reading of some Hebrew manuscript he had seen but which he did not have in front of him at the time.

---

138 Kelly: p. 285f. For the theory that *Ep.* 106 was a literary fiction and Sunnia and Fretela figments of Jerome's imagination, see D. De Bruyne: 'La lettre de Jérôme à Sunnia et Fretela sur le Psautier', in *ZNTW* 28 (1929) 1-13. Replies to this theory are given in A. Allgeier: 'Der Brief an Sunnia und Fretela und seine Bedeutung für die Textherstellung der Vulgata', in *Biblica* 11 (1930) 80-107, and J. Zeiller: 'La lettre de saint Jérôme aux Goths Sunnia et Fretela', in *Comptes-Rendus de l'Académie des Inscriptions et Belles Lettres* (1934) 338-350.

139 This translation, and those used for headings *infra* are taken from the R.S.V.

140 *Ep.* 106, 18 (*CSEL* 55, 257): Pro quo in Latinis codicibus legebatur: in pauore meo, et nos iuxta Graecum transtulimus: ἐν τῇ ἐκστάσει μου, id est, 'in excessu mentis meae'; aliter enim ἔκστασιν Latinus sermo exprimere non potest nisi 'mentis excessum'. aliter me in Hebraico legisse noueram: in stupore et in admiratione mea.

2. Ps. 35:10: 'All my bones shall say: "O Lord, who is like thee?"'
Jerome's comment on this phrase is:

> '"*Omnia ossa mea dicent, domine*". Here, you say, you have found in the Greek the word "*domine*" twice. It is to be noted, however, that there are many Hebrew copies which have the word "*dominum*" not even once.'[141]

This is the first explicit reference in this letter to 'Hebrew exemplars' which Jerome has consulted. The Greek texts read by the two Goths had κυριε twice, and some Septuagintal texts do have this reading, including some witnesses of the Lucianic Recension.[142] When we come to the 'many Hebrew copies' which omit the divine name, there are no extant Hebrew manuscripts which can confirm Jerome's statement. The Hebrew Psalter reads: *Omnia ossa mea dicent, Domine, quis similis tui?*

3. Ps. 50:22: '"...lest I rend, and there be none to deliver".'
Jerome has:

> '"*ne quando rapiat et sit, qui eripiat*". You say that you have found in the Greek: et non sit, qui eripiat, which I also have translated thus, and is to be found that way in our codices. So I wonder why you blame the translator for the negligence of a sleepy *librarius*, unless perchance the reading is: *ne quando rapiat nec sit, qui eripiat*, so that he wrote *et* for *nec*.'[143]

Although Jerome does not mention what he read in Hebrew texts, this passage is of interest because it shows that he was aware of the dangers of copyists' errors. Here, he asserts that negligence on the part of a 'sleepy *librarius*' who may have read *et* for *nec*, has resulted in the faulty reading which the two Goths have. The Hebrew Psalter has a quite different reading: *ne forte capiam, et non sit qui liberet.*

4. Ps. 68:24: 'Thy solemn processions are seen, O God, the processions of my God, my King, into the sanctuary.'
As part of a very extended comment on this Psalm, Jerome writes:

---

141 *Ep.* 106, 20 (*CSEL* 55, 257): Omnia ossa mea dicent, domine: Pro quo in Graeco bis 'domine' inuenisse uos dicitis. sed sciendum, quod multa sint exemplaria apud Hebraeos, quae ne semel quidem 'dominum' habeant.

142 L', Theodore of Mopsuestia and Codex Alexandrinus. See *Septuaginta*, ed. A. Rahlfs, Göttingen 1931, ad. loc.

143 *Ep.* 106, 30 (*CSEL* 55, 261f): ne quando rapiat et sit, qui eripiat. et in Graeco repperisse uos dicitis: et non sit, qui eripiat, quod et a nobis uersum est et in nostris codicibus sic habetur. et miror, quomodo uitium, librarii dormitantis ad culpam referatis interpretis, nisi forte fuerit hoc: ne quando rapiat nec sit, qui eripiat, et ille pro 'nec' 'et' scripserit.

'*viderunt ingressus tui, deus*', for which you say your Greek has; '*visi sunt ingressus tui, deus*'. The Hebrew has 'rachua alichatach', which Aquila, Symmachus, Theodotion and the Fifth and Sixth editions have translated *uiderunt itinera tua, deus*, and what follows: *itinera dei mei regis, qui est in sancto*. So we should read: *uiderunt ingressus tuos, deus*, and not imitate the mistake of the transcriber who put the nominative instead of the accusative, although in the Septuagint and in the Hexapla I have found ἐθεώρησαν αἴ πορεῖαι σου, ὁ θεός, and for ἐθεώρησαν, that is, '*uiderunt*', in many texts ἐθεωρήθησαν is found, and custom has preserved this reading.'[144]

There are several points of interest in this passage. First, it is clear that the LXX text Jerome was using was that of the Hexapla. Second, Jerome again blames the transcriber (*scriptor*) for the faulty reading, based on an incorrect grammatical case. Third, although he refers briefly to the Hebrew reading, it is the Greek manuscripts to which Jerome turns for his decisive reading. Even after having completed the Hebrew Psalter, Jerome was still prepared to accept the authority of the other versions of the Psalter, and especially if 'custom' – i.e. the custom of the liturgical use of the Psalms in Church – dictated a specific reading, even though that reading may not be the most accurate one. The Hebrew Psalter reads: *Uiderunt itinera tua, Deus: itinera Dei mei, regis mei in sancto*.

5. *Ps. 74:1: 'O God, why dost thou cast us off forever?'*
Jerome offers the following comments:
'*Ut quid, deus, reppulisti in finem?*, for which the Greek with an awkward word-order says: *ut quid reppulisti, deus?* In the same: *quanta malignatus est inimicus in sancto*! (vs 3) I wonder who has corrected a mistake into your codex by substituting *sanctis* for *sancto?*, since my codex also has the form *in sancto*. In the same: *incendamus omnes deis festos dei a terra*, for which the Greek has καταπαύσωμεν, and I translated: *quiescere faciamus omnes dies festos*

---

144 *Ep.* 106, 41 (*CSEL* 55, 266): uiderunt ingressus tui, deus, pro quo in Graeco scriptum sit: uisi sunt ingressus tui, deus. in Hebraeo ita habet: 'rachua alichatach', quod Aquila et Symmachus et Theodotio et quinta sextaque editio interpretati sunt: uiderunt itinera tua, deus, et, quod sequitur: itinera dei mei regis, qui est in sancto. ergo a nobis ita legendum est: uiderunt ingressus tuos, deus, et scriptoris uitium relinquendum, qui nominatiuum posuit pro accusitiuo, licet in Septuaginta et in Ἑξαπλοῖς ita repperim: ἐθεώρησαν αἴ πορεῖαι σου, ὁ θεός, et pro eo, quod est ἐθεώρησαν, hoc est 'uiderunt', in multis codicibus habet ἐθεωρήθησαν, quod et obtinuit consuetudo.

dies a terra. I wonder why some rash person has thought that the note: "the correct form is not καταπαύσωμεν, as some think, but κατακαύσωμεν, that is, *incendamus*," which was placed by me in the margin for the guidance of the reader, should be put into the body of the text... Thus, whenever anything has been added in the margin for the sake of note-taking, this should not be put into the body of the text, in order not to corrupt the original translation according to the whim of the copyists.'[145]

Once again, Jerome lays the blame for a variant reading at the feet of the transcribers, this time for writing *sanctis* instead of *sancto*. The language of the codex Jerome mentions is, of course, Latin, and not Hebrew. Perhaps the most interesting point about this long passage is the note concerning the inclusion of a marginal note of Jerome's into the text of a manuscript. This is the only reference in Jerome's writings to his practice of making marginal notes.[146] The accidental changing of κατακαύσωμεν to καταπαύσωμεν would be a very easy mistake for a scribe to make, and extant LXX manuscripts attest to this confusion. Jerome cannot help laying down regulations for copyists about not including marginal notes into the text of manuscripts.

6. *Ps. 80:9: '...it took deep root and filled the land.'*
Jerome's brief comment is as follows:
'*et plantasti radices eius hinc*. You say that '*hinc*' does not occur in the Greek. That is good, for it does not occur in our codices either, and so, I am wondering which unskilled man has falsified your books.'[147]

---

[145] *Ep.* 106, 41 (*CSEL* 55, 269f): Ut quid, deus, reppulisti in finem: pro quo male apud Graecos legitur ordine commutato: ut quid reppulisti, deus? in eodem: quanta malignatus est inimicus in sancto! miror, quis in codice uestro emendando peruerterit, ut pro 'sancto' 'sanctis' posuerit, cum et in nostro codice 'in sancto' inueniatur. in eodem: incendamus omnes dies festos dei a terra. pro quo in Graeco scriptum est καταπαύσωμεν et nos ita transtulimus: quiescere faciamus omnes dies festos dei a terra. et miror, quomodo e latere adnotationem nostram nescio quis temerarius scribendam in corpore putauerit, quam nos pro eruditione legentis scripsimus hoc modo: non habet καταπαύσωμεν, ut quidam putant, sed κατακαύσωμεν, id est incendamus... Unde, si quid pro studio e latere additum est, non debet poni in corpore, ne priorem translationem pro scribentium uoluntate conturbet.
[146] For the practice in antiquity of marginal notation, see B.M. Metzger: *The Text of the New Testament*, Oxford 1968, pp. 17-21.
[147] *Ep.* 106, 52 (*CSEL* 55, 274): et plantasti radices eius hinc. et dicitis, quod in Graeco 'hinc' non habeat; et bene, nam et in nostris codicibus non habetur; et miror, quis inperitorum uestros libros falsauerit.

This explicit reference to O.T. manuscripts is to Latin copies. Again, as in the majority of the explicit references to O.T. manuscripts, Jerome lays the blame for variant readings on faulty copying by scribes. None of the extant Hebrew manuscripts read *hinc*, and the Hebrew Psalter has: *et stabilisti radices eius, et impleuit terram*. Jerome makes no explanation of why '*hinc*' came to be in the text.

7. Ps. 116:2: *'Therefore I will call on him as long as I live.'*
Commenting on Sunnia's and Fretela's query on Gallican Psalter 114:2 (Hebrew Psalter 116:2), Jerome says:
> '*et in diebus meis inuocabo te*. You say that '*te*' is not in the Greek, and that is good. Hence it should be erased from your codices.'[148]

This brief comment has interest because Jerome agrees with Sunnia's and Fretela's reading at this point, and actively encourages them to amend their codices. The Hebrew Psalter also omits the '*te*'.

8. Ps.116:2: *'All nations surrounded me; in the name of the Lord, I cut them off.'*
In reply to Sunnia's and Fretela's minor query, Jerome has:
> '*et in nomine domini, quia ultus sum in eos*. You say that *quia* is not found in the Greek codices. It should be added, however, in the Latin under an asterisk.'[149]

Here, the 'Greek codices' refer to the LXX copies which the Goths have, but none of the extant LXX manuscripts witness to this reading. The LXX reads καὶ τῷ ὀνόματι κυρίου ἠμυνάμην αὐτούς.

Jerome's explicit references to N.T. manuscripts

When we come to discuss Jerome and the manuscripts of the N.T., we must again restrict ourselves to his explicit references to manuscripts, either Greek or Latin, of the N.T. B.M. Metzger's article[150] has discussed

---

148 *Ep*. 106, 73 (*CSEL* 55, 285): et in diebus meis inuocabo te. dicitis, quod in Graeco non sit 'te', et bene; e uestris quoque codicibus eradendum est.
149 *Ep*. 106, 74 (*CSEL* 55, 285): et in nomine domini, quia ultus sum in eos. dicitis 'quia' in Graecis codicibus non inueniri; sed et in Latinis sub asterisco legendum est.
150 Published originally in *Text and Interpretation: Studies in the New Testament presented to Matthew Black*, ed. E. Best and R. McL. Wilson, Cambridge 1979, 179-190; republished in B.M. Metzger: *New Testament Studies: Philological, Versional, Patristic*, Leiden 1980, 199-210.

some 27 explicit references in Jerome's works to manuscripts of the N.T.,[151] but this list is incomplete. We will discuss below a further eight examples of Jerome's explicit references to N.T. manuscripts. These will be given (following Metzger) in canonical order.

1. Matt. 5:25: 'Make friends quickly with your accuser, while you are going to court...'
Jerome says, in *Comm.Matt.*, that 'in Latin codices we have *consentiens*, which in Greek writing is εὐνοῶν, which means 'benevolent' or 'benign'.[152] Here, the 'Latin codices' must refer to O.L. texts, most of which read '*consentiens*'.[153] The Vulgate also reads *consentiens*.

2. Matt. 22:3: 'He sent his servants to call those who had been invited to the marriage feast...'
Jerome comments that 'if we read *servos*, as most copies have, it refers to the prophets'.[154] Jerome has here chosen the minority reading, (*servum suum*) as the correct one, even though he knows that 'most copies' have the plural *servos suos*. In reading the singular at this point, Jerome may be trying to harmonise this verse with the singular reading in Luke 14:17, the parallel version of the story of the wedding feast. Although the singular is preferred by Jerome here, the Vulgate reads *servos suos*. It is interesting to note that, in his application of the plural reading to the prophets, Jerome is following Origen, who prefers the plural reading δουλοί.[155]

---

[151] B.M. Metzger's list consists of the following references: Matt. 5:22 (*Adv. Pel.* II, 7; *Comm.Matt.* 5, 22); 6:25 (*Comm.Matt.* 6, 25); 11:19 (*Comm.Matt.* 11, 19); 11:23 (*Comm.Matt.* 11, 23); 13:35 (*Comm.Matt.* 13, 35); 16:2-3 (*Comm.Matt.* 16, 2f); 21:31 (*Comm.Matt.* 21, 31); 24:36 (*Comm.Matt.* 24, 36); Mk. 16:9 (*Ep.* 120, 3); 16:14 (?); Lk. 14:27 (*Ep.* 127, 6); 22:43f (*Adv. Pel.* II, 16); Jn. 7:53-8:11 (*Adv. Pel.* II, 17); Acts 15:29 (*Comm.Gal.* 5, 2); Rom. 12:11 (*Ep.* 27, 1); Rom. 16:25-7 (*Comm.Ephes.* 3, 5); I Cor. 9:5 (*Adv.Iovin.* 1, 26); 13:3 (*Comm.Gal.* 5, 25); 15:51 (*Ep.* 119, 2); Gal. 2:5 (*Comm.Gal.* 2, 5); 3:1 (*Comm.Gal.* 3, 1); Eph. 3:14 (*Comm.Ephes.* 3, 14); Eph. 5:22 (*Comm.Ephes.* 5, 22); Col. 2:18 (*Ep.* 121, 10); I Tim. 1:15 and 3:1 (*Ep.* 27, 3); Heb. 2:9 (?).
[152] *Comm.Matt.* 5, 25 (*CCL* 77, 29): Pro eo quod nos in latinis codicibus habemus consentiens, in graecis scriptum est εὐνοῶν, quod interpretatur beniuolus aut benignus.
[153] See S.C.E. Legg: *Novum Testamentum Graece*, Oxford 1940; A. Jülicher: *Itala: I Matthäus – Evangelium*, Berlin 1938.
[154] *Comm.Matt.* 22, 3 (*CCL* 77, 200): Si autem seruos legerimus ut pluraque habent examplaria, ad prophetas referendum est.
[155] Origen: *In Matt.* XVII, 15 (*GCS* 40, 628).

3. Luke 22:37: '...and he was reckoned with transgressors...'
In the *Comm.Gal.*, while discussing the matter of Christ's sinlessness even though he was born 'under the Law' (Gal. 4:4), Jerome refers to Lk. 22:37b, a quotation from Isa. 53:12: 'He was reckoned among the transgressors'. Concerning this verse, Jerome says that the Latin codices may be misleading because the word used for 'transgressor' in Latin – *iniquus* – is inadequate for translating the Greek ἄνομος. The correct Greek word for what 'we have in the Latin volumes' would be ἄδικος, for ἄνομος means 'he who is without the Law', while ἄδικος means 'truly unjust'.[156] Although this is perhaps more of a linguistic comment than a text-critical one, it is still worthy of mention here, because it shows that Jerome was fully aware of the textual critic's duty to transmit accurately what was read in his exemplars, even though he may have occasion to doubt that the best textual reading in a secondary language (Latin manuscripts rather than Greek) may not always transmit accurately the precise meaning intended by the original author. No extant Greek or Latin manuscript supports Jerome's reading. The Vulgate reads *Et quod cum iniustis deputatus est*.

4. John 1:45: 'We have found... Jesus of Nazareth, son of Joseph.'
In his treatise *Adv.Helvid.*, on the perpetual virginity of the Blessed Virgin Mary, Jerome makes the following remark in castigating Helvidius' understanding of the scriptural passage where Mary and Joseph are referred to as Jesus' parents:

> 'As you are foolish enough to persuade yourself that the Greek manuscripts are corrupt, perhaps you will plead the variety of readings. I come therefore to the Gospel of John, where it is plainly written: "Philip found Nathaniel and said to him: 'We have found him of whom Moses in the Law and also the Prophets wrote, Jesus of Nazareth, son of Joseph'". You will certainly find this in your manuscript.'[157]

Jerome uses this passage to show Helvidius that, just as this reference to Jesus' father could not mean his *real* father (who was God in the person of the Holy Spirit), so the reference to Jesus' 'brothers' (Matt. 13:55; Mk. 6:3) should not be understood literally. It is difficult to know what Jerome may have meant by his rather vague reference to 'the Greek manuscripts'. Extant manuscripts witness no difficulty with Jn. 1:46, and while in Matt. 13:55 some witnesses read Ἰωσῆς for Ἰωσῆφ, it seems very unlikely that this is what Jerome is referring to. It may just

---

156 *Comm.Gal.* 4, 4f (*PL* 26, 398D).
157 *Adv.Helv.* 16 (*PL* 23, 211A).

be possible that Jerome is referring to the variant in Mk. 6:3, where some witnesses (including ℵ, A, B, C, D, K, fl, p⁴⁵) read τέκτονος, ὁ υἱός, – 'Is not this *the son* of the carpenter, the son of Mary.', instead of 'Is not this the carpenter, the son of Mary...'. Jerome refers to this passage earlier in the passage just quoted. Certainly, as early as the time of Celsus, non-Christians derided Jesus' occupation as a carpenter, and the variant reading was probably included to lessen the effect of this criticism.[158]

5. Gal. 3:13: 'Cursed be everyone who hangs on a tree'

In the *Comm.Gal.*, Jerome cites an otherwise unknown variant for 'Cursed be everyone who hangs on a tree' (Deut. 21:23 as quoted in Gal. 3:13). What is interesting about this variant is that Jerome claims to have read it in the (now lost) *Altercation between Papiscus and Jason*. The variant, as Jerome remembers it, (*memini me*) reads: λοιδορία θεοῦ ὁ κρεμάμενος, *id est, maledictio Dei qui appensus est*. After a lengthy discussion of the meaning of the word *maledictum*, Jerome concludes by rejecting the variant which includes the divine name, because it must have been added in order to bring disgrace to Christians:

> '...in our codices, the name of God is added by someone, so that disgrace is branded on us.'[159]

Because Jerome uses the plural – 'our codices' – it may be that the variant which Jerome says he read in the *Altercation* had corrupted other manuscripts current in Jerome's day but not now extant.

---

[158] See Origen: *C.Celsum* VI, 34 and 36. Origen replied erroneously 'In none of the Gospels current in the churches is Jesus ever described as a carpenter'. B.M. Metzger suggests that Origen may not have remembered Mk. 6:3, or the text of this verse in copies known to him had already been assimilated to the Matthean parallel. (*A Textual Commentary on the Greek New Testament*, London 1971, p. 89.)

[159] *Comm.Gal.* 3, 13 (*PL* 26, 388C): in nostris codicibus ab aliquo Dei nomen appositum, ut infamiam nobis inureret... Jerome also mentions the *Altercation between Papiscus and Jason* in *QHG* 1, 1 (*CCL* 72, 3), where he says that, at Gen. 1:1, it read: 'In filio fecit Deus caelum et terram', which Jerome rejects, noting that Tertullian in *Adversus Praxean* and Hilary in '*expositione cuiusdam psalmi*' give the reading found in the *Altercation*. Jerome is, in fact, incorrect in his attribution to Tertullian and Hilary. The *Altercation* was known to Origen (*C.Celsum* IV, 52), and, according to Maximus the Confessor (*Scholia in Lib. de Mystica Theologia* I [*PG* 4, 421-2]), also to Clement of Alexandria, who, in the sixth book of the *Hypotyposes* (now also lost), attributed it to Luke the evangelist. J.E. Bruns claims to have rediscovered a portion of the *Altercation* in the work of the seventh century writer, Anastasius the Sinaite. See *Theological Studies* 34 (1973) pp 287-294.

6. *Gal. 5:7: 'You were running well; who hindered you from obeying the truth?'*

In the *Comm.Gal.* on this verse, Jerome makes the following comment:
> 'Now the Latin translator has put: "*veritati non obedire*" here, as it is written in Greek, τῇ ἀληθείᾳ μὴ πείθεσθαι; so in the above place it is to be translated, *non credere veritati* (Gal. 3:1). But because we do not have it in the ancient codices, we may make a mark in that place, for the Greek exemplars have made this error.'[160]

This passage shows well Jerome's good text-critical practice, for one of the basic principles of textual criticism is that the older the text, the higher the probability that it exhibits a text close to the original.[161] Here, Jerome rejects the reading 'not to obey the truth' for Gal. 3:1 because it is not included in the 'ancient codices'. Jerome also suggests that, in manuscripts which do include the reading, an emendation should be made in order to show readers that it is an addition to the original text. Jerome is presumably thinking of the *sigla* which Origen used in his *Hexapla*. The addition of τῇ ἀληθείᾳ μὴ πείθεσθαι to Gal. 3:1 (from 5: 7) is attested by many manuscripts, including the Textus Receptus, following C, D^c, K, L, P, Ψ, and most minuscules. The Vulgate at Gal. 3:1 does not include the phrase.

7. *Gal. 5:9: 'A little leaven leavens the whole lump.'*

In his commentary to this verse, Jerome gives the reading 'A little leaven leavens (*fermentat*) the whole dough (*conspersionem*)', and then comments:
> 'In our codices we wrongly have: "A little leaven corrupts (*corrumpit*) the whole lump", and the interpreter preferred his own thought to the words of the Apostle.'[162]

This expression may well have been a proverbial one, and Jerome reports correctly that the reading *corrumpit* in 'our codices' is incorrect. In some texts with Western characteristics, Ζυμοῖ is replaced by δολοῖ (D*, it^d, goth, Marcion, Marius Victorinus and Ambrosiaster). Tertullian (*De Pudic.* 13, 25 and 18, 8) reads *desipiat consparsionem*. This reading may be explained by saying that if it was a proverbial saying,

---

160 *Comm.Gal.* 5, 7 (*PL* 26, 428D).
161 See B.F. Westcott and F.J.A. Hort: *The Greek New Testament* II, pp. 4-11; 44; B.M. Metzger: *The Text of the N.T.*, p. 209.
162 *Comm.Gal.* 5, 9 (*PL* 26, 429C): Modicum fermentum totam conspersionem fermentat. Male in nostris codicibus habetur: 'Modicum fermentum totam massam corrumpit', et sensum potius interpres suum, quam verba Apostoli transtulit.

then there may well have been another (negative) form of it. The same reading occurs in Western witnesses at 1 Cor. 5:6, where Paul quotes from the text again. The Vulgate at both verses reads *modicum fermentum totam massam corrumpit*.

8. *Titus 3:10: 'As for a man who is factious, after admonishing him once or twice, have nothing more to do with him.'*

The chief interest of this passage is Jerome's reference to Athanasius. He says:

> 'We read in Latin codices (which also Bishop Athanasius approved of as the true reading): After reproaching him once and another time, for it is evidently not sufficient to reform him to such a degree only once...'[163]

Textually, the reading which Jerome prefers at this point is slightly different from almost all the extant manuscripts. Jerome reads *alter* instead of *secundus*, which would translate the Greek ἕτερος, rather than the δευτέρος of all Greek manuscripts. We may be led to believe from this that some Latin codices which Jerome had seen, and which he knew that Athanasius had also seen, read *alter* in the text, and so presupposed an underlying Greek exemplar which read ἕτερος rather than δευτέρος. None of the extant Greek witnesses reads ἕτερος and Jerome is alone in his attestation. Athanasius, although he quotes the verse twice, never cites this reading,[164] and the Vulgate reads *post unam et secundam correptionem*.

Conclusions

We have studied in some detail the methods and techniques utilised by Jerome in his textual criticism of the Bible. It is quite clear, from every page of his commentaries, that the first task of the exegete must be to establish the most accurate scriptural text possible. This is possible for Jerome only by detailed examination of a number of manuscripts. These, where possible, should be in the original language – Hebrew or Greek – but if these are not available then the most reliable versions from other languages should be used.

---

163 *Comm.Titum* 3, 10 (*PL* 26, 633B): Legitur in Latinis codicibus (quod verum Papa quoque Athanasius approbabat): 'Post unam et alteram correptionem', quod scilicet non sufficiat tantum semel eum corrigi...

164 Athanasius (c A.D. 295-373) both times reads δευτέρος (*Ep. ad Max.Phil.* 1; *Ep. ad Adel. Episc.* 2 [*PG* 26, 1085; 1073]).

We have shown that Jerome took over some of the principles of textual criticism – especially the use of critical *sigla* – from Origen (who had, in turn, adapted these from classical usage). Jerome, however, went further than Origen in his principles of textual criticism. He certainly used Origen's *sigla*, but he was more thorough-going in his use of these *sigla*, because Origen had used them simply in order to establish his Hexaplaric text, while Jerome utilised them as an aid to his exegesis. In his commentaries and letters, Jerome often used the critical *sigla* at the beginning of his comment on a passage, in order to establish the correct text. Only after he has done this will Jerome continue with a discussion of the meaning(s) of the passage. This practice of Jerome's is so frequent that we need cite only one example, from *Ep.* 106:

> 'Ps. 17: *Grando et carbones ignis*, and you ask why in the Greek text it does not have this little verse a second time two lines later. It is to be noted, however, that this one has been added in the Septuagint, under an asterisk from the Hebrew and the text of Theodotion... In the same (Psalm): *uiuit dominus et benedictus deus meus*. You say that in the Greek *"meus"* is lacking. This has not been added under an asterisk, but has been translated from the Hebrew by the very translators of the Septuagint, and all translators agree on this point.'[165]

In our discussion of Jerome's use of the methods and techniques of textual criticism, we have already seen clearly the principles he enunciates. For instance, Jerome is clear that the older a manuscript is, the more likely it is to contain a correct reading. Also, in connection with judging the authenticity of a particular writing or author, Jerome is guided by three criteria:[166]

a) *the character or style of writing.* Jerome, as a great stylist himself would be quick to see the importance of this for judging authenticity.

b) *the sense of a passage.* By this, Jerome means that the ideas expressed in a book or passage are characteristic of an author. If, therefore, when comparing two works, opposing ideas are evident, it is unlikely that the same author was responsible for both works.

---

165 *Ep.* 106, 9 (*CSEL* 55, 253): Septimo decimo: grando et carbones ignis. et quaeritis, cur Graecus istum uersiculum secundum non habeat interpositis duobus uersibus, sed sciendum, quia de Hebraico et Theodotionis editione in septuaginta interpretibus sub asterisco additum sit... in eodem: uiuit dominus et benedictus deus meus. et dicitis in Graeco non haberi 'meus'. quod non sub asterisco, sed ab ipsis Septuaginta de Hebraica ueritate translatum est; et cuncti interpretes in hac parte consentiunt.

166 See above, p. 39f, on the authorship of the *Epistle of the Hebrews* and its possible connection with the *Epistle of Clement of Rome to the Corinthians*.

c) *the word order.* Again, like the characteristic ideas in a passage, the order of words which a particular author used may be characteristic, and thus can be used as a criterion to determine authenticity.

Jerome nowhere states explicitly his principles of textual criticism, but we have attempted to show in this chapter that Jerome was acutely aware of these principles, and that he used them in a way that enhanced his exegesis. For Jerome, the practice of textual criticism was fundamental to any discussion of the meaning of a passage, for without a sound text on which to work, it would be pointless to attempt an exegesis of the scripture. Another issue of fundamental importance for Jerome as an initial step towards the exegesis of scripture was a knowledge of the original languages of the Bible, Hebrew and Greek, and his use of the Hebrew canon of the O.T. This will be our concern in the next chapter.

3. Jerome and the Hebraica Veritas

Jerome astonished the fourth century Christian world in his attempt to re-establish the Hebrew text of the O.T. as authoritative for exegesis, in opposition to the Greek version, the Septuagint, which had been hallowed by three centuries of Christian use. Jerome's persistence with his belief in the correctness and authenticity of what he termed the *Hebraica veritas* (that is, the Hebrew text and the meaning conveyed by it, which is the truth), in the face of considerable criticism, is a memorial to his scholarly integrity and resolute convictions. In the course of this chapter, we will trace the reasons behind Jerome's decision to read the *Hebraica veritas*, and the two important manifestations of this – his acceptance of the biblical canon of the Jews, and his decision to translate and interpret the O.T. direct from the Hebrew. We shall also ask whether Jerome knew the Aramaic language.

Jerome and the Septuagint

The roots of Christianity are buried deep within the rich soil of Judaism. It is natural, therefore, that the scriptures to which the apostles and their followers appealed should be those of Judaism. The predominance of the Gentile element within Christianity meant that it was to the *Greek* version of Jewish scripture that Christians went for inspiration and guidance. In fact, the Septuagint (LXX) was appropriated with such enthusiasm by the early Christian Church that there were serious ramifications for Judaism.[1] One of the principal uses to which the LXX was put was in Christian anti-Jewish polemic. Two famous examples of this were at Isa. 7:14 and Ps. 96:10 (LXX 95:10). In the Isaiah passage, the word עלמה had been translated as παρθένος which, as the Christians correctly held, was not a Christian mistranslation, but had originated with the Jewish translators themselves. The Jews also correctly rejected it as an inaccurate translation. In the text of Ps. 96:10, a Christian hand had added the words 'from the tree' to the Hebrew original, 'The Lord

---

[1] See B.J. Roberts: *The Old Testament Text and Versions*, Cardiff 1951, pp. 117-9.

reigns'. Justin Martyr believed that this additional phrase was original and accordingly accused the Jews of having maliciously excised it.[2] Further, the use of the LXX by Christians eventually led to a discrediting of the Greek bible among Jews, which in turn led to a revival of interest among scholarly Jews in the Hebrew text. This Hebrew text quickly became important and even Diaspora Jews, who could no longer read Hebrew, disregarded the LXX.[3]

The LXX was not, however, the only Greek version of the O.T. The existence of different Greek versions and of recensions of the LXX is attested both by Origen and Jerome.[4] Origen's ambitious enterprise of compiling a six-column *Hexapla*, comprises of 1) the current Hebrew text, 2) a transliteration of this in Greek letters, 3) Aquila's version, 4) Symmachus' version, 5) his own revised LXX text and 6) Theodotion's version. It is appropriate here to say a little about each of these Greek versions and also the recensions mentioned by Jerome.

The version of Aquila arose in part because of the Christian appropriation of the LXX.[5] It was felt by some Jews that a Greek version which would give an accurate reflection of the Hebrew text was required. Aquila, who was probably a proselyte from Pontus in Asia (d. c A.D. 150),[6] provided this in an extremely literal translation of the Hebrew. Influenced by R. Akiba and his school of strict exegesis, where every particle and detail of the Hebrew text was sacred, Aquila attempted to reproduce the Hebrew word for word in Greek, with no regard for Greek grammar or syntax. Some scholars have attempted to identify Aquila with Onqelos, the reputed compiler of the Targum to the Pentateuch,[7] while D. Barthélemy identifies Aquila with Onqelos but denies that he was responsible for an Aramaic Targum. Barthélemy argues that the Greek leather scroll of the Minor Prophets found at Mu-

---

[2] Justin: *Dial.* 71, 81. S. Jellicoe: *The Septuagint in Modern Study*, Oxford 1968, p. 75; F.G. Kenyon & A.W. Adams: *The Text of the Greek Bible*, London 1975, p. 17.

[3] H.B. Swete: *Introduction to the Old Testament in Greek*, Oxford 1902, p. 462; Jellicoe: *op.cit.*, pp. 74-6.

[4] For Origen, see particularly on the Hexapla, F. Field: *Origenis Hexaplorum quae supersunt*, 2 Vols, Oxford 1875; Jerome: cf for example, *Ep.* 32, 1 (*CSEL* 54, 252); *Comm.Isa.* 49, 5f; *Comm.Osee.* 2, 16f (*CCL* 73A, 536f; 76, 28f); *Praef. in Paral.* (*PL* 28, 1392f).

[5] Jellicoe: *op.cit.*, p. 76.

[6] Epiph.: *De mens. et pond.* 14ff; Ps. Athan.: *Syn.script.sacr.* 77; *Dial. between Timothy and Aquila*, xxvff; Jer.: *De VirIllus.* 54 (*PL 23, 702)*; cf Swete: *op.cit.*, pp. 31-42; Jellicoe: *op.cit.*, pp. 76-83.

[7] Notably A.E. Silverstone: *Aquila and Onkelos*, Manchester 1931.

rabba'at bears witness to an antecedent revision (named *Kaigé* by Barthélemy) of the LXX toward the Hebrew text that Aquila both knew and used.[8]

Jerome was impressed by Aquila's fidelity to his task of providing a literal translation.[9] He made occasional use of Aquila's interpretation of obscure Hebrew words, and in a few cases borrowed readings from him direct.[10]

H.St.J. Thackeray described Theodotion as 'a successful plagiarist... best known for his habit of transliteration, in other words for the evasion of the translator's function'.[11] As with Aquila, details of the life and person of Theodotion are scanty. Irenaeus says that Theodotion came from Ephesus and was a proselyte to Judaism,[12] while Jerome says that he was an Ebionite.[13] Scholars now think it more likely that Theodotion was a Jew of the Diaspora who for a time became loosely attached to Christianity (hence the origin of the Ebionite tradition) but whose Jewish training, too strong to be permanently overcome, finally brought him back to his native faith.[14] Barthélemy identifies Theodotion with Jonathan ben 'Uzziel.[15]

Theodotion's version of Daniel supplanted the LXX version early in the Christian era. The reason for this supercession of the LXX was unknown to Jerome, who comments on the matter and adds: 'This one thing I can affirm – that it differs widely from the original, and is rightly rejected.'[16]

It now seems certain that this second century Theodotion was preceded in his work of revision by a person in the first century B.C. or A.D., termed 'Ur-Theodotion' by modern scholars. This is because 'Theodotionic' readings have been evidenced in writings which antedate the time of the second century Theodotion.[17] One recent scholar has said that the Theodotionic revision of the book of Exodus is to be identified with the *Kaigé* recension discovered by Barthélemy.[18] Barthélemy him-

---

8 D. Barthélemy: *Les Devanciers d'Aquila*, Leiden 1963, pp. 148-154, 246-252.
9 E.g. *Comm.Isa.* 49, 5f (*CCL* 73A, 536f).
10 E.g. *Ep.* 57, 11 (*CSEL* 54, 524); F. Field: *op.cit.*, Vol. 1, p. xxivf; Jellicoe: *op.cit.*, p. 80f.
11 *The Septuagint and Jewish Worship: A Study in Origins*, 2nd Ed., London 1923, p. 14.
12 *Haer.* iii, 21, 1; cf Eus.: *HE* V, 8, 10.
13 *De Vir.Illus.* 54 (*PL* 23, 702).
14 Jellicoe: *op.cit.*, p. 84.
15 *Op.cit.*, pp. 148-154.
16 *Praef. ad Dan.* (*PL* 28, 1357); cf *Apol.* 2, 33 (*CCL* 79, 70).
17 See the discussion in Jellicoe: *op.cit.*, pp. 84ff.
18 K. O'Connell: *The Theodotionic Revision of the Book of Exodus*, Cambridge Mass. 1972.
19 *Op.cit.*, p. 156f.

self raises the possibility that the readings assigned to Theodotion in the Minor Prophets derive from neither the traditional Theodotion nor from an Ur-Theodotion, but from some other translator altogether.[19]

The third of the Greek versions of the O.T. is that of Symmachus. Epiphanius says that he lived in the time of Severus (A.D. 193-211) and speaks of him as a Samaritan who submitted to recircumcision and became a Jewish proselyte.[20] Eusebius says he was an Ebionite[21] and Jerome also has this tradition[22], which is borne out by the existence of the Ebionite commentary on Matthew's Gospel bearing his name, along with the references in Ambrosiaster and Augustine to the Ebionite sect, the Symmachians.[23]

Symmachus' version is marked, as Jerome noted,[24] by a much more elegant style than either Aquila or Theodotion, and it is thought that Symmachus intended to recast Aquila's very literal translation into idiomatic Greek with a free use of other sources, including the LXX and Theodotion. Against this view, Barthélemy argues that Symmachus is more faithful to the Hebrew text than is Aquila or Theodotion, and, at least for the Minor Prophets, is probably not dependent on Aquila for his translation, although Barthélemy does not dispute Symmachus' knowledge of Aquila in 'certain other books'.[25]

In addition to the Hexapla of Origen, Jerome mentions two other recensions of the LXX current in his day, by Lucian and Hesychius. The Lucian whom Jerome mentions was probably a presbyter at Antioch who suffered martyrdom in A.D. 311 or 312. Born at Samosata c A.D. 240 of Christian parents, he studied at Edessa and Antioch. He was for a time suspected of Adoptionism, but was restored and eventually became leader of the Antiochene exegetical school.[26]

Lucian's recension is characterised by its lucidity, comprehensiveness and tendency towards stylistic purity by replacing Hellenistic forms of Greek by Attic. Because it often revises the LXX in favour of better Greek style and includes reading from various sources, the Lucianic text often has 'double readings'. The sources of these revised readings are, however, of unequal worth. In the Prophets, the text seems to be no

---

20 *De mens. et pond.* 15.
21 *HE* VI, 17.
22 *De Vir.Illus.* 54 (*PL* 23, 702); cf *Comm.Hab.* 3, 13 (*CCL* 76A, 641).
23 Ambrosiaster: *Comm.Gal.*: Prol.; Aug.: *C.Faustum Manich.* XIX, 4.
24 E.g. *Comm.Amos* 3, 11 (*CCL* 76, 250f).
25 *Op.cit.*, pp. 261-5.
26 Some of this data is disputed by some scholars. See the discussion in Jellicoe: *op.cit.*, p. 157f, and Jerome: *Praef. in Paral.* (*PL* 28, 1392f).

more than an expansion of the Hexapla text with further insertions from Aquila, Theodotion, and (especially) Symmachus. In Samuel, however, the Lucianic text appears to preserve elements of great antiquity, so that Barthélemy has argued that in certain parts of Samuel-Kings, the Lucianic text is essentially only the ancient LXX text debased and corrupted.[27] Some scholars have traced the existence of 'Lucianic' readings which antedate the historical Lucian, and this has occasioned the hypothesis of an Ur- or Proto-Lucian.[28]

The Hesychius mentioned by Jerome[29] is commonly thought to have been the Egyptian bishop of that name who, according to Eusebius,[30] was martyred at Alexandria, presumably during the persecution of Diocletian in the first decade of the fourth century. However, Jerome speaks of him with less respect than one would expect for a martyr-bishop, and, as a Hesychian text is not extant as such, the subject is surrounded by speculation and controversy.[31] Also debated is the extent to which existing manuscripts preserve the Hesychian recension. Some scholars believe that the Hesychian recension is primarily extant in Codex Vaticanus, while others have taken Codex Marchalianus as the primary representative.

In addition to these recensions mentioned by Jerome, it is now clear that other revisions, both pre- and post-hexaplaric, existed in the early centuries. M.L. Margolis, in his work on the text of Joshua, discovered evidence of another recension which was apparently popular in Constantinople and Asia Minor.[32] Similarly, A. Rahlfs isolated two recensions in Ruth, Judges and Samuel-Kings.[33]

This, then is the background against which we must study Jerome's attitude to the LXX. Jerome makes a number of interesting comments about the LXX, and it will be useful to examine some of these briefly.

In the preface to the translation of Chronicles (LXX) in A.D. 389, Jerome says:

'In the Greek and Latin manuscripts this book of names is so de-

---

[27] *Op.cit.*, p 126f; cf Jellicoe: *op.cit.*, p. 170f.
[28] E. Tov: 'Lucian and Proto-Lucian – Toward a new Solution of the Problem', in *RB* 79 (1972) 101-113.
[29] *Praef. in Paral.* (*PL* 28, 1392f).
[30] *HE* VIII, 13.
[31] For a full discussion, see Jellicoe: *op.cit.*, pp. 146-156.
[32] M.L. Margolis: *The Book of Joshua in Greek*, 4 Vols, Paris 1931-8 and other works mentioned in Jellicoe: *op.cit.*, p. 278-280.
[33] A. Rahlfs: *Das Buch Ruth griechisch als Probe einer kritischen Handausgabe der Septuaginta*, Stuttgart 1922; *Septuaginta-Studien*, 3 Vols, Göttingen 1904-1911.

fective that one would think that it was compiled of barbarian and Sarmatian names rather than Hebrew ones. But this is not because of the Seventy translators, who, filled with the Holy Spirit, transcribed the true text, but to the faults of the copyists.'[34]

Here, even after having studied Hebrew for some years, Jerome defends the divine inspiration and authority of the LXX, ascribing its errors to copyists.

In the same year (A.D. 389) Jerome wrote his first biblical commentary. This commentary on Ecclesiastes is an important milestone in the history of exegesis, for it is the first Latin commentary to be based on the Hebrew text. In the preface Jerome says:

'...here briefly reminding you that I have not followed anyone's authority, but, translating from the Hebrew, I have preferred to conjoin myself to the Seventy interpreters only in those places where they have not diverged greatly from the Hebrew. I have sometimes referred to Aquila, Symmachus and Theodotion so as not to deter the reader's interest by too much novelty, nor, on the other hand, to follow the streams of opinions, omitting, against my conscience, the source of truth.'[35]

This shows that Jerome has a somewhat ambivalent attitude towards the LXX. He was prepared to base his first commentary on the Hebrew text (the 'source of truth'), but still believes the LXX to be of great importance. Jerome was both a great scholar, who knew that the Hebrew text was the original one, and also a great churchman, who had been brought up to believe that the LXX was the inspired scripture. In the other extracts we shall quote below, we will see that this ambivalent attitude is never really resolved in Jerome's mind.

In the preface to the *Qaest.Heb. in Gen.*, written in A.D. 391, Jerome discusses the origins of the LXX and gives sound historical reasons for being cautious in the use of the LXX.[36] Some parts of the LXX are more reliable than others with respect to the fidelity of their translation.

---

[34] *PL* 29, 424: ...et in Graecis et Latinis codicibus hic nominum liber vitiosus est, ut non tam Hebraea quam barbara quaedam, et Sarmatica nomina congesta arbitrandum sit. Nec hoc Septuaginta Interpretibus, qui Spiritu Sancto pleni, ea quae vera fuerant, transtulerunt, sed scriptorum culpae ascribendum.
[35] *CCL* 72, 249: ...hoc breuiter admonens, quod nullius auctoritatem secutus sum; sed de hebraeo transferens, magis me septuaginta interpretum consuetudini coaptaui, in his dumtaxat, quae non multum ab Hebraicis discrepabant. Interdum Aquilae quoque et Symmachi et Theodotionis recordatus sum, ut nec nouitate nimia lectoris studium deterrerem, nec rursum contra conscientiam meam, fonte ueritatis omisso, opinionum riuulos consectarer.
[36] *CCL* 72, 2.

Jerome still implies the divine inspiration of the LXX, when he attempts to explain the mistakes in the translation by the original translators' fear for the welfare of the Jews during the reign of Ptolemy. It is clear from this preface that Jerome has been under attack for his use of Hebrew. He frequently feels the need to justify his work of translation from the Hebrew text, and it is an indicator of the widespread reaction which his allegiance to the *Hebraica veritas* caused.

In the preface to the translation of the Pentateuch, written in A.D. 403, Jerome questions the story of the origins of the LXX put forward by the so-called *Letter of Aristeas*:

> 'I do not know who was the first author whose lie constructed seventy cells in Alexandria in which they (i.e. the translators) were separated and yet all wrote the same words; whereas Aristeas... and long after him, Josephus, have related nothing of the sort, but write that they were assembled in one magnificent building and conferred together, not that they prophesied... What then? Do we condemn the ancient texts? Certainly not, but we work in the Lord's house as best as we can, after the studies of our predecessors.'[37]

Jerome here shows an almost modern critical acumen when he demonstrates that the myth of LXX beginnings had no basis in fact.[38] But, although he is highly critical of its historical beginnings, he does not disparage the value of the LXX. He believes the Hebrew text gives a more original version of the O.T., but the Greek text is still useful, for each interpreter or translator must necessarily build on the work of his predecessors.

Right to the end of his life, Jerome continued to cite the text of the LXX alongside that of the Hebrew in his commentaries, sometimes basing the spiritual interpretation on it. In the preface to his translation of Chronicles (A.D. 395), Jerome mentions that the sermons he preached and the instructions he gave in the monastery at Bethlehem were based on the LXX. Jerome, therefore, never discarded the LXX in favour of the *Hebraica veritas*, as many scholars have implied. The situation was not as simple as that. Jerome continued to use both the LXX and the

---

37 *PL* 28, 181-3: Et nescio quis primus auctor septuaginta cellulas, Alexandriae mendacio suo exstruxerit, quibus divisi eadem scriptitarent, cum Aristeas... et multo post tempore Josephus, nihil tale retulerint; sed in una basilica congregatos, contulisse scribant, non prophetasse... Quid igitur? Damnamus veteres? minime: sed post priorum studia, in domo Domini quod possumus, laboramus.
38 For a discussion of the modern scholarly appraisal of LXX origins, see Jellicoe: *op.cit.*, pp. 29-73.

Hebrew text throughout his career, but gave primacy of importance to the Hebrew text, for, as a scholar, he recognised its precedence. Jerome used the LXX because it was the Church's scripture. The ambivalence of Jerome's attitude towards the LXX, of which we have written, is a consequence of an ambivalence within Jerome's own personality. He could do none other than use both the LXX and the Hebrew text, for he was both churchman and scholar.

Jerome's acceptance of and allegiance to the *Hebraica veritas* manifested itself in two distinct ways. First, he accepted the canon of the Jews, refusing to accept as canonical any book which they did not accept. Secondly, he accepted the precedence of the Hebrew text over the Greek one, and based his translation and exegesis of the O.T. on this *Hebraica veritas*. We shall now study these two facets.

Jerome and the biblical canon

The starting point for any modern student of Jerome's attitude to the canon of scripture must be H.H. Howorth's extended study in the *Journal of Theological Studies*.[39] In this important work, Howorth traced the influence of Jerome on the canon of the Western Church. He put forward the thesis that Jerome's views on the extent on the Christian O.T. underwent a decisive change. Jerome's early career mirrored the attitudes of the Western Church as expressed in the Council of Rome in A.D. 382, where the 'apocryphal' books were included as canonical. Howorth bases this view on the fact that Jerome, in 382, worked for Pope Damasus as his secretary, and that he was probably in sympathy with the pronouncements of the Council as regards the O.T. canon. He suggests that Jerome may have drafted the list of O.T. books for the Council. Further, Howorth argues, Jerome translated the O.T. from the Greek text.[40] Later, at Bethlehem, Jerome became interested in the Hebrew text as the basis of the O.T. scripture. This led him to accept only the Jewish canon, which in turn led him to undertake a new translation of the O.T. from the Hebrew.[41] Howorth believed he could trace this change of attitude to the years 390-1, Jewish influence on Jerome being partly responsible, and his conflict with the supporters of Origen also affecting his attitude.

---

39 'The influence of St. Jerome on the Canon of the Western Church', in *JTS* 10 (1908) 481-496; 11 (1909) 321-347; 13 (1911) 1-13.
40 *JTS* 11 (1909) pp. 321-5.
41 *JTS* 11 (1909) pp. 325ff; 10 (1908) p. 493.

Howorth has been followed in his view by A.C. Sundberg[42] and recently by J. Braverman.[43] His theory is, however, open to objections. One such objection has been raised by P.W. Skehan in his scholarly article on 'St. Jerome and the canon of the Holy Scriptures'.[44] Howorth's chronology, on which he bases part of his argument, is open to serious doubt. Skehan shows that Jerome only became involved in the Origenist controversy in 393, and that Jerome's attitude to the canon cannot have changed as a result of this in 390-1, as Howorth suggests.[45]

This is not the only criticism which can be levelled at Howorth's thesis. As we have seen above, he argues that Jerome was probably in sympathy with the list of canonical books of the Council of Rome in 382, and that he may have drafted the list for the Council. Now, it is certain that Jerome came to Rome in 382.[46] It is also the case that Jerome took some part in the Council; later, in the heat of controversy, Rufinus reports that Damasus had asked Jerome to draft a statement of belief which Apollinarians would have to sign before being admitted to communion.[47] But Jerome, in his reply, dismisses this report as mere gossip, but makes the general statement that Damasus had delegated to him 'the dictation of letters on Church affairs' (*ille ecclesiasticas epistulas dictandas credidit*).[48] There is no evidence, however, to connect Jerome with the composition of the list of canonical books for the Council, nor is there any explicit acceptance of the list in Jerome's writings. Howorth's unsubstantiated suggestion must, therefore, be rejected.

This discovery leads us to question whether, in fact, Jerome's attitude to the O.T. canon changed. To answer this, we will need to make a study of Jerome's quotations from the apocryphal books. For our purpose there is no need to go further than Jerome's epistles. In his very first epistle, written in 374, Jerome uses the story of Susannah, who was freed by the judge to escape death by the sword, to contrast with the story of the pious Christian woman condemned because of her faith, but who could not be killed with the executioner's sword.[49] In *Ep.* 3, 1, also

---

[42] A.C. Sundberg: *The O.T. of the Early Church* (Harvard Theological Studies XX), Cambridge, Mass. 1964.
[43] J. Braverman: *Jerome's Commentary on Daniel* (CBQ Monograph Series 7), Washington D.C. 1978.
[44] In *A Monument to St. Jerome*, ed. F.X. Murphy, New York 1952, 259-287.
[45] Skehan: *art.cit.*, p. 263; cf Kelly: p. 195; Cavallera: *Saint Jérôme* I, pp. 193-286; II,31-43.
[46] *Ep.* 127, 7 (written in 413) (*CSEL* 56, 150).
[47] Rufinus: *De Adult.lib.Orig.* 13 (*CCL* 20, 15).
[48] *Apol.c.Ruf.* 2, 20 (*CCL* 79, 56).
[49] *Ep.* 1, 9 (*CSEL* 54, 6). See *Susannah* 45.

written in 374, Jerome refers to *Bel and the Dragon* (33-6), wishing that he could be transported to Rufinus the Monk as quickly as Habakkuk was transported to Daniel in the den of lions.

During the years 375-7, Jerome lived in an ascetic community in the desert of Chalcis. While here, as we shall see later, Jerome began his study of Hebrew. He also wrote several epistles. In only one of these, however, does he quote from apocryphal material. In *Ep.* 14, 6, he quotes from Wisdom 1:11, and at 14, 9 he quotes from Wisd. 6:6 and alludes to *Sus.* 45. These references have the air of proverbs or wise sayings, rather than being commented on or referred to as scripture.

In 384, Jerome made, at the request of Pope Damasus, a revision of the Four Gospels. In the preface to this revision, Jerome argues that it is better to go back to the original Greek language. He says:

'...why not go back to the original Greek and correct the mistakes introduced by inaccurate translators, and the stupid alterations of confident but ignorant critics, and further all that has been inserted or changed by copyists who were more asleep than awake? I am not discussing the O.T., which was turned into Greek by the Seventy elders and has reached us by a descent of three steps. I am not asking what Aquila and Symmachus think, or why Theodotion takes a middle course between the ancients and moderns. I am willing to let that be the true translation which had apostolic authority.'

Going on to speak of Matthew's gospel, which he thought was originally written in Hebrew, Jerome says:

'We must confess that, as we have it in our language, it is marked by discrepancies, and now that the stream is distributed into different channels, we must go back to the source.'[50]

Two letters written at this time to Marcella are very important for our purpose here. In *Ep.* 32, 1, explaining why the letter is so brief, Jerome says:

'...for some time past I have been comparing Aquila's version of the O.T. with the scrolls of the Hebrew, to see if the synagogue has changed the text, because of their hatred of Christ, and, speaking candidly to a friend, I have found several variations which confirm our faith. After having exactly revised the prophets, Solomon, the Psalter, and the books of Kings, I am now working on Exodus... and when I have finished this, I shall go on to Leviticus.'[51]

---

50 *Pref. to Four Gospels* (*PL* 29, 559).
51 *CSEL* 54, 252.

In *Ep.* 34, Jerome answers two specific questions on Psalms, comparing the readings of the LXX, Aquila, Symmachus and Theodotion with the Hebrew, and choosing the Hebrew as the original reading. These three passages, all dating from 384, are of great importance in determining whether (and if so, when) Jerome's attitude to the canon changed. We shall come back to them when we have completed our review of Jerome's use of the apocryphal books in his letters.

The next epistle of Jerome which quotes from an apocryphal book is *Ep.* 48, written to Pammachius in 393. In section 14, he quotes from Esther 14: 11, but the short quotation is only one of a number of quotations (from Exodus and Job) which illustrate the same point, and it does not have any great importance for Jerome. The same thing is found for all the remaining quotations from or allusions to apocryphal books in Jerome's letters,[52] with the exception of two quotations. These occur in *Ep.* 108, 21, written in 404 to Eustochium, and *Ep.* 118, 1, written in 407 to Julian. In the former epistle, Jerome quotes briefly from Ecclus. 13:2, 'Do not burden yourself beyond your strength', but prefaces it with the phrase, 'Does not scripture say...'. In *Ep.* 118, 1, Jerome quotes from Ecclus. 22:6, 'A story out of season is like music in mourning', and prefaces it with 'Holy scripture says...'. To these two interesting examples, we must return in a moment.

First, however, it will be interesting and useful to compare Jerome's use of apocryphal writings with his quotation of and allusion to secular literature in his letters. The story of Jerome's important dream is too well-known to need recapitulation here. Before this dream, or rather nightmare,[53] Jerome had spent much time reading, and building up a library of secular literature. The dream was understood by Jerome as a warning concerning his priorities in life, and he vowed never again to read another piece of non-Christian literature. This vow, however, was broken almost immediately. We can see that the frequency of quotation of secular literature in Jerome's letters after the dream varies only fractionally from its frequency beforehand.[54] Jerome quotes secular litera-

---

[52] The remaining quotations are as follows: *Ep.* 51, 6 (A.D. 393) (Wisd. 2:23); 58, 1 (A.D. 395-6) (Wisd. 4:9); 71, 3 (398) (Ecclus. 13:1); 75, 2 (399) (Wisd. 4: 11-14); 77, 4 (399) (Baruch 5:5); 79, 5 (399) (Ecclus. 3:30); 108, 16 (404) (Ecclus. 3:30); 108, 23 (404) (Wisd. 9:15); 125, 19 (412) (Ecclus. 27:25); 127, 6 (413) (Ecclus. 7:36); 133, 2 (414) (Ecclus. 10:9).
Allusions are as follows: 52, 13 (394) (Wisd. 8:7); 54, 2 (394) (Wisd. 4:13); 77, 6 (399) (Ecclus. 11:25); 79, 10 (399) (Judith 13).
[53] See Cavallera: *op.cit.*, I, p. 29; Kelly: p. 41. The story of the dream is recounted in *Ep.* 22.
[54] See the scholarly work of H. Hagendahl: *Latin Fathers and the Classics*, Göteborg 1958.

ture all through his long literary career, and his dream had a minimal effect.

From the review we made above of Jerome's use of apocryphal material, we can see a somewhat parallel situation. Jerome quotes apocryphal material right through his epistles, not just before 390-1, as Howorth suggests. It is also noticable that Jerome makes much less use of the apocrypha than he does of secular literature in his letters. If we return now to discuss Jerome's preface to the Four Gospels of 384, and his statements in *Epp*. 32 and 34, we may be able to suggest an alternative to Howorth's thesis.

Jerome's words in the preface to his revision of the Four Gospels have always been understood as meaning that Jerome believed unreservedly in the authority of the LXX (and hence the Greek canon, which included the apocrypha), ('I am not discussing the O.T., which was turned into Greek by the Seventy elders'), and that he believed that version which had apostolic authority ('I am willing to let that be the true translation which had apostolic authority'). But if we take seriously what Jerome says in *Epp*. 32 and 34, (and there is no reason to doubt what he says there), that he had been comparing Aquila's version with the original Hebrew (*Ep*. 32) and choosing Hebrew readings as opposed to those of the LXX, or any of the Greek versions (*Ep*. 34), then it is plausible to put another interpretation on his words in the preface to the Four Gospels. His statement that he is not discussing the O.T. which was translated by the Seventy elders, is not an important statement in the context of his revision of the Four Gospels, that is to say, it is not the subject which he is now discussing. Because the O.T. is not his main subject, he passes over it quickly and in so doing uses the standard contemporary phrase to refer to the Christian O.T. The statement should not therefore be taken to mean that Jerome affirms the LXX as the only authoritative scripture. Similarly, his affirmation that he believes in 'that version which had apostolic authority' does not refer to the O.T., i.e. the LXX, but is a general statement directed to Pope Damasus, to whom Jerome dedicated this revision. Jerome is sycophantically saying that he will, as a good churchman, believe in whichever version of the bible the Pope, as successor of the chief apostle Peter, affirmed.

We are left now with the two quotations from Ecclus. which Jerome prefaced with the words 'Does not scripture say...' and 'Holy scripture says' in *Epp*. 108 and 118 respectively. Both of these quotations are used at a time when Jerome's commentaries were based on the Hebrew text of the O.T. and not the LXX, and hence when he affirmed the Hebrew canon rather than that of the Greek O.T. How, then, can he refer to Ecclus. as 'Holy scripture'? A simple solution is plausible: Jerome, in these two quotations, was very probably quoting from memory and did not take the time to check them in a manuscript copy, especially as, with all his quotations from the apocryphal books, he was merely using them to illustrate a minor point in his overall argument.

It is to be hoped that the evidence which has been set out above has made it clear that Howorth's thesis that Jerome's attitude to the canon of the O.T. changed radically in 390-1 is not tenable. We do not see any real change in Jerome's attitude to the canon. The scanty evidence which exists from the time before Jerome began his sojourn in the desert of Chalcis shows nothing. After this time (375-7), he began to use the Hebrew text for his exegesis, even though he continued to quote from the apocrypha (just as he continued to quote from secular literature after his dream).

Jerome makes apparently contradictory statements about the O.T. canon at different times in his life. In the prologue to his *Comm. Abacuc*, composed in 392, Jerome makes the following statement about the canonicity of *Bel and the Dragon*: '...although among the Hebrews this story is not read. Therefore, if anyone accepts this as scripture, or if he does not...' (*quamquam apud Hebraeos haec ipsa non legatur historia. Igitur siue quis recipit scripturam illam, siue non recipit...*).[55] Jerome makes this statement in passing, and it seems plain that he intended it as a scholarly note and did not wish to make any other point from it.

Also at about this time (392-3), Jerome had begun working on his translation of the O.T. from Hebrew. In the famous *Prologus Galeatus*,[56] Jerome sets out the principles he used in his translations from Hebrew into Latin. He begins by explaining that the Hebrew alphabet has 22 letters: 'As, then, there are 22 characters by which we write Hebrew... and the compass of the human voice is contained within their limits, so we count 22 books, by which, as by the alphabet of the doctrine of God, a righteous man is instructed in gentle infancy...' Jerome continues by listing the books in the Hebrew canon, and then says:

> 'This prologue to the scriptures may serve as a 'helmeted introduction', to all the books we have translated from Hebrew into Latin, so that we may know that whatever is not on our list should be placed among the apocryphal writings. Wisdom, therefore, which is usually called Solomon, and the book of Jesus, son of Sirach, and Judith and Tobit and the Shepherd (of Hermas) are not in the canon. I have found the first book of Maccabees to

---

55 *Comm.Hab.*: Prol. (*CCL* 76A, 580).
56 *PL* 28, 600-601.

be Hebrew, but the second Greek, as can be proved from its style.' Having said this, Jerome might be thought to have left the ancient tradition of the Church, but immediately after enouncing this fine scholarly principle, he continues:

> 'I beg you, brother, not to think that my work is in any way meant to debase the old translators. Each one offers the service of the tabernacle of God what he can; some gold and silver and precious stones, others linen and blue and purple and scarlet; we shall do well if we offer skins and goats' hair.'

Here, Jerome offers what is probably his longest and most balanced statement on the relation between his translation from the Hebrew and the older Greek translations. He believes that God has given different gifts to be used to glorify him. In his own case, Jerome believes he has been given a scholarly mind and a certain linguistic ability. Jerome uses these gifts to study the bible in the original languages and to communicate the fruits of this learning through a translation and his many commentaries.

In *Ep.* 53, 8,[57] written in 395, Jerome records a list of O.T. books which he considers canonical. This list is interesting in that it includes all the books in the Hebrew canon, but the order in which they are recorded has been influenced by the LXX canon in two ways. First, the minor prophets are placed before the other prophets, and second, Daniel is placed at the end of the prophets, ostensibly as one of them.[58] This is a good example of Jerome's ambivalent attitude to the canon; the scholar is influenced by the original Hebrew canon, but the churchman cannot stray too far from the revered tradition of the LXX canon.

It is instructive to compare Jerome's views on the O.T. canon with those of Origen. The Alexandrian theologian shows the same ambivalence in his attitude to the canon as does Jerome. He was forced to study the question of the canon when he noticed that the LXX contained material which was not found in the Jewish canon, which consisted of 22 books.[59] The only extant canonical list of Origen's is found in Eusebius' *Church History* VI, 25. Origen says that this list is the one handed down by the Hebrews:

> 'It should be known that there are 22 canonical books, as the Hebrews have handed them down; the same as the numbers in their alphabet...'[60]

---

57 *CSEL* 54, 455-462.
58 This point is noticed in J. Braverman: *op.cit.*, p. 48.
59 *Comm. on Ps.* 1 (*PG* 12, 1084). See R.P.C. Hanson: *Origen's Doctrine of Tradition*, London 1954, p. 133.
60 *LCL* 265, p. 72.

It has been noted by H.B. Swete and others[61] that two problems exist in Origen's list. First, he omits the book of the twelve minor prophets, and second, he includes 1 Esdras and the Ep. of Jeremiah, neither of which was recognised by the Jews as canonical. A.C. Sundberg has suggested that the omission of the twelve minor prophets was due to an error on Origen's part, since his list of Hebrew names amounts to only 21. Sundberg suggests that Origen received from his Jewish informants only the Hebrew names of the books and their meanings, but not their Greek titles. Origen correlated the 22 book Hebrew canon with the equivalent Greek names of LXX – Christian usage. If this was the case, then Origen's inclusion of 1 Esdras and the Ep. of Jer. was probably his guess as to the books which the Jews included under the title Ezra and Nehemiah.[62]

Origen's purpose in heeding the Hebrew canon was not because he thought it to be the original canon, but rather the practical one of polemic against the Jews. In his *Ep. ad Africanum*, which is largely an attempt to justify the canonicity of some of the books found in the LXX (e.g. Susannah and Tobit) which were not found in the Hebrew bible, he makes this quite plain:

> 'I make it my endeavour not to be ignorant of their various readings, lest in my controversies with the Jews I should quote what is not found in their copies, and that I may make some use of what is found there, even though it should not be in our scriptures.'[63]

Origen here makes a clear distinction between 'their scriptures' and 'our scriptures'. It is also clear that Origen believed Susannah to be genuinely canonical.[64] Tobit and Judith were considered canonical by Origen, although they were not by the Jews:

> '...and Tobit as well as Judith, we ought to notice, are not used by the Jews. They are not even found in the Hebrew hidden books (ἐν ἀποκρύφοις ἑβραϊστί) as I learned from the Jews themselves. However, since the churches use Tobit...'[65]

This makes it clear that the most important factor in determining whether or not a book was canonical was its use in the Church. In *Contra Celsum* 5, 54 Origen excluded Enoch from the canon, 'for he (Celsus) does not appear to have read the passages in question, or to have been

---

61 E.g. by Swete: *op.cit.*, pp. 222, 266-7; Braverman: *op.cit.*, p. 38.
62 A.C. Sundberg: *op.cit.*, p. 135.
63 *Ep. ad Afric.* 5 (*PG* 11, 60f).
64 *Ibid.*; cf *Comm.Matt.* 2, 61.
65 *Ep. ad Afric.* 13 (*PG* 11, 80f).

aware that the books which bear Enoch's name do not all circulate in the churches as divine'.[66]

It can be seen, therefore, that points of contact exist between Origen and Jerome as regards the canon, as well as differences. Both were scholars as well as churchmen. Both used the Hebrew canon, but they did so for different reasons: Origen for practical considerations in his debates with Jews, Jerome because it was the authentic biblical canon.[67] Jerome also went beyond Origen in his view that the Hebrew canon should be normative for the Christian Church.[68] Both continued to use books which were not in the Hebrew canon, because, as good churchmen, they felt obliged to remain faithful to the tradition of the Church.

As regards the N.T. canon, Jerome's views are relatively straightforward. He affirms the books which are now in the N.T. canon, with the possible exception of 2 John.[69] He did much to stabilise the opinion of the Western Church as to the canonicity of the epistle to the Hebrews and the book of Revelation. He recognised that various sections of the Church rejected these books because of the doubt concerning their apostolic authorship, but says that he was influenced 'not so much by the custom of his own time as by the authority of the ancients and so I receive them both'.[70] Of the epistle of James, long disputed in the Church,[71] Jerome says that some disputed its authorship, but as time

---

66 *GCS* Orig. Werke III, p. 58. Origen, however, changed his views on the canonicity of Enoch. Earlier, in the *De Princ.*, he quotes from it three times without commenting on its status (I, 33, and twice at IV, 48). In *Comm.Iohan.* 6, 42 he refers to the book, adding the phrase 'if anyone cares to receive the book as holy'.
67 Jerome does say, however, that in controversy with the Jews, use of the Hebrew scriptures would leave the Jews no place of retreat or subterfuge, so that they 'may be struck down most effectively by their own sword' (*Apol.* 3, 25: ut, siquando aduersum eos christianis disputatio est, non habeant subterfugiendi diuerticula, sed suomet potissimum mucrone feriantur [*CCL* 79, 97]. This is not his primary motivation for using the Hebrew canon, for, in the same sentence, Jerome says that the Hebrew canon contained the actual copies of the scriptures, meaning that they were more original than the LXX, which was only a translation.
68 *Apol.* 3, 25 (*CCL* 79, 97).
69 In his *Book of Hebrew Names* (c 390), Jerome omits any mention of this epistle, but this is presumably because it does not contain any names. At *De Vir. Illus.* 9 (c 392), Jerome expresses some doubt about the authorship of 2 and 3 John (whether they were written by John the Apostle or John the Presbyter), but includes both in the canon (*PL* 23, 654-5).
70 *Ep.* 129, 3 (written c 414) (*CSEL* 56, 167).
71 For the interesting history of this epistle in the Church, see the commentaries of J.E.B. Mayor and J.H. Ropes.

went by it gradually became accepted.⁷² Of the epistle of Jude, Jerome notices that, because it quotes from Enoch, many reject it, but he considers it canonical because of its age and authority.⁷³

Jerome several times refers to an extra-canonical gospel, which he calls 'the gospel of the Nazareans' or the 'gospel according to the Hebrews'.⁷⁴ This was a Jewish-Christian gospel and is also attested by Eusebius and Epiphanius.⁷⁵ Jerome refers to it to impress his readers and does not think of it as canonical. He also mentions various works supposedly written by the apostle Peter but rejects them as apocryphal.⁷⁶

Jerome and the Hebrew language

In 375 Jerome took his first steps along the path which, more than anything else, made him unique among the Fathers of the Western Church. As we shall see, he was the only Father, in either the Eastern or Western Church, to gain a good working knowledge of Hebrew. In this section, we shall enquire as to how much Hebrew Jerome knew, and to learn this, it will be instructive to compare Jerome's Hebrew knowledge with that of Philo and Origen. We shall also ask whether or not Jerome learned any other Semitic languages. First, however, we must ascertain what Jerome actually says about his Hebrew studies.

After the completion of his secular studies in Rome, Jerome felt guided toward the ascetic life,⁷⁷ and for this purpose he joined, in A.D. 375, a community in the desert of Chalcis in Syria,⁷⁸ in order to draw close to God. This was thought to be possible by a life of denial of bodily pleasures and desires; 'here I rejoice to throw off the burden of

---

⁷² *De Vir.Illus.* 2 (*PL* 23, 639).
⁷³ *De Vir.Illus.* 4 (*PL* 23, 646).
⁷⁴ Reference may be found in R. McL. Wilson (ed.): *N.T. Apocrypha*, Vol. 1, London 1963, pp. 126-136; see G. Bardy's important article: 'Saint Jérôme et l'Évangile selon les Hébreux' in *Mélanges de Science Religieuse* 3 (1946) pp. 5ff. We shall come back to this work in a later chapter.
⁷⁵ See Wilson: *op.cit.*, pp. 120-6.
⁷⁶ *De Vir.Illus.* 2 (*PL* 23, 642).
⁷⁷ *Ep.* 3 shows that Jerome envies his friend Bonosus, who had already taken up the ascetic life.
⁷⁸ The exact location of the community is not known, but various notes in Jerome's letters give us clues to the general area. Chalcis was near the border of Northern Syria and an area West of the Euphrates overrun by the Saracens, about 50 miles East of Antioch. See *Epp.* 5, 1; 7, 1; 15, 2.

the flesh and rise to the pure radiance of heaven'.[79] It was here that Jerome first learned Hebrew. Writing much later, he gives his reason for taking up the study of this language:

> 'When I was a young man walled in by the loneliness of the desert, I was unable to resist the temptations of vice and the hot passions of my nature. Although I tried to crush them with repeated fasting, my mind was in a turmoil with [sinful] thoughts. To bring it under control, I made myself the pupil of a Christian convert from Judaism. After the *acumina* of Quintilian, the *fluvii* of Cicero, the *gravitas* of Fronto and the *lenitas* of Pliny, I set myself to learn an alphabet and strove to pronounce hissing, breathtaking words.'[80]

But this rhetorical piece is written with the benefit of hindsight, and we would do well to heed James Barr's caveat that Jerome's natural intellectual curiosity and his perception of the place of the Hebrew text in exegesis probably played a part in his decision to learn Hebrew.[81]

Another possible reason for learning Hebrew was to be able to combat the Jews, who, according to Jerome, derided the Christians on their inferior knowledge of the Law. He says:

> 'The Jews are proud of their knowledge of the Law and parade the fact that they can repeat correctly by heart all the biblical names. As, however, these are foreign to us and we do not know their etymology, we pronounce them incorrectly. When we happen to make a mistake in the accent and lengthen a short syllable or shorten a long one, they laugh at our ignorance especially if the mistake is in an aspirate or a guttural. If we do not pronounce these peculiar surnames and the language generally – which is barbarous to us – in exactly the same way as the Jews do, they break out into loud laughter and swear that they cannot understand what we say.'[82]

---

79 *Ep.* 14, 10; nescio quid plus lucis aspicio. libet sarcina carnis abiecta ad purum aetheris uolare fulgorem (*CSEL* 54, 60).
80 *Ep.* 125, 12 (written in 411): Dum essem iuuenis et solitudinis me deserta uallarent, incentiua uitiorum ardoremque naturae ferre non poteram; quae cum crebris ieiuniis frangerem, mens tamen cogitationibus aestuabat. ad quam edomandam cuidam fratri, qui ex Hebraeis crediderat, me in disciplinam dedi, ut post Quintiliani acumina Ciceronisque fluuios grauitatemque Frontonis et lenitatem Plinii alphabetum discerem, stridentia anhelantiaque uerba meditarer. (*CSEL* 56, 131).
81 J. Barr: 'St. Jerome's Appreciation of Hebrew', in *BJRL* 49 (1966) p. 286.
82 *Comm.Titum* 3, 9 (*PL* 26, 630): Proprie pulsat Iudaeos, qui in eo se jactant et putant legis habere notitiam, si nomina teneant singulorum: quae quia barbara

The 'Christian convert from Judaism' who taught Jerome may well be the same man of whom he speaks in *Ep.* 18A, 10 saying that he was regarded by the Jewish authorities as being a Chaldean, because he had so refined the Hebrew language. Jerome says that he learned a great deal from this man.

It is clear from Jerome's account that he found Hebrew a difficult language to learn. This difficulty is evident when we remember that the structure of Hebrew was very different from Latin, and that no grammars, concordances or dictionaries of Hebrew existed to assist Jerome in his studies. The language must, therefore, have been taught orally and the sounds of the consonants and the vocabulary memorised. Presumably Jerome practised writing the Hebrew characters by copying out manuscripts.[83] Of his Hebrew studies, Jerome says: 'What labour I spent on this task, what difficulties I went through, how often I despaired and how often I gave up and in my eagerness to learn started again.'[84]

Jerome's eagerness to master Hebrew continued long after his return from Chalcis in A.D. 377-8, and several times he mentions his Jewish teachers. Before he translated the book of Chronicles, he received assistance from a Doctor of the Law from Tiberias and went carefully through the whole book.[85] For the book of Job, Jerome obtained the help, at no inconsiderable expense, of a certain renowned Jew from Lydda as a tutor.[86] Only one of Jerome's Hebrew teachers is named – at both Jerusalem and Bethlehem, Jerome employed a certain Bar-Hanina, or *Baranina* as Jerome calls him.[87] Jerome says that it was only after

---

sunt, et etymologias eorum non novimus, plerumque corrupte proferuntur a nobis. Et si forte erraverimus in accentu, in extensione et brevitate syllabae, vel brevia producentes, vel producta breviantes, solent irridere nos imperitiae, maxime in aspirationibus in quibusdam cum rasura gulae litteris proferendis... Si igitur a nobis haec nominum et linguae idiomata, ut videlicet barbara, non ita fuerint expressa, ut exprimuntur ab Hebraeis, solent cachinnum attollere, et jurare se penitus nescire quod dicimus.

[83] See E.F. Sutcliffe: 'St. Jerome's Hebrew Manuscripts', in *Biblica* 29 (1948) 195-204.

[84] *Ep.* 125, 12 (*CSEL* 56, 131): quid ibi laboris insumpserim, quid sustinuerim difficultatis, quotiens desperauerim quotiensque cessauerim et contentione discendi rursus inceperim.

[85] *PL* 29, 423A.

[86] *PL* 28, 1141A. In *Comm.Hab.* 2, 15ff (*CCL* 76A, 610), he reports a story told to him by a Jew from Lydda, quite possibly the same man. Jerome calls him *sapiens* and δευτερώτης.

[87] Jerome says (*Lib.Nom.Heb.* [*CCL* 72, 87]) that he often omits the aspirate in writing.

considerable trouble and expense on his part that he persuaded this man to teach him, and even then Bar-Hanina would only come at night, like another Nicodemus, because he was afraid of what his fellow Jews might say.[88]

Jerome thought, along with the rest of the ancient Jewish and Christian world, that Hebrew was the world's original language. He says:

> 'The beginning of speech and general conversation and all that we say is the Hebrew language, in which the O.T. is written. So universal tradition reports. But after the imposition of diversity of tongues because of the offense to God in erecting the tower (of Babel) a variety of speech was spread over all nations.'[89]

Regardless of the antiquity of Hebrew, however, it was, for Jerome, having been steeped in the cultured world of Latin and Greek, a barbarous language which affected his Latin style. In the preface to his *Comm.Gal.* III, Jerome apologises for his unliterary style, blaming it partly on eye trouble, and problems with copyists, but also on his study of Hebrew:

> 'I leave it to others to judge how far my unflagging study of Hebrew has profited me; what I have lost in my own language, I can tell.'[90]

Again, in the *Comm.Haggai* 2, 21-4, Jerome apologises for his deficient style, which is due to his prolonged study of Hebrew.[91]

Is it possible to know exactly how good Jerome's knowledge of this 'barbarous' language was? One way which has been used to judge this is to study Jerome's etymological works, noticing especially the instances in which he given a fantastically incorrect meaning, and attempting to

---

88 *Ep.* 84, 3: rursum Hierosolymae et Bethleem quo labore, quo pretio Baraninam nocturnum habui praeceptorem! timebat enim Iudaeos et mihi alterum exhibebat Nicodemum. (*CSEL* 55, 123). S. Krauss (*Jewish Encycl.* 7 [1904] p. 116) misunderstands this passage, thinking that Baranina was sometimes too afraid to come himself, and sent a certain Nicodemus.

89 *Ep.* 18A, 6: initium oris et communis eloquii et hoc omne, quod loquimur, Hebraeam linguam, qua uetus testamentum scriptum est, uniuersa antiquitas tradidit. postquam uero in fabricatione turris per offensam dei linguarum diuersitas adtributa est, tunc sermonis uarietas in omnes dispersa est nationes (*CSEL* 54, 82).

90 *PL* 26, 427: Quod autem profecerim ex linguae illius infatigabili studio, aliorum judicio derelinquo: ego quid in mea amiserim, scio. Just before this comes – Sed omnem sermonis elegantiam, et Latini eloquii venustatem, stridor lectionis Hebraicae sordidavit.

91 *CCL* 76A, 746.

discover the reasons for his mistakes. Very many of Jerome's explanations are correct, but a sizeable minority of these meanings are taken from the Bible itself, and so these are no real guide to the extent or quality of Jerome's Hebrew knowledge. We shall take a number of examples from the *Liber Interpretationis Hebraicorum Nominum*.

1. Bamoth
Jerome gives two meanings for this word – *in morte siue excelsa*.[92] The second of these is the correct one, for בָּמוֹת means 'high places'.[93] He cannot have found the first explanation in the Bible, so we must look elsewhere. It is very interesting to discover that the great Alexandrian exegete, Origen, had also explained this word as 'the coming of death' (*adventus mortis*) in his twelfth homily on Numbers.[94] He presumably understood Bamoth as a combination of the two words בּוֹא, 'to come in', and מָוֶת, 'death'.

2. Chanaan
As one of the meanings of this word Jerome gives σάλος, (*hoc est motus*).[95] That the meaning 'motion (of the sea)' attached to Canaan had had a long heritage can be seen when it is pointed out that Philo Judaeus also gave this meaning to Canaan in the first century,[96] deriving it from the verb נוּעַ, 'to move', and כְּ, 'as, like'. In the LXX, this verb is occasionally translated by σαλεύω.

3. Cherubim
Jerome gives as the meaning of this word *scientia multiplicata* ('abundance of knowledge'). Again, we find that Philo had also given this explanation – 'Cherubim, or as we would call them, full knowledge and much science'.[97] It is not certain where this etymology arose, but it is also attested by Clement of Alexandria (ἐπίγνωσις πολλή) and by Augustine (*plenitudo scientiae*). It may possibly derive from the verb of root נכר, giving Hiphil הִכִּיר and הַכֵּר. Therefore, 'the cherubin' would be hakker plus rubin (הַכְּרוּבִין), = 'much knowledge'.

---

[92] *Lib.Heb.Nom.* (*CCL* 72, 79).
[93] Num. 21:19f.
[94] *PG* 12, 663.
[95] *Lib.Heb.Nom.* (*CCL* 72, 63).
[96] *De Sobrietate* 44.
[97] *De Vita Mosis* II, 97: Χερουβίμ, ὡς δ'ἂν Ἕλληνες εἴποιεν, ἐπίγνωσις καὶ ἐπιστήμη πολλή. *LCL* Philo VI, p. 496.

4. *Lamech*
Jerome gives the explanation *humiliatus* for this word.[98] This interpretation can also be traced back to Philo, who etymologised Lamech as ταπείνωσις, 'humbleness',[99] presumably deriving it from the verb מכך, 'to sink', and the preposition of direction, לְ.

5. *Nachor*
Jerome's explanation of this word is *requies luminus*.[100] This etymology is also found in Origen's *Fragments on Genesis* (on 22:20), Ναχὼρ ἀνάπαυσιν φωτός, 'refreshment of light'.[101] Origen probably took this from נוח, which means 'rest', plus אוֹר, 'light'.

6. *Noe*
The meaning assigned to this name by Jerome is *requies*, 'rest'.[102] He rejects the biblical meaning given in Gen. 5:29, of נחם, 'comfort', and instead chooses נוח, 'rest', which can be traced back to Philo, who gave ἀνάπαυσις as the meaning of Noah.[103]

7. *Raguhel*
According to Jerome, this word means 'God's shepherd' (*pastor dei*).[104] This is a very interesting example, for it does not appear in the Massoretic Text,[105] but only in the Greek bible. If we look at Origen's explanation of this word, we find the solution to this puzzle. Origen interprets Raguel as φίλος ἰσχυρός, ἢ ποιμανσία θεοῦ,[106] 'strong friend, or shepherd of God', certainly deriving it from the root רעה, 'to observe or tend', giving the nouns רֵעַ, 'friend' and רֹעֶה, 'shepherd', plus אֵל, 'God'.

8. *Rebecca*
Jerome gives the meaning of this name as *multa patientia*,[107] which is

---

98 *Lib.Heb.Nom.* (*CCL* 72, 68).
99 *De Post.Cain.* 41.
100 *Lib.Heb.Nom.* (*CCL* 72, 70).
101 *PG* 12, 117.
102 *Lib.Heb.Nom.* (*CCL* 72, 69).
103 *Leg.Alleg.* III, 77.
104 *Lib.Heb.Nom.* (*CCL* 72, 71).
105 The Hebrew text of Num. 10:29 has רְעוּאֵל, although the Revised Version here reads 'Raguel', presumably being influenced by the LXX, which has Ῥαγουήλ.
106 *Frag. on Gen.* (on 25:1-4) (*PG* 12, 121).
107 *Lib.Heb.Nom.* (*CCL* 72, 70).

also the etymology Origen gives.¹⁰⁸ This explanation probably derives from רַב, 'much', plus 'qah' taken from תִּקְוָה, 'hope', which is rendered as *patientia* in Vulgate Jer. 29:11 and elsewhere.

9. *Salmona*
The meaning of this word is *umbra portionis*,¹⁰⁹ according to Jerome. Again, we find that Origen gave this meaning to the word: *Selmona, quid interpretatur umbra portionis*,¹¹⁰ undoubtedly deriving it from צֵל, 'shadow', plus מָנָה, 'part, portion'.

10. *Salomi*
Jerome gives the meaning of this word as *pax mea*, 'my peace'.¹¹¹ Origen also gives the same meaning to the word – εἰρηνή,¹¹² obviously linking this personal name with שָׁלוֹם, 'wholeness, peace'.

These ten examples of Jerome's name explanations make interesting reading. All of them show that the meaning which Jerome attaches to these words had already been put forward previously by other writers. We are not attempting to prove that Jerome read only Philo and Origen's etymologies: this would be impossible because of the proliferation of etymologies in the early centuries.¹¹³ We do want to show, however, that, on some occasions (notably with *Raguel* above), Jerome has merely copied out the etymological meanings of other authors without thinking or checking their correctness.

This fact has important ramifications for our study of the extent and quality of Jerome's Hebrew knowledge. Judgement must not be made on this matter until a number of factors have been taken into account. Among these are the following:
a) Jerome copied some of his etymologies from other authors;
b) he worked very quickly, and thus did not check his work;
c) he was a child of his time in believing that *every* word and name had a meaning. If a meaning could not be found for a Hebrew word, an etymology from a like-sounding Hebrew word or words was const-

---

108 *Hom. on Num.* 12 (*PG* 12, 658).
109 *Lib.Heb.Nom.* (*CCL* 72, 85).
110 *Hom. on Num.* 27 (*PG* 12, 798).
111 *Lib.Heb.Nom.* (*CCL* 72, 85).
112 *Hom. on Jer.*, fragment 60 (*GCS*, Orig. Werke III, p. 227, 26).
113 The detailed and careful study of F. Wütz: *Onomastica Sacra* (TU 41, 1914) has shown that Jerome's word lists went back to the third century at least, and that Jerome did not necessarily go direct to Philo and Origen's writings to obtain his word explanations.

ructed. Similarly, if a meaning was required for a Greek word, Jerome felt no compunction about supplying an etymology, by treating it as if it were a Hebrew word.[114] He even acknowledges that some of his etymologies are incorrect,[115] but still persists in the exercise.

These factors, then, must be taken into consideration when attempting to judge Jerome's Hebrew knowledge. At first glance, and judging Jerome by modern standards, it may appear that his Hebrew knowledge was slight. But when the context of Jerome's age, when the science of philology was almost unknown, and Jerome's eclectic method of writing (his use of previous authors and etymologies), and his pace of study are all taken into account, then a more favourable judgement may be possible.

We can only judge Jerome's knowledge of Hebrew by comparing him with his predecessors, rather than with modern standards. It will be instructive in this regard to look briefly at the extent of the Hebrew knowledge of Philo and Origen, and then compare their knowledge with that of Jerome.

Some older scholars of Philo thought that the Alexandrian philosopher had a considerable knowledge of Hebrew. C. Siegfried, for example, wrote that 'Philo understood Hebrew... in accordance with those traditions concerning the rules and vocabulary of the sacred language which had been brought to Alexandria by Palestinian Jews and indeed had already been accepted there for some considerable time'.[116] But more recently, the tendency among scholars has been to deny that Philo knew any Hebrew. In 1929, E. Stein amassed evidence to show that, among other things, Philo apparently did not know that κύριος was the equivalent of יהוה and θεός to אֱלֹהִים.[117] Stein showed that Philo was dependent on the LXX for his knowledge of the Pentateuch and that he drew conclusions from translations in the LXX which have no support in the Hebrew.

The most recent scholarship, however, has reached a more balanced position concerning the extent of Philo's Hebrew knowledge. V. Nikiprowetzky has said that 'Philo's knowledge (of Hebrew) was very gen-

---

114 On this see J. Barr: *art.cit.*, pp. 298-300.
115 E.g. *Comm.Isa.* 7, 14 on *Almah*. Jerome says he includes its false etymology in order to 'give the Jews a laugh' (*ut risum praebeamus Iudaeis*) (*CCL* 73, 103).
116 C. Siegfried: *Philo von Alexandria als Ausleger des A.T.*, Jena 1875, p. 144.
117 E. Stein: *Die allegorische Exegese des Philo aus Alexandria*, Giessen 1929, p. 20f.

eral',[118] and that he was ignorant of the *realia* of Judaism.[119] S. Sandmel came to the conclusion that 'there is, then, no compelling evidence that Philo himself knew any Hebrew, even though his writings reflect some knowledge of it', and that, if he knew any Hebrew, 'he used it, if at all, so little that his knowledge of it was at best useless'.[120] The modern scholarly consensus, then, is that Philo may have known a little Hebrew, and this he used to compile his etymologies from earlier sources. Philo's knowledge of Hebrew was a quantitative one. He was able to recognise Hebrew words and use them to compile an etymology from previous written sources, but had no real conception of Hebrew grammar, and no extensive vocabulary.

Eusebius of Caesarea[121] states that Origen made a thorough study of Hebrew. Writing about the *Hexapla*, he says that ('so accurate was the study which Origen brought to bear on the words of scripture, that he even made a thorough study of the Hebrew language, and made the original writings in Hebrew characters, which were used among the Jews, his own.') Eusebius was followed in this opinion by Jerome,[122] who says that Origen's Hebrew learning is common knowledge. In *Ep.* 39, 1, Jerome compares Blesilla with Origen, saying that '...in a few months, or rather days, she so completely mastered the difficulties of Hebrew as to emulate her mother's zeal in learning and chanting the Psalms'.[123] Some older commentators apparently took this to refer to Origen's mother, whom they understood to be Jewish, and that she taught Origen Hebrew at an early age. But, as N.R.M. de Lange has recently pointed out,[124] the subject of the sentence is Blesilla and *cum matre* refers to Paula. It does, however, show that Jerome believed that Origen had learned Hebrew.

From Origen himself we gain a different picture. His language at several places, employed to refer to various Jewish traditions, makes it clear that Origen derived these particular pieces of information from another source, and that he was not particularly conversant with Hebrew.

---

[118] V. Nikiprowetzky: *Le commentaire de l'Écriture chez Philon d'Alexandrie*, Thesis, Paris 1970, published by Service de réproduction de thèses, Université de Lille 1974, p. 59.
[119] *Ibid.*, p. 70.
[120] S. Sandmel: *Philo's Place in Judaism*, Cincinnati 1956, pp. 12ff.
[121] *HE* 6, 16, 1.
[122] *De Vir.Illus.* 54 (*PL* 23, 699).
[123] *CSEL* 54, 294: ...in paucis non dico mensibus, sed deibus ita Hebraeae linguae uicerat difficultates, ut in ediscendis canendisque psalmis cum matre contenderet.
[124] *Origen and the Jews*, Cambridge 1976, p. 23.

He says, for instance, that the name of God *is said* to be written differently in Hebrew when the true God is meant and when a false god is meant.[125] Again, we find the telling phrase, 'Those who are expert in Hebrew matters say...'.[126]

Again, if Origen knew Hebrew well, we should expect him to quote from the Hebrew bible frequently. But, as de Lange has shown,[127] he often relies on the LXX when he might be expected to use the Hebrew bible, and, when he does comment on the Hebrew text, he is vague and hesitant and most often incorrect. For the *Hexapla*, Origen probably relied on help from Jewish colleagues. We must conclude that Origen could read Hebrew only with great difficulty, if at all, and his vocabulary was not extensive. As with Philo, then, Origen's knowledge of Hebrew was quantitative and superficial.[128]

The knowledge of Hebrew which Jerome portrays is on a quite different level from that of either Philo or Origen. Whereas their knowledge of the language is slight and superficial, Jerome has a much more extensive and profound knowledge. James Barr rightly notes[129] that Jerome also has the same quantitative use of Hebrew as does Origen, 'but he added to it a qualitative use of Hebrew as a guide to the right *meanings*'.

This qualitative use of Hebrew manifests itself in various ways. Of these, we will look briefly at four: translation, vocalisation, appreciation of Hebrew linguistic features, and Jerome's ability to teach Hebrew. First, the very fact that Jerome undertook to translate the books of the O.T. from the original Hebrew must surely be taken as proof of a high degree of ability in Hebrew. Even bearing in mind that he had the previous Greek translations of Theodotion, Symmachus and especially of Aquila, which must have been of considerable value to him, Jerome's own translation from the Hebrew was quite a remarkable achievement, especially when it is noticed that it is generally a good and faithful translation. We shall return to Jerome's translation technique in another chapter.[130]

Second, the vocalisation which Jerome employs can be used as

---

125 *Hom. on Num.* 14.
126 *Comm. in Ps.* 24, 10.
127 *Op.cit.*, p. 22.
128 See G. Bardy's conclusion: 'We must simply conclude that if Origen had learnt enough Hebrew to read it and transcribe it, yet he never possessed more than a superficial knowledge of the language.' ('Les traditions juives dans l'Oeuvre d'Origène', in *RB* XXXIV [1925] 217-252).
129 *Art.cit.*, p. 282.
130 See Chapter 4.

evidence of a high degree of Hebrew knowledge. We have already noted that the Hebrew text with which Jerome worked was unpointed, and that Jerome was very probably taught Hebrew orally. This means that distinctions in meaning could be brought about by different vocalisations of the same consonants. A study of Jerome's vocalisation will, therefore, bring us close to the knowledge of Hebrew which he must have had.

A passage from the *Comm.Hier.* is often quoted in this context:
> 'The Hebrew word, which is written with the three letters "d-b-r" (it has no vowels in it) according to the natural progression of the passage and the judgement of the reader, if "dabar" is read it means "word"; if "deber", it means "death"; and if "dabber", it means "speak".'[132]

In this example, Jerome is combatting the incorrect translations of this word which appeared in the Greek versions, which implied different vocalisations. The LXX omitted the word; the *Hexapla* had θανάτῳ; Aquila had λάλησον, as did Symmachus.[133] It seems unlikely that Jerome was here influenced by the Jewish 'al-tiqre' (do not read) interpretation, as Prof. Barr suggests,[134] for if he had done, one would have thought that he would have used the different possibilities of vocalisation in his interpretation. It is more likely that Jerome is merely revelling in his knowledge of Hebrew, and showing off to his Christian readers by exhibiting his mastery of the language.[135]

Third, Jerome shows occasionally that he can recognise various features of Hebrew style, especially assonance. In the *Comm.Isa.*, he notes the word plays between משפט and משפה, and צדקה and צעקה, obvious in Hebrew, but which do not come across in translation – 'judgement' and 'bloodshed', and 'justice' and 'shouting'.[136] This gives Jerome the opportunity once more to show off the extent of his Hebrew knowledge, and he takes some little time explaining the word plays, showing the difference which was caused in each case by the change of one letter. Another example of this is seen at the famous passage of the

---

131 J. Barr: *art.cit.*, p. 293.
132 *Comm.Hier.* 9, 22 (not 9, 21 as Prof. Barr says – *art.cit.*, p. 293) (*CCL* 74, 99): Verbum Hebraicum, quod tribus litteris scribitur 'daleth, beth, res' – uocales enim in medio non habet – pro consequentia et legentis arbitrio si legatur 'dabar', 'sermonem' significat, si 'deber', 'mortem', si 'dabber', 'loquere'.
133 J. Barr: *art.cit.*, p. 293.
134 *Ibid.*
135 This is also the case elsewhere, e.g. at *Comm.Isa.* 2, 22 (*CCL* 73, 39f).
136 *Comm.Isa.* 5, 7 (*CCL* 73, 68).

call of Jeremiah[137] where he explains the word play between שָׁקֵד (saced; *nux*; 'nut-tree') and שֹׁקֵד (soced; *uigilia*; 'watch'). Jerome would not have been able to show off like this (for he does not use these explanations of the word plays in his exegesis) unless he had a good knowledge of the language.

Finally, that Jerome had an extensive knowledge of Hebrew is shown by the fact that, not content with learning the language himself, he, in turn, became a teacher of Hebrew so that, under his tutelage, Paula and her daughter Eustochium became so versed in Hebrew that they could chant the Psalms in Hebrew and speak the language without a trace of Latin accent.[138] Jerome may have been exaggerating to some extent here, as he wrote this in his eulogy of Paula. But that she and Eustochium actually learned Hebrew is not disputed. In many of the letters Jerome wrote to them, he discusses exegetical points based on the Hebrew text, as, for example, *Ep.* 28, which discusses the meanings of the Hebrew word 'Selah'; *Ep.* 29, which explains the Hebrew words 'Ephod bad' (1 Sam. 2:18) and 'Teraphim' (Judges 17:5); and *Ep.* 30, in which Jerome expounds the mystical meaning of the Hebrew alphabet. These epistles were written in A.D. 384 in Rome, and, although we do not know that Jerome continued with his Hebrew lessons, the fact that he began to teach others may imply that he also continued to study with a Hebrew teacher in order to deepen his own knowledge of the language.

Jerome and Aramaic

Jerome speaks several times as if he were fluent not only in Hebrew but also in Syriac and Aramaic. In the desert in Chalcis, he writes of the barbarous language which his fellow ascetics speak. Replying to a letter of Chromatius and two other friends, Jerome says that he experienced great joy when he received their letter, because it was the only contact he now had with the Latin language, 'for here one must either learn a barbarous language at an advanced age or else say nothing'.[139] This barbarous language was not Hebrew but very probably Syriac, the local dialect of Aramaic, used by the simple, uneducated hermits who inhabited caves in the desert of Chalcis.[140] From a knowledge of

---

[137] *Comm.Hier.* 1, 11 (*CCL* 74, 7).
[138] *Ep.* 108, 26: ...ut psalmos Hebraeice caneret et sermonem absque ulla Latinae linguae proprietate resonaret (*CSEL* 55, 345).
[139] *Ep.* 7, 2 (*CSEL* 54, 27): Hic enim aut seni sermo discendus est aut tacendum est.
[140] See A. Festugière: *Antioche paienne et chrétienne*, Paris 1959, pp. 245-356.

Jerome's personality, we may conjecture that he would have found it impossible to remain silent for the duration of his stay in the ascetic community, and so we would expect Jerome to have some knowledge of Syriac. Indeed, in a letter written to the presbyter Mark, a leader in the ascetic community at Chalcis, Jerome answers various accusations which have been made against him. Among these is apparently one which suggests that Jerome might say damaging things about the Church, to which he replies:

> 'You are afraid, I suppose, that a man as eloquent in both Syriac and Greek as I, will travel round the churches, seduce the people into error and form a schismatic group.'[141]

If we take these words at their face value, Jerome must have been very proficient in Syriac, if some of the hermits thought him capable of seducing whole churches into schism. On the other hand, Jerome may be exhibiting one of his characteristic displays of sarcasm – if Jerome knew only a little or no Syriac, he would not be able to seduce anyone into schism, and so the accusation against him is worthy only of contempt.

Is there any way of ascertaining the extent of Jerome's knowledge of Syriac? If he knew Syriac well, we should suppose that biblical Aramaic would not pose any great difficulty for him. But in the preface to his translation of Daniel, we find the following passage:

> 'As for myself, when in my youth, after having read the flowery rhetoric of Quintilian and Cicero, I vigorously began to study this language [Aramaic], the expenditure of much time and effort allowed me to utter the puffing and hissing sounds. I appeared to be walking in a kind of underground chamber with only a few scattered rays of light shining on me; when at last I met with Daniel, such a sense of weariness came over me that, in despair, I could have counted all my previous work as useless. But a certain Hebrew encouraged me... and so, conscious that among Hebrews I was only a smatterer, I once more began to study Chaldean. And, to tell the truth, even today I can read and understand Chaldee better than I can pronounce it.'[142]

The preface to Jerome's translation of Tobit tells us that he did not translate direct from Aramaic, but employed a person who rendered the Aramaic into Hebrew, whereupon Jerome translated simultaneously from Hebrew into Latin.[143] The only reason why Jerome did not

---

141 *Ep.* 17, 2 (*CSEL* 54, 72): Plane times ne eloquentissimus homo in Syro sermone uel Graeco ecclesias circumeam, populos seducam, scisma conficiam.
142 *Pref. to Daniel* (*PL* 28, 1357-60).
143 *PL* 29, 23-26. See also above p. 29.

translate directly from Aramaic into Latin himself would be that he did not know enough to accomplish the task.

The conclusion that Jerome's statement – that he was fluent in Syriac – cannot be taken literally, and must be dismissed as sarcasm, seems unavoidable when a study is made, first of Jerome's comments on the O.T. passages written in Aramaic, and second, of other passages where Aramaic names or words are encountered. If Jerome knew Syriac or Aramaic well, we should reasonably expect a certain amount of extended comment on various facets of the language, as we have seen to be the case for Hebrew.[144]

At Dan. 2:4a, the beginning of the Aramaic passage of that book, Jerome merely says that from this place, the visions Daniel had were written in Hebrew characters but the language used was 'Chaldean', which is called Syriac.[145] At the end of the Aramaic section (7:28b), Jerome merely mentions that the rest of the volume is in Hebrew.[146] Jerome did not compose a commentary on Ezra, and the preface to his translation of this book makes no reference to or comment on the Aramaic sections (4:8-6:18; 7:12-26). Similarly, on the Aramaic gloss at Jer. 10:11, Jerome is silent.

Scattered throughout Jerome's commentaries, and, more frequently, as we would expect, in the *Liber Interp.Heb.Nom.*, are a number of observations that such-and-such a word is Aramaic or Syriac and not Hebrew, of which the following are examples:

Acheldemach ager sanguinis. Syrum est, non Hebraeum.[147]
Barrabban filium magistri eorum. Syrum est, non Hebraeum.[148]
Golgotha caluaria. Syrum est, non Hebraeum.[149]
Rabbi magister meus. Syrum est.[150]
Audiamus cetera: lingua Hebraea et Syra Baal interpretatur ἔχων, *id est habens.*[151]

---

[144] *Ep.* 17, 2. See footnote 141 above.
[145] *CCL* 75A, 785: Hucusque quae lecta sunt, sermone narrantur hebraeo; ab hoc loco usque ad uisionem anni tertii regis Baldasar quam Daniel uidit in Susis, hebraicis quidem litteris sed lingua scribuntur chaldaica, quam hic syriacam uocat.
[146] *CCL* 75A, 850: Cetera quae sequuntur, usque ad finem uoluminis, hebraice legimus.
[147] *Lib.Heb.Nom.* (*CCL* 72, 134).
[148] *Ibid.* (*CCL* 72, 135).
[149] *Ibid.* (*CCL* 72, 136).
[150] *Ibid.* (*CCL* 72, 138).
[151] *Comm.Osee* 2, 16f (*CCL* 76, 28).

Bariona filius columbae. Syrum est pariter et Hebraeum. Bar quippe lingua syra filius, et iona columba utroque sermone dicitur.[152]

These examples show that Jerome had some knowledge of the vocabulary of Aramaic or the dialect of Syriac, but nowhere in Jerome's works do we find any kind of detailed knowledge of the language. While he can recognise some instances where etymological meaning is important for the interpretation, as at *'Bariona'*, at other times the interpretation is already given in the Bible, as with *Aceldemach* (Matt. 27:8). In the former cases, we may conjecture that Jerome got this information from his Jewish teachers.

It may be thought strange that Jerome who, as we have seen, was so competent in the Hebrew language, did not also have at least a reasonable grasp of Aramaic. But the reason for this is simple. Jerome was not interested in languages for their own sakes: he learned Hebrew because this was the language in which the O.T. was written, and to understand this correctly, it was necessary to study the original language. Aramaic, on the other hand, was not, except for a few parts, the language of scripture. Jerome, therefore, had no intrinsic motivation for having more than an acquaintance with the language. From the information available to us, we must conclude that Jerome's knowledge of Aramaic was minimal. He could recognise words in this language, but no more.

Conclusions

In this chapter, we have charted the acceptance by Jerome of the *Hebraica veritas* and its two main manifestations in his work, the acceptance of the Jewish biblical canon, and the use of the Hebrew language as the basis of his O.T. interpretation. Jerome's acceptance of the *Hebraica veritas*, however, was not accepted by other Christians. Evidence of the difficulties Jerome encountered is extant in the form of letters between Jerome and his younger contemporary, Augustine, who initiated the correspondence.

In *Ep.* 28, 2,[153] Augustine boldly (this was his first letter to Jerome) asks Jerome not to translate the holy scriptures unless he uses the same

---

152 *Lib.Heb.Nom.* (*CCL* 72, 135).
153 *Ep.* 56 in Jerome's correspondence. For the details of the correspondence, see P. Auvray: 'Saint Jérôme et saint Augustin: La controverse au sujet de l'Incident d'Antioche', in *RSR* 29 (1939) 594-610; and D. De Bruyne: 'La correspondance échangée entre Augustin et Jérôme', in *ZNTW* 31 (1932) 233-248.

methods as he did for his translation of Job, i.e. from the LXX, and to use Origen's critical signs to indicate its difference from the Hebrew. For Augustine could not understand why anyone would wish to go back to the Hebrew manuscripts after the Seventy translators had made such a good translation.

In another letter (*Ep.* 71, 3f) Augustine puts forward more reasons why Jerome should abandon the Hebrew and translate from the LXX. Augustine had heard that Jerome had translated the book of Job afresh from the Hebrew, but was perplexed not to find any critical marks indicating differences between the Hebrew and LXX texts, as he had done in his other translation of Job. Again, Augustine was afraid that, if Jerome's version from the Hebrew is read in the churches, then differences will inevitably arise between the Latin and Greek churches, since the Greek churches would continue to use the LXX. Another reason Augustine gives is that Jerome may have made mistakes in his new version, and that the Jews, if consulted for the meaning of the Hebrew text, might give a different answer than Jerome, and no-one else would know which answer was correct. Further, Augustine cites an example of a disturbance which had broken out at Oea (Tripoli) when the local bishop, who had adopted Jerome's new version, read out an unfamiliar word from the story of Jonah (4:6 - 'ivy' for 'gourd'). The disturbance was so great, denouncing the translation as false, that the bishop was forced to ask some local Jews their opinion, who 'out of ignorance or spite' answered in favour of the LXX, and the bishop had to change the translation.

Jerome characteristically took little notice of these arguments of Augustine, and did not alter his convictions with regard to the *Hebraica veritas*. At the end of his life, he was as firmly convinced as he had been many years before when he began his Hebrew studies, of the precedence and authority of the Hebrew text of scripture. We have seen that his attitude to the biblical canon did not undergo a decisive change, as some scholars have argued, and that he had a good command of written Hebrew. The question of whether or not Jerome could speak Hebrew cannot be answered because of lack of evidence. If, however, we reason from such evidence as the preface to Tobit, which, as we have seen, cannot be taken at face value, it must be doubted that Jerome was a fluent Hebrew speaker. It is more likely that his conversations with Jews were conducted in Greek, still the *lingua franca* of the Empire. As for Aramaic and Syriac, we must conclude that Jerome's knowledge was superficial, amounting only to the ability to recognise Aramaic words and the retention of some vocabulary.

4. Jerome as a Translator

Introduction

The most profound and lasting influence which Jerome has had on the history of Christianity has been his translation of the Bible into Latin, transforming a morass of divergent textual readings into what we know as the Vulgate.[1] Jerome's background and education made him especially suited for the task of translating the Bible, for he was, as he himself says, a *vir trilinguis*, knowing Hebrew, Greek and Latin.[2] His connection with Pope Damasus brought the initial impetus and opportunity to undertake this mammoth task, and the Vulgate is a monument to Jerome's labour, perseverance and natural aptitude for linguistic study. A survey of his work as translator is also of fundamental importance for our wider investigation of Jerome's exegesis, for he saw it as part of the exegete's task in explaining the word of God to Christian people to have an easily understood text in the common language. This translation was a necessary preliminary to the explanation of the deeper meaning of the Bible.

In order to discuss aright Jerome's principles and practice of the art of translation, it will be necessary first to say a little about the theories of translation in ancient times, and also to place Jerome in the context of the nature of Christian translation and translations in the fourth century.

The nature of language and linguistic phenomena was a matter of importance and speculation for the ancients. The first extended discussion of the nature of language is found in Plato's *Cratylus*, which asks the question whether language was a natural growth or an arbitrary conven-

---

1 Jerome's version was not officially known as the 'Vulgate' until the Council of Trent. The term appears to have been used first by Faber Stapulensis at the end of the Middle Ages. Cf E.T. Sutcliffe: 'The name "Vulgate"', in *Biblica* 29 (1948) 345-352; A. Allgeier: '"Haec vetus et vulgata editio". Neues Wort – und begriffsgeschichtliche Beiträge zur Bibel auf dem Tridentinum', in *Biblica* 29 (1948) 353-390. When Jerome used the term 'vulgata', he referred, of course, to the existing Latin version(s), which we know as the Old Latin (henceforth O.L.).
2 *Apol.c. Ruf.* III, 6 (*CCL* 79, 79): '...*hebraeus, graecus, latinus, trilinguis*'.

tion. This question gave rise to a controversy which raged for several centuries between two opposing schools of thought, the Analogists and the Anomalists. The former school maintained first that nouns and verbs were capable of classification into declensions and conjugations on the basis of similarity of form (ἀναλογία), and secondly, that the names of things derive from a natural and necessary connection between the things themselves and their names. The latter school, on the other hand, by observing the great number of irregularities (ἀνωμαλίαι) in the use of language, believed that no such orderly classification could be made, and that the names of things had no necessary connection with the things they signified, but were largely the result of chance and convenience.

This Analogist-Anomalist controversy manifested itself in both the Greek- and Latin-speaking worlds. Among the Greeks, the grammarians of Alexandria produced several eminent Analogists, for example, Aristarchus[3] and Dionysius Thrax,[4] and also Anomalists, like the Stoic Chrysippus[5] and Crates of Mallos.[6] Among the Latins, the Scipionic circle of writers were generally in favour of the Analogical view of language, with their use of *latinitas* and *purus sermo*. Caesar wrote a treatise called *De Analogia*, in favour of this linguistic approach.[7] Cicero, on the other hand, inclined towards the Anomalist school,[8] as did Horace[9] and Quintilian,[10] giving great importance to the claims of *consuetudo*.

---

[3] Aristarchus lived c 217-145 B.C., was tutor to Ptolemy VII Eupator, head of the Alexandrian library (c 153 B.C.) and the author of many works of criticism and commentary. His work covered the wide range of grammatical, etymological, orthographical, literary and textual criticism. He founded a school at Alexandria which lasted until the Roman imperial period, and which had many distinguished pupils.

[4] Dionysius Thrax (c 170-90 B.C.) was a pupil of Aristarchus. His only extant work, Τέχνη γραμματική, is an epitome of pure grammar as developed at Alexandria; it classifies accents, stops, letters and syllables, defines the various parts of speech with their subdivisions, and gives paradigms of inflection. Many commentaries were written on this work, which remained popular until the Renaissance.

[5] Chrysippus (c 280-207 B.C.) was head of the Stoa, succeeding Cleanthes in 232 B.C. He wrote numerous works, among them four books called Περὶ Ἀνωμαλίας. Only fragments of his literary output are extant.

[6] Crates of Mallos, contemporary of Aristarchus, was the first head of the library at Pergamum, and wrote on Hesiod, Aratus, Euripides and Homer.

[7] Aulus Gellius: *Attic Nights* I, 10, 4.

[8] See especially *Orat.* 155-162.

[9] See *Ars Poetica* 70-72.

[10] See *Institutes* I, 6.

The Jewish people operated with a different linguistic philosophy, which neither influenced nor was influenced by the Anomalist-Analogist controversy. The Jewish view of the nature of language was not speculative or analytical, but was a logical consequence of their doctrine of creation. Language for them was a gift from God, who had created all things, and therefore there was no need to speculate about the origin of language. In early Mishnaic times, the Hebrew language of the scriptures and the Hebrew of the rabbis was referred to as לְשׁוֹן הַקֹּדֶשׁ, the 'holy tongue', as contrasted with all other languages, which were described as לְשׁוֹן חוֹל, the 'common tongue'.[11] The Jews (as well as Latin classical writers) were also intensely interested in allegorising[12] and in giving meaning to the names of people and places. We have already seen that this practice of etymology was carried on by the Church Fathers.[13]

The Church Fathers were influenced to a much greater degree by the Jewish conception of the nature and origin of language than by the Anomaly-Analogy philosophical debate. That is not to say, however, that this philosophical debate had no influence on the Church Fathers. The *Contra Eunomium II* of Gregory of Nyssa, composed c 380, includes a discussion of the origin of language and the question of whether names are given by human perception or by divine direction. Gregory argues forcefully against Eunomius that God is not the creator of languages and names, but rather they are human creations, coming into being through 'conception' (ἐπίνοια, an operation of the mind). Although this polemical work has little bearing on the subject of translation, it does show that the Anomaly-Analogy debate was still alive in the fourth century A.D. Gregory apparently read this work to Gregory of Nazianzus and Jerome at the Second Ecumenical Council at Constantinople in 381,[14] but Jerome never discusses it or its subject matter anywhere else in his works.

Jerome himself seems to have been influenced little by the Anomalist-Analogist controversy, but rather was convinced of the variety of the Judaeo-Christian conception of language. Nowhere in his works does Jerome discuss the nature of language, except that, several times, he follows the Jewish idea that Hebrew was the original language of the world.[15]

---

11 M.H. Segal: *A Grammar of Mishnaic Hebrew*, Oxford 1927 (reprinted 1980) p. 2; cf *Sota* VII, 1f; cf S.P. Brock: 'Aspects of translation technique in antiquity', in *Greek, Roman and Byzantine Studies* 20 (1979) 69-87, esp. p. 75.
12 See above, Chapter 1.
13 See above, Chapter 3.
14 Jerome: *De Vir.Illus.* 128 (*PL* 23, 754).
15 Cf *Gen.R.* XVIII, 4; *Cant.R.* iv, 12, 1. It is worthy of note that Herodotus (*Hist.* 2, 2) thought that Phrygian was the original language of the world.

It is very probably true to say that Jerome was one of the two most important Christian translators of the fourth century, the other being Rufinus.[16] A great deal of their literary activity was given over to the pursuit of the practical objective of giving Christians in the West the opportunity of reading and learning from the writings of the Greek Fathers. However, as G. Bardy emphasises in his interesting article,[17] Jerome and Rufinus were not the only two Christian translators at this time. Several others assisted in the same enterprise with similar objectives. Hilary of Poitiers, for instance, at the end of his *De Synodis*, translated all the Greek documents relative to the Arian controversy,[18] and in the *De Trinitate*, he translated a letter of Arius.[19] In these two instances, Hilary's objectives were practical ones – to show Latin readers the complexity of the problems involved in the contemporary theological debate, and to show, from first-hand evidence, the true character of Arius' heresy.

There are few other instances from the fourth century which show that there were Latin writers, other than Jerome and Rufinus, who were active in translating Greek words, using 'translation' here in the modern sense of the word.[20] If, however, we use the word more loosely, it is possible, as Bardy demonstrates, to show that Jerome and Rufinus were not alone in their objective of giving the Latin-speaking world the opportunity of knowing Greek Christian works. Hilary and Ambrose, for example, in their exegetical works, were influenced to a great extent by Origen, and it is possible to see this influence as a kind of 'translation' of Greek ideas into the Latin-speaking Church. Taken in this sense, almost every Latin Christian writer may be said to have translated some Greek Christian ideas into Latin. But it is chiefly to Jerome and Rufinus that we owe the development of the idea of translation in the modern sense, for they thought it worthwhile to translate *in toto* the works of several Greek Christian writers. The reason for this is probably that they were more profoundly influenced by Greek writers than their predecessors.

---

[16] Cf G. Bardy: 'Traducteurs et Adaptateurs au IVe Siècle, in *RSR* 30 (1940) p. 270; also G. Bardy: *La Question des Langues dans l'Église Ancienne*, Paris 1948, p. 247.
[17] Cf the previous footnote.
[18] Cf *De Synodis* 9.
[19] Cf *De Trin*. IV, 12-13. There are several differences in Hilary's Latin translation from Athanasius' Greek version (*De Synodis* 16).
[20] But see Augustine: *Conf.* 8, 2, 3, where Victorinus is said to have translated Platonist writers.

F. Blatt[21] went so far as to say that Jerome initiated 'a new principle of translation' – the word for word translation of the Bible. This is probably going too far, for it lays too much stress, as we shall see below, on what Jerome says, and not enough stress on what Jerome actually does in his translations. But Blatt is certainly correct to see Jerome (and, perhaps to a lesser extent Rufinus) as the major figure in the fourth century in connection with the art of translation. It is the intention of this chapter to show first, the range and amount of literature which Jerome translated, and second, the techniques he used in these translations.

Jerome's translations

While Jerome was living in Constantinople between 379 and 382,[22] he took the first step in an important aspect of his career as a biblical exegete, the scholarly activity of translation. Jerome gives us no firm indication of his reasons for turning to this activity in the preface to his first translation, made in 380, of Eusebius of Caesarea's *Chronicle*. We may conjecture, however, that, having now spent several years learning from the works of Greek theologians and steeping himself in Greek theology, he was anxious that the Latin-speaking world should have the opportunity of benefitting from the scholarship of Greek Christians. Perhaps also his immediate attraction to Eusebius' *Chronicle* was that, as Kelly suggests,[23] the work offered a panoramic picture of a whole sweep of world history, the like of which had never been seen before in the Western world.

Eusebius had composed his *Chronicle* as an apologetic work, attempting to show that the Jewish-Christian tradition was older (and therefore worthy of more respect) than the traditions of many other people. Most of the work consists of a series of synchronistic tables of dates (including the dates of kings' and emperors' reigns) set out in parallel columns, with other noteworthy events catalogued along with them.[24] He began with the birth of Abraham, which he dated in 2016

---

21 F. Blatt: 'Remarques sur l'histoire des traductions latines', in *Classica et Medievalia* 1 (1938) p. 220.
22 Cavallera I, pp. 59-72; II, pp. 20-22.
23 Kelly: p. 73.
24 Following Helm (*GCS* 47, xxxiiif), most scholars argue that, although there were two separate columns at the beginning of the work, by the time Eusebius reached the rebuilding of the Temple in 520 B.C., the two columns had become interspersed.

B.C., and ended in the twentieth year of the reign of Constantine, 325 A.D.[25]

The apologetic nature of the *Chronicle* would, however, have meant little to Jerome, as Christianity had, by this time, become the religion of the Empire, having now no need to justify its own antiquity and superiority. Eusebius, however, had little interest in events or personalities in the West, so Jerome, in translating it for a western audience, felt obliged to make changes in the original. He omitted Eusebius' introductory essay on the comparative systems of dating used by the Chaldeans, Assyrians, Hebrews, Greeks and Romans,[26] and made many additions, mostly concerned with Roman history, literature and scholarship. He also added a section at the end of the *Chronicle*, which brought it from 325 to 379 A.D. Jerome speaks of these changes, and his sources, in the preface:

> 'The truth is that I have partly discharged the office of translator and partly that of a writer. I have with the utmost fidelity rendered the Greek portion, and at the same time have added certain things which seemed to me to have been allowed to slip, especially in the Roman history, which Eusebius... only glanced at; not so much because he was ignorant, for he was a learned man, but because, writing in Greek, he thought them of little importance to his countrymen. So from Ninus and Abraham right up to the captivity of Troy, is translated simply from the Greek. From Troy to the twentieth year of Constantine there is much which I have gleaned with great diligence from Tranquillus and other famous historians. Sometimes I have set this down separately and sometimes it is intermingled (with the original). Moreover, the section from the aforementioned year of Constantine to the sixth consulship of the Emperor Valens and the second of Valentinianus is entirely my own.'[27]

---

[25] Some scholars posit an earlier edition, which ended at 303 A.D. See D.S. Wallace-Hadrill: 'The Eusebian Chronicle: the Extent and Date of Composition of its early editions', in *JTS* N.S. 6 (1955) 248-253.

[26] *GCS* 47, 8.

[27] *GCS* 47, 6-7: Sciendum etenim est me et interpretis et scriptoris ex parte officio usum, quia et Graeca fidelissime expressi et nonnulla, quae mihi intermissa uidebantur, adieci, in Romana maxime historia, quam Eusebius... non tam ignorasse ut eruditus, sed ut Graece scribens parum suis necessariam perstrinxisse mihi uidetur. Itaque a Nino et Abraham usque ad Troiae captiuitatem pura Graeca translatio est. A Troia usque ad uicesimum Constantini annum nunc addita, nunc admixta sunt plurima, quae de Tranquillo et ceteris inlustribus historicis curiosissime excerpsi. A Constantini autem supra dicto anno usque ad consulatum Augustorum Ualentis sexies et Ualentiniani iterum totum meum est.

Jerome's translation was a great success. He had, in effect, provided the western world with a history of the world as it was then known and understood. His friend Vincentius, who was one of the two men to whom the translation was dedicated,[28] and who became closely involved with Jerome's literary efforts from now on, suggested that he ought to turn his attention to translating the works of Origen into Latin, in order 'to make available to Roman ears the man who, according to Didymus, who was blind but yet clear-sighted, is second only to the apostles as a teacher of the Church'.[29] Jerome was apparently interested in translating a large number, if not all, of Origen's works into Latin, but, as he explained to Vincentius,[30] was prevented from carrying out his wish by one of his frequent bouts of illness – a painful eye irritation caused by constant reading; and also by lack of copyists, owing to a shortage of money.[31] For these reasons, Jerome had to be content with translating only a few of Origen's homilies, of which there were originally about six hundred. In 380-1, Jerome was to translate fourteen of Origen's homilies on Jeremiah, fourteen on Ezekiel and nine on Isaiah. Later, in 383-4, he translated two homilies of Origen on the Song of Songs, and between 389-392, thirty nine homilies on the Gospel of Luke. In his preface to the translation of the homilies on Jeremiah, Jerome admits to having translated them *confuso ordine*,[32] omitting some of the original homilies which he believed to have been contaminated with Origen's suspect doctrine. He managed to retain the direct simplicity of Origen's homiletic style. The nine homilies on Isaiah were transmitted without the name of the translator, but they are today attributed to Jerome, because he uses them later in the *Comm.Isa.*, because they are written in his style, and also because Rufinus testifies that Jerome had translated certain homilies of Origen on Isaiah, citing a passage from the first of these, which is verbally identical with the translation.[33]

In 383-4, a few years after translating the homilies on Jeremiah, Ezekiel and Isaiah, Jerome explained to Pope Damasus that he should very

---

On the unsolved problem of who the 'famous historians' were, see R.M. Grant: *Eusebius as Church Historian*, Oxford 1980, p. 4, and Kelly: p. 74, n. 24, and the literature cited there.

28 The other was Gennadius; cf Jerome's preface to Eusebius' *Chronicle*.
29 Preface to translation of Origen's *Hom.Ezek.* (*GCS* 33, 318).
30 *Ibid.*
31 Kelly: p. 76, sees in this lack of money a hint that Jerome's family estates in Stridon may have been taken over by the Goths, and that consequently he could not rely on them for any more money.
32 Pref. to translation of Origen's *Hom.Ezek.* (*GCS* 33, 318).
33 Rufinus: *Apol.c.Hier.* 2, 27: see W.A. Baehrens: *GCS* 33, pp. xlii-xlvi.

much have liked to translate Origen's *Comm. on Song of Songs*. However:

> 'I have left that work on one side, since it would require almost boundless leisure, labour and money to translate so great a work into Latin, even if it could be worthily done; and I have translated these two short treatises which he wrote in the form of daily lectures...'[34]

The 'two short treatises' were the two homilies on the Song of Songs, originally intended for catechumens and written in a very simple style. Jerome's translation again retains the simplicity of the original and the result is a very elegant rendering.

Jerome's purpose in translating thirty nine of Origen's homilies on Luke in 389-390 was not merely to give the Latin-speaking West the benefits of Greek theology. He says in his preface that Paula and Eustochium had begged him to translate Origen's homilies because they had been so disgusted by a commentary on this gospel which they had been reading. Its author, Jerome says, was 'an evil croaking raven', (*sinistro oscinem coruum audiam crocitantem*), which, darkness itself, was decked out in bright colours stolen from other birds.[35] It appears, from what Rufinus says later,[36] that the author of this work was none other than the revered Bishop of Milan, Ambrose, whose *Expositio Euangelii secundum Lucam libri decem* had been published in 388-9. It was a sprawling mass of material, containing sermons, extensive borrowing of Origen's work, and a revision of Eusebius' *Quaestiones Euangelicae*.

Kelly[37] is correct to stress the significance of Jerome's decision to translate these homilies of Origen. Although Hilary of Poitiers had made extensive use of Origen's exegesis in his *Tractatus in Psalmos*,[38] Jerome's translations of Origen's homilies provided one of the first opportunities that Latin-speaking Christians had of experiencing Origen's exegesis in homiletical form. Jerome is also responsible for having preserved a number of Origen's homilies which would not otherwise be extant today. The main characteristics of Jerome's translations of Origen and other Greek works, and their fidelity to the originals, will be discussed in the next section of this chapter.

---

34 Pref. to translation of Origen's *Hom. on Song of Songs* (*GCS* 33, 26).
35 Pref. to translation of Origen's *Homs. on Luke* (*GCS* 49, 1f).
36 Ruf.: *Apol.c.Hier.* 2, 23.
37 Kelly: p. 77.
38 Written between Hilary's return from exile in 361 and his death in 367/8. For a recent assessment of this work and its place in Hilary's exegetical output, see G.M. Newlands: *Hilary of Poitiers: A Study of Theological Method* (European University Studies 108), Bern 1978, pp. 134ff.

Jerome was also responsible for the translation of at least one other Greek theological work. In 384, at the request of Pope Damasus, he began translating Didymus the Blind's treatise *De Spiritu Sancto*. Ambrose had used the Greek text in 381 as the basis for his own work *De Spiritu Sancto*, and, in the preface to his translation of Didymus, Jerome accuses Ambrose of plagiarism. The Greek text of Didymus is now lost, and Jerome's translation is the only version of this work which is extant.

In summer 382, Jerome returned to Rome, the city of his schooldays. He says that 'urgent business of the Church brought me to Rome along with the venerable Bishops Paulinus and Epiphanius'.[39] This 'urgent business' was brought about by 'certain dissensions between the Churches',[40] when certain western Bishops, under the leadership of Ambrose of Milan, expressed grievances over the decisions reached at the Council of Constantinople the previous year.[41] It is very probable that Paulinus and Epiphanius brought Jerome with them in order that he could act as their translator.

Jerome also used his ability to translate from Greek into Latin during his involvement in the Origenist Controversy. In its initial phases, when Epiphanius, Bishop of Salamis and John, Bishop of Jerusalem were embroiled in controversy over Origen's heretical doctrines, Epiphanius requested Jerome to translate into Latin a letter he (Epiphanius) had written to John in 394. Epiphanius had accused John of being an Origenist, and had also encroached upon John's episcopal authority by ordaining Jerome's brother, Paulinian, in order that the monastery at Bethlehem might be served by an anti-Origenist priest, thus making it independent of John's influence. John naturally resented Epiphanius' actions and complained to him. This letter (*Ep.* 51 in Jerome's corpus) is Epiphanius' attempt to explain his actions. When Jerome had translated it, he was criticised for having made errors and deliberate changes in the original. It was these changes which prompted him to compose *Ep.* 57,[42] *De optimo genere interpretandi*, which we shall discuss in detail later in this chapter.

Jerome's acrimonious personal battle with Rufinus in the Origenist Controversy reached its nadir over the issue of the translation of Orig-

---

[39] *Ep.* 127, 7 (*CSEL* 56, 150), (written in 413): ...cum et me Romam cum sanctis pontificibus Paulino et Epiphanio ecclesiastica traxisset necessitas...

[40] *Ep.* 108, 6 (*CSEL* 55, 310): ecclesiarum dissensiones.

[41] See Theodoret: *HE* 5, 9, 1-18; Sozomen: *HE* 7, 11.

[42] See *Ep.* 57, 2 (*CSEL* 54, 505). Jerome translated several other letters, including the paschal letter of Theophilus (*Ep.* 100).

en's *De Principiis*. Rufinus travelled from Jerusalem to Rome in 397, possibly with the intention of making Origen's (and other Greek theologians') works known to Roman Christians.[43] While in Rome, he made a translation of Origen's Περὶ Ἀρχῶν. Later, he recorded[44] that he was led to do this by a certain Macarius, who wished to learn about Origen's opinion on the difficult problems of divine providence. Macarius apparently wanted to refute the fatalism of the then prevalent astrology. Rufinus told Macarius of Pamphilus' *Vindication of Origen*, which dealt with these issues and, again under pressure from Macarius, translated it into Latin.

In order to avoid criticism of his translation of Pamphilus, Rufinus wrote a preface to it,[45] including a short profession of faith, hoping that his critics would be assured of his own orthodoxy. He also composed another work, *The falsification of the works of Origen*,[46] in which he propounded the novel thesis that Origen's writings had been subject to interpolation on a large scale by heretics, and that this accounted for the unorthodox passages. He referred to a letter of Origen which claimed that a heretic had falsified the report of a discussion he had had, and (Rufinus) cited several examples of ecclesiastical writings which had been tampered with, including one example in which Jerome was involved.[47] Rufinus then translated the Περὶ Ἀρχῶν, and it was completed after Easter 398.[48]

Jerome's friends at Rome, especially Marcella and Pammachius, were outraged by some of Rufinus' statements and his translation, and wrote to Jerome at Bethlehem asking for information about his views on Origen.[49] In reply, Jerome made a literal translation of Περὶ Ἀρχῶν and sent it, along with a letter[50] in which he was concerned to justify and define exactly his attitude to Origen, playing down his early enthusiasm for Origen, appealing to his own commentaries on Ecclesiastes and Ephesians, and criticising Origen's heretical opinions as well as Pamphilus' *Vindication*. It will be interesting to make a comparison of Jerome's and Rufinus' translation techniques in the next section of this chapter.

---

[43] Kelly: p. 227-8. Rufinus also translated some of the writings of Basil of Caesarea, Gregory of Nazianzus, Gregory of Nyssa, Evagrius of Pontus and others.
[44] *Apol.c.Hier.* 1, 11.
[45] *Prol. in Apol.Pamph.Mart. pro Orig.* (*CCL* 20, 233-4).
[46] *De Adult.Lib.Orig.* (*CCL* 20, 7-17).
[47] See Jer.*Apol.* 2, 20; Kelly: p. 82, and, on the question of literary frauds in antiquity, G. Bardy: 'Faux et fraudes litteraires dans l'antiquité chrétienne', in *RHE* (1936) 5-23; 275-302.
[48] Pref. to *De Princ.* (*CCL* 20, 245-8).
[49] Jer.: *Ep.* 83.
[50] *Ep.* 84.

We have now seen that Jerome spent considerable time and effort in the translation of Greek theological works and important letters. He is probably best remembered, however, for his work of translating the Bible into Latin. He, more than any other single person, was responsible for fixing the literary form of the Bible of the entire western Church.[51] The story of Jerome's involvement in the scheme begun by his patron, Pope Damasus, is a complicated one, having exercised the minds of many scholars, but one which it is necessary for us to understand before we can move on to discuss Jerome's technique of translation.

In 383, Damasus came to the conclusion that, because of the proliferation of variant readings in the Latin Bible of the day, a thorough revision was a desideratum. For this task, he commissioned Jerome. Although we do not have the actual words of his commission, we get a very clear idea of his wishes from Jerome's preface to the four gospels. He says:

> 'You urge me to compose a new work from the old, and, as it were, to sit in judgement on the copies of the scriptures which are now scattered throughout the world; and, inasmuch as they differ from one another, you would have me decide which of them agree with the Greek original. The labour is one of love, but at the same time dangerous and presumptuous; for in judging others I must be content to be judged by all; and how can I change the language of the world in its old age, and carry it back to its early childhood? Is there a man, learned or unlearned, who will not, when he takes the volume in his hands, and sees that what he reads does not suit his settled tastes, break out immediately into violent language and call me a forger and a profane person for having had the audacity to add anything to the ancient books, or to make any changes or corrections in them.'[52]

Jerome, however, was prepared to risk castigation in this way for two

---

[51] B.M. Metzger: *The Early Versions of the New Testament*, Oxford 1977, p. 332.

[52] *Pref. to Four Gospels* (R. Weber: *Biblia sacra iuxta Vulgatam versionem II*) p. 1515. Novum opus facere me cogis ex veteri, ut post exemplaria Scripturarum toto orbe dispersa quasi quidam arbiter sedeam et, quia inter se variant, quae sint illa quae cum graeca consentiant veritate decernam. Pius labor, sed periculosa praesumptio, iudicare de ceteris ipsum ab omnibus iudicandum, senis mutare linguam et canescentem mundum ad initia retrahere parvulorum. Quis enim doctus pariter vel indoctus, cum in manus volumen adsumpserit et a saliva quam semel inbibit viderit discrepare quod lectitat, non statim erumpat in vocem, me falsarium me clamens esse sacrilegum, qui audeam aliquid in veteribus libris addere, mutare, corrigere? = (*PL* 29, 557f).

reasons. First, he explains, is the Pope's command. Second, was the terrible diversity of O.L. manuscripts. He exclaims that there were 'almost as many forms of text as there are manuscripts'.[53] Jerome's younger contemporary, Augustine, confirms this fact when he laments:

> 'Those who translated the scriptures from Hebrew into Greek can be counted, but the Latin translators are out of all number. For in the early days of the faith, every man who happened to gain possession of a Greek manuscript (of the N.T.) and who imagined he had any facility in both languages, however slight that might have been, dared to make a translation.'[54]

A question is raised by these two statements. How much of a deterioration had taken place in the pre-Jerome Latin version of the Bible? Do Jerome and Augustine exaggerate in their estimation of the number of divergent forms of text? In order to understand Jerome's decision to revise the existing Latin Bible, it will be necessary to discuss briefly the history of the text of the Latin Bible before Jerome's time.

The history of what is referred to as the Old Latin version is extremely confused and unclear. There is no one single manuscript containing a complete Bible (or even N.T.) in the O.L. version. Most copies are fragmentary and many are palimpsests.[55] This difficult textual situation is made more complicated by the fact some O.L. readings are preserved in Vulgate texts, as marginal annotations in Vulgate manuscripts, and also as biblical quotations in Latin Christian authors as late as the 6th century. It is certain that no one person was responsible for the entire work. The O.L. is not a uniform whole, and each book appears to have been translated a number of times. These facts make it extremely difficult to determine with any accuracy when the O.L. Bible was translated, although a theory may be built up from scattered indications.[56]

It is likely that the O.L. Bible began to take shape in the same kind of fashion as did the Aramaic Targums. The biblical text would be read in Greek (LXX for O.T.) and then repeated in the vernacular. Originally, the vernacular rendering would have been oral, but, as time went by, just as with the Targums, they began to be written down for continued

---

53 *Ibid.*: Tot sunt (exemplaria) paene quot codices.
54 Aug.: *De Doct.Christ.*: II, 16. See also Aug.: *Retract.* I, 21, 3, where he refers to 'the endless vanity and multitude of Latin translators'.
55 See E.A. Lowe: 'Codices rescripti: a list of the oldest Latin palimpsests with stray observations on their origins' in *Mélanges Eugène Tisseront V* (Studi e Testi CCXXXV), Vatican City 1964, 67-113.
56 Further details may be found in B.M. Metzger: *op.cit.*, pp. 286-293.

use in the liturgy. Finally, the reading of the Bible in Greek died out and the only version used was the vernacular Latin translation.

Because the O.L. very probably began as a spoken version in order to explain the Bible readings to the common Christians, the language of the O.L. is much more akin to popular spoken Latin than to the classical language.[57] Latin Christians prided themselves in the face of pagan charges of unsophistication, their *sermo humilis*.[58] In addition to being close to contemporary spoken Latin, the language of the O.L. also created a considerable amount of new vocabulary, reflecting the central themes of the Christian faith. New words, frequently taken over from Greek (e.g. *apostolus, baptisma, ecclesia*) and sometimes from Hebrew (e.g. *pascha, amen, alleluia*) were coined; old words changed their meaning (e.g. *confessio*).[59]

According to B.M. Metzger,[60] the textual affinities of the O.L. are with the Western text type. He also asserts that 'the diversity among the Old Latin witnesses is probably to be accounted for on the assumption that scribes, instead of transmitting the manuscripts mechanically, allowed themselves considerable freedom in incorporating their own and others' traditions'.[61] This attitude on the part of scribes has led to the confusing textual position of the O.L. At many passages, there is a bewildering number of variant readings. At Luke 24:4f, for instance, there are no fewer than 27 variant readings. The O.L. also witnesses some very interesting additions to the text. For example, at Matt. 3:15, when Jesus 'was baptised, a tremendous light flashed forth from the water, so that all who were present feared'.[62]

Jerome's and Augustine's statements would appear, then, not to be mere hyperbole, but based on sound factual information. Jerome's statement concerning the many text-types of the O.L. would also seem to be substantiated, for the modern scholarly consensus distinguishes

---

57 See L.K. Palmer: *The Latin Language*, London 1954, pp. 148-205.
58 Augustine's words: 'melius est reprehendant nos grammatici quam non intelligant populi', (*In Ps.* 138, 70) express the Christian view of pagan criticism of the O.L. translation.
59 More examples will be found in H. Rönsch: *Itala und Vulgata*, Marburg 1875, esp. pp. 434-455; W. Matzkow: *De Vocabulis quibusdam Italae et Vulgatae christianis*, Berlin 1933. See also C. Mohrmann: 'Traits caractéristiques du latin des chrétiens' in *Miscellanea Giovanni Mercati I* (Studi e Testi CXXI), Vatican City 1946, pp. 437ff.
60 *Op.cit.*, p. 325.
61 *Ibid*.
62 Other examples are given by Metzger: *op.cit.*, p. 326.

four text-types among O.L. manuscripts: African, European, Italian and Spanish.[63]

Faced with a great array of variant readings and different text-types, Jerome prepared to carry out Pope Damasus' wish to revise the Latin Bible and create (or re-create) a uniform text. Naturally enough, he began his revision with the four gospels. Pope Damasus did not commission Jerome to make a *fresh translation* of the Bible,[64] but Jerome found himself checking the accuracy of the Latin text by referring constantly to the Greek original. He was conscious, however, of his commission to *revise* the existing O.L. version, and changed this text only when it was necessary. He finished his revision of the four gospels and presented it to the Pope in 384, shortly before the latter's death.

That Jerome revised the four gospels is certain. Less certain, however, is how much of the remainder of the O.L. N.T. Jerome revised. In *De Vir.Illus.* and elsewhere, he claims to have 'restored the N.T. to its Greek original'.[65] Scholars have expressed opposing views on Jerome's statement. Some, notably Dom J. Chapman,[66] have believed that Jerome did, in fact, revise the whole of the N.T. Chapman argued that Jerome's quotations from Paul in *Ep.* 27 show his intention of publishing soon a revision of the Pauline epistles, that the lack of prefaces to the N.T. other than the gospels can be explained easily – because the Pope, for whom Jerome was making the revision, died soon after the gospels had been revised, Jerome did not wish to write prefaces to anyone else. Chapman also attempts to explain why Jerome's quotations from the Pauline epistles often differ from those in the Vulgate: he often quotes readings with which he disagrees and he may have thought a certain reading to be a fairly good one, his own suggestion being meant only to explain the real force of the Greek, not to serve as a tolerable Latin rendering. Jerome is often inconsistent anyway, and the differences between the Vulgate readings and those found in Jerome's works do not necessarily prove that he was not the author of the Vulgate of the Pauline epistles. Chapman cites examples from the gospels which vary from the Vulgate. Those who argue that Jerome did not revise the text

---

63 See the discussion in Metzger: *op.cit.*, pp. 326-8.
64 It is not clear from Jerome's language whether Pope Damasus commissioned him to revise the whole Bible, or only the N.T. It is probable, however, that, since he tackled the Latin Psalter not long after he had finished the four Gospels, Pope Damasus had wished the revision of the entire Bible.
65 *De Vir.Illus.* 135; *Ep.* 71, 5; 112, 20 (*PL* 23, 758; *CSEL* 55, 5; 389).
66 J. Chapman: 'St. Jerome and the Vulgate New Testament', in *JTS* 24 (1922-3) 33-51; 113-125; 282-299.

of the Pauline epistles because his quotations differ from the Vulgate, must also conclude that he did not revise the text of the gospels, *quod est absurdum*. Stylistically, he says, the Vulgate N.T. is the work of a single author and that author must be Jerome. Furthermore, Jerome is always accurate when enumerating his own works, so when he says he had revised the whole N.T., he must have done. Chapman dates the revision of the complete N.T. to 391 A.D.

This traditional belief that Jerome revised the text of the complete N.T., has been seriously questioned by other scholars. Fr. Cavallera made a detailed study of the Vulgate of Acts, the Pauline epistles and Revelation,[67] and noted especially the discrepancies between the Vulgate and quotations in Jerome's works. Sometimes Jerome employs a text which coincides more or less with the Vulgate, but more often he quotes one which differs. Sometimes he rejects readings which are found in the Vulgate. It is very important in this context that, in his commentaries on Galatians, Ephesians, Philemon and Titus, written c 387, shortly after his supposed revision of these letters, he never attributes the Latin text he uses to himself, but, on the contrary, often uses the phrase '*Latinus interpres*' of the translator. He sometimes disagrees with their readings. Recently, J.N.D. Kelly[68] has stated his opinion that the style of the Vulgate of Acts is against Jerome's authorship. Kelly has also asserted categorically that 'the only tenable conclusion is that Jerome, for whatever reason, abandoned the idea of revising the rest of the N.T. (if indeed he ever entertained it at all) once he had completed the gospels'.[69]

Before he left Rome in 385, after having revised the text of the gospels, Jerome revised the Latin text of the Psalter according to the LXX. He says that he revised this book very quickly, but made substantial changes.[70] This revision used to be identified as the 'Roman Psalter', but recent work has indicated that, while the Roman Psalter is not the version which Jerome made at Rome in 384, it may well represent the text on which he worked and which he corrected.[71] A few years later (c 387-8), Jerome made another translation of the Psalms, this time using Origen's Hexaplaric LXX text as his basis. This version is known as the 'Gallican Psalter', as it was first accepted for use in the churches

---

[67] F. Cavallera: 'Saint Jérôme et le Vulgate des Actes, des Épîtres, et de l'Apocalypse', in *Bulletin de littérature ecclésiastique* (1920) 269-292.
[68] Kelly: p. 88.
[69] *Ibid.*
[70] Pref. to transl. of Psalms from Hebrew (*PL* 29, 121f).
[71] See. D. De Bruyne: 'Le problème du Psautier romain', in *RB* 42 (1930) 101-126; A. Vaccari: *Scritti di erudizione e di Filologia I*, Rome 1952, pp. 211-221.

of Gaul. It also remained in greater use than his later translation of the Psalms from Hebrew, and so became included in the official Vulgate edition of the Bible, ratified by the Council of Trent. In this 'Gallican Psalter', Jerome included Origen's diacritical signs, which were intended to show where the LXX text differed from the Hebrew original.

In the same period, Jerome also translated the books of Job, 1 & 2 Chronicles, Proverbs, Ecclesiastes and Song of Songs.[72] The Psalter, Job (in two manuscripts) and (in only one manuscript[73]) Song of Songs, are all that remain of this translation of parts of the O.T. from Origen's critical Hexaplaric LXX text. The other books are not now extant. In 416, when Augustine asked to consult Jerome's revised LXX, the latter had to inform the African Bishop that, due to someone's deceit, he no longer had a copy of the other books.[74]

In the last chapter, we traced the reasons behind Jerome's desire to use the *Hebraica veritas*, rather than to rely on the Greek translation of the O.T. By 390, he had become convinced of the necessity to make a fresh translation of the O.T. from the Hebrew text, and, encouraged by friends and the desire to demolish the arguments of the Jews,[75] he began to translate each of the books of the Hebrew canon, a task which was not completed until 405.

It is probable that Jerome began this new translation with the books of Samuel and Kings. After explaining that the Hebrew canon has three divisions, Law, Prophets and 'Hagiographa', Jerome goes on to say:

> 'This preface to the scriptures may serve as a "helmeted" introduction to all the books which I translate from Hebrew into Latin... Read first, then, my Samuel and Kings; mine, I say, mine. For whatever by careful translation and cautious correction I have learnt and comprehended, is my very own. And when you understand anything of which you were ignorant before, either (if you are grateful) consider me a translator, or (if ungrateful) a paraphraser, although I am not at all conscious of having deviated from the Hebrew original.'[76]

---

72 See the prefaces to these books – translation from Hebrew (Weber: pp. 730, 957).
73 Discovered by A. Vaccari in the early 1950's. See Vaccari: *op.cit.*, Vol. II, pp. 121-146.
74 *Ep.* 134, 2 (*CSEL* 56, 262).
75 *Pref. to Psalms* (Weber: p. 768); *Pref. to Isaiah* (Weber: p. 1096). Augustine (*De Civ. Dei* 18, 43), whilst not in favour of Jerome's new translation, admitted that, although the Jews found the LXX to be full of errors, they acknowledged the accuracy of Jerome's revision.
76 *Pref. to Sam. and Kings* (Weber: p. 365).

It sounds as if Jerome is writing this preface as a general introduction to his whole translation of the O.T., discussing the contents and limits of the O.T. canon. He refers to the preface as 'helmeted' (*galeatus*) because he arms himself in advance to defend himself from the critics he knows will rise up against him.

Soon after he had finished the translation of Samuel and Kings, Jerome started on Job, the Psalter and the Prophets. His friend Sophronius made an 'elegant Greek translation' of Jerome's rendering of Job and the Psalter,[77] and in *Ep.* 49, composed in 393-4, he informs Pammachius that he has translated the sixteen prophets (thus including Daniel) and Job, of which he will be able to borrow a copy from his cousin Marcella. Of this book, Jerome says:

> 'Read it both in Greek and Latin, and compare the old version with my rendering. You will then see clearly that the difference between them is that between truth and falsehood.'[78]

He also tells Pammachius that he has translated Samuel and Kings. The omission of Psalms must have been an oversight on Jerome's part. Ezra, Nahum and Chronicles were translated in 394-5.

It was not until late 404 and early 405 that Jerome translated any more of the Hebrew O.T. He gives no reason for the long delay in completing the project, but it is very probably due to his involvement in the Origenist Controversy from 393 till 402-3, and also to the fact that he wrote several commentaries in this period. He first translated the Pentateuch, having been asked to by his friend Desiderius.[79] His preface makes it clear that he thinks there is still a good deal to be done before his translation of the O.T. would be complete.

Next, he translated Joshua, Judges and Ruth, in early 405. In the preface, he expresses his relief at having finished the Pentateuch:

> 'Having at last finished Moses' Pentateuch, I feel like a man released from a crippling load of debt.'[80]

The rest of the O.T. books were completed by early 406, thus bringing a labour of some fourteen years to an end.

---

[77] *De Vir.Illus.* 134 (*PL* 23, 755).
[78] *Ep.* 49, 4 (*CSEL* 54, 349): Lege eundem Graecum et Latinum et ueterem editionem nostrae translationi conpara, et liquido peruidebis, quantum distet inter ueritatem et mendacium.
[79] *Pref. to the Pentateuch* (Weber. p. 3).
[80] *Pref. to Joshua, Judges, Ruth* (Weber: p. 285).

Jerome's translation technique

Having now reviewed the chronological occurrence of the different genres of translation which Jerome undertook throughout his long career, we must now enquire into some of the characteristics of these translations and the techniques which he used when translating Greek and Hebrew into Latin. It is of great importance in this context to remind ourselves that, when studying Jerome's statements concerning his principles of translation, we must always take into account the context in which his statements occur. His statements about the principles involved almost always occur in polemical situations, when defending his translations and the method of which he has made use in them, against his enemies, who often accused him of falsifying the original. It is important to take these polemical contexts into account because almost all modern scholars conclude that Jerome is inconsistent in his translation technique, making general statements about the nature and technique of translation in one place, which he contradicts in his own translations. Some of these contradictions, although by no means all, may be resolved when the context of the statement is taken into consideration.

Jerome's most important statement concerning his principles of translation is *Ep.* 57, known as *De Optimo Genere Interpretandi*. Composed in 395, this little treatise is a direct response to a severely critical charge made by an unnamed person (Jerome believed that Rufinus instigated the charge) that Jerome's translation of Epiphanius' letter to John of Jerusalem (*Ep.* 51 in Jerome's corpus) did not give a true indication of the original letter. Jerome, therefore sets out in this treatise to explain and justify his methods of translating.

The title of the letter was chosen by Jerome himself, in all probability consciously borrowing from the title of Cicero's treatise, *De optimo genere oratorum*.[81] Jerome begins (para. 1) by quoting St. Paul, who, when he appeared before King Agrippa, expressed his gladness for the opportunity to discuss all the things of which he was accused. Jerome is similarly glad to be able to answer his critic, and to explain to Pammachius, to whom the letter is addressed, the 'true order of the facts' (*rei ordinem*).[82] He continues by explaining the background of the situation – how Epiphanius sent a letter to John of Jerusalem; how Jerome was asked by a monk to translate it, in order that this monk could read

---

[81] Jerome refers to the latter by this title several times. See *Comm.Mal.* 3, 1 (*CCL* 76A, 928); *Comm.Ionah*: Prol. (*CCL* 76, 377); *Ep.* 112, 20 (*CSEL* 55, 390f).
[82] *Ep.* 57, 1 (*CSEL* 54, 504).

it; how this private translation was stolen after eighteen months, probably by a bribed monk; how the robbers accuse Jerome of falsifying the original by failing to translate it word for word (para. 2). Next, Jerome asks his critics how they got hold of a copy of the letter in question: he could take legal proceedings against them for theft. He cites examples of this from history (para. 3). He insists that every man has the right to privacy; he had every right to translate the letter in the way he did, because it was a private document. His enemy should argue with the author of the letter, not Jerome (para. 4).

Paragraph 5 contains Jerome's major argument. He admits that he has made alterations in the letter, and that any simple translation may contain unintentional errors. But, he says, it can plainly be seen that he has not changed the sense of the letter in his translation; he has made no additions or doctrinal emendations. He continues:

> 'I not only admit but proclaim freely that when translating from Greek (except in the case of holy scripture, where even the order of the words is a mystery) I translate sense for sense and not word for word.'[83]

For this principle (*sensum exprimere de sensu*), Jerome cites precedents from the writings of Cicero, who is quoted as saying in the preface to his translation of Aeschines and Demosthenes the Attic orators:

> 'I have translated the noblest speeches of the two most eloquent of the Attic orators... but I have rendered them not as a translator but as an orator, keeping the sense but altering the form by adapting both the metaphors and the words to suit our own language.'[84]

Jerome also cites the example of Horace, who, in his *Art of Poetry*, advised the translator not to render word for word; and also Terence, Plautus and Menander. Jerome also quotes from the preface he himself had written to his translation of Eusebius' *Chronicle*, composed in 381-2, his first work of translation, saying that even then the same kind of charges were made against him.

In paragraph 6, Jerome continues to cite precedents for his principles of translation. He now cites examples of Christian translators who have eschewed the word for word method in favour of translating the sense. He quotes from the translator's preface to Athanasius' *Vita Antonii*.

---

[83] *Ep.* 57, 5 (*CSEL* 54, 508): Ego enim non solum fateor, sed libera uoce profiteor me in interpretatione Graecorum absque scripturis sanctis, ubi et uerborum ordo mysterium est, non uerbum e uerbo, sed sensum exprimere de sensu.

[84] *Ep.* 57, 5 (*CSEL* 54, 509). Only a small portion of this preface is extant elsewhere.

Although Jerome does not mention the translator's name, we know it was the one made by Evagrius of Antioch, who translated this work into Latin not later than 375, in an almost paraphrastic rendering of the original.[85] He refers also to the translations of Hilary of Poitiers (homilies on Job, and 'several treatises' on the Psalms).

Paragraphs 7 and 8 again continue the amassing of precedents for translating sense for sense rather than for literal rendering. Even the translators of the LXX, the apostles and evangelists have done the same thing in dealing with the sacred writings. Jerome gives many examples where readings in the gospels (in the O.L. version, which was considered to be the inspired version) disagree with either the LXX or the Hebrew or both. He notes instances where the gospels have made additions to the O.T. passages they quote, or have attributed a passage to the wrong O.T. book.

Jerome moves on to give his reason for noting the places where the gospel writers have made incorrect quotations or attributions (para. 9):

> 'I refer to these passages, not to convict the evangelists of falsification... but to bring home to my critics their own lack of knowledge.'[86]

If Jerome is to be condemned for not having translated this letter (*Ep.* 51) word for word, then the apostles and evangelists must also be condemned. Jerome gives several more examples of errors of this nature in the gospels.

This point is obviously a very strong one for Jerome, as, in the next paragraph (10), he cites still more examples of incorrect citations in the Gospels. In paragraph 11, he says it would be tedious to enumerate all the incorrect translations in the LXX. The Jews, he says, laugh at the Christian version of Isaiah because it contains so many incorrect translations of the Hebrew. Yet he believes that the Church is right to read the LXX, because it was the first of all the versions, because it was read by the apostles and also because it is much better than the extremely literal version of Aquila. Literal versions are pedantic and often do not make sense:

---

85 For a succinct discussion of the translations of this work, see J. Quasten: *Patrology* III, pp. 39ff. Jerome makes no mention of the very literal translation of this work, a copy of which was discovered in the 1930's by A. Wilmart in the Chapter Library of St. Peter's, Rome. In *De Vir.Illus.* 87 and 88, Jerome mentions that Athanasius was the author of this work, and, in *De Vir.Illus.* 125, he says that his friend Evagrius translated Athanasius' *Vita Antonii* from Greek into Latin (*PL* 23, 731; 751).

86 *Ep.* 57, 9 (*CSEL* 54, 518): Haec replico, non ut euangelistas arguam falsitatis... sed ut reprehensores meos arguam inperitiae et inpetrem ab eis ueniam.

> 'There are many phrases which are charming in Greek, which, if translated word for word, do not sound well in Latin; and conversely there are many which are pleasing to us in Latin which – assuming that the word order is not altered – would not please in Greek.'[87]

In paragraph 12, Jerome's biting sarcasm comes to the fore against his critics and the petty errors they found. He sets down the first sentence of the letter, comparing his translation with the Greek. How many errors there are, says Jerome, mocking his critics, in the first line! Ἀγαπητός means 'loved' and not 'dearly beloved', and so on, as Jerome shows how fastidious and ridiculous are the criticisms of his enemies.

Finally, in the *peroratio*, (para. 13), Jerome exhorts Pammachius to compare the Greek and Latin, when he will see for himself how insulting and valueless are his detractors' claims.

Ep. 57, while being the most important explanation of Jerome's principles of translation, is not the only place where he speaks about this important topic. As we mentioned briefly above, Jerome discusses the subject for the first time in the preface to his translation of the *Chronicle* of Eusebius, composed in 381-2. The background to this preface seems to be that Jerome has not yet been criticised for his translation, but he definitely anticipates much criticism, for he says:

> 'I am well aware that there will be many who, with their usual fondness for universal slander – the only escape from them is never to write anything – will drive their fangs into this book. They will disapprove of the dates, change the order, doubt the accuracy of events, sift the syllables, and, as is very frequently the case, will impute copyists' errors to the author.'[88]

He begins the preface by noting that translation is an ancient art, of which Cicero was a master, but it is an extremely difficult one:

> 'It is an arduous task to preserve beauty and grace undamaged in a translation.'[89]

One must take many things into account when translating, including

---

[87] *Ep.* 57, 11 (*CSEL* 54, 524): Quanta enim apud Graecos bene dicuntur, quae, si ad uerbum transferamus, in Latino non resonant, et e regione, quae apud nos placent, si uertantur iuxta ordinem, apud illos displicebunt!

[88] Pref. to transl. of Eusebius' *Chron.* (*GCS* 47, 5-6): Nec ignoro multos fore, qui solita libidine omnibus detrahendi huic uolumini genuinum infigant. Quod uitare non potest nisi qui omnino nil scribit. Calumniabuntur in tempora, conuertent ordinem, res arguent, syllabas euentilabunt et, quod accidere plerumque solet, neglegentiam librariorum ad auctores referent.

[89] *Ibid.* (*GCS* 47, 2): Arduum, ut quae in alia lingua bene dicta sunt eundem decorem in translatione conseruent.

'the ins and outs of transposition, the variations in cases, the diversity of metaphors, and lastly the peculiar... idiom of the language'.[90] Because of these factors,

> 'a literal translation sounds absurd; but if, on the other hand, I am forced to change either the order or the words themselves, then I shall appear to have forsaken the duty of a translator.'[91]

Jerome goes on to discuss the various translations of the Bible, and especially those made by Aquila, Symmachus and Theodotion. Each of these applied different principles to the Hebrew original, and the result was to give:

> 'a totally different character to one and the same work; one strove to give word for word, another the general meaning, while the third wanted to avoid any great divergence from the ancients.'[92]

Jerome, throughout his life, felt obliged to attempt to justify his principles of translation. This is clear from the many passages, in addition to those already quoted, where he comments on the subject. Again and again, the same basic points emerge. He repeatedly approves of a sense for sense translation as opposed to a literal, word for word translation.[93] This kind of translation is necessary because a literal translation results in stylistic absurdities,[94] or in obscurity.[95] At one place, Jerome implies the impossibility of a word for word translation:

> 'We should not conclude that Latin is a poor language because it is not possible to translate word for word.'[96]

The exception which Jerome made to this rule of translating sense for sense was the translation of the Bible. We have already seen that, because even the order of the words of holy scripture was a mystery,[97]

---

[90] *Ibid.* (*GCS* 47, 2): Accedunt hyperbatorum amfractus, dissimilitudines casuum, uarietas figurarum, ipsum postremo suum et... uernaculum linguae genus.
[91] *Ibid.* (*GCS* 47, 2): Si ad uerbum interpretor, absurde resonat: si ob necessitatem aliquid in ordine, in sermone mutauero, ab interpretis uidebor officio recessisse.
[92] *Ibid.* (*GCS* 47, 3): Quam ob rem Aquila et Symmachus et Theodotio incitati diuersum paene opus in eodem opere prodiderunt, alio nitente uerbum de uerbo exprimere, alio sensum potius sequi, tertio non multum a ueteribus discrepare.
[93] See *Ep.* 112, 20; 18A, 15; 121, 2 (*CSEL* 55, 390f; 54, 95; 56, 10); *Pref. in Lib. Iob* (Weber: p. 731-2).
[94] See quote from pref. to Eusebius' *Chron.* above, p. 92.
[95] See *Ep.* 121, 10 (*CSEL* 56, 43); *Apol.c.Ruf.* 1, 22 (*CCL* 79, 21f).
[96] *Ep.* 106, 3 (*CSEL* 55, 250): Nec ex eo quis Latinam linguam angustissimam putet, quod non possit uerbum transferre de uerbo.
[97] See *Ep.* 57,5. quoted above, p. 105.

Jerome believed that a word for word translation of the Bible was vital. This conclusion was forced on Jerome by his doctrine of scriptural inspiration: every word of the Bible was written by God himself, therefore, in translating the Bible, the translator had to take great care to retain not only the meaning of each individual word, but even the order of the words in the original language. So Jerome had two sets of principles for translating literature into Latin: one for the Bible, where a word for word rendering was required, and one for other literature, where a sense for sense translation was needed. These mutually exclusive principles of translation pose no conceptual problems for Jerome in theory, and, in studying Jerome as a translator, we must always bear in mind that, when he translated the Bible, one set of principles applied, and when he translated other literature into Latin, another set applied. If this is not remembered, then, of course, Jerome will appear to be arbitrary in his principles, which is not in fact the case. As a translator, he was by no means arbitrary, although he was not altogether consistent.

When we come to studying Jerome's practice in translating, we sometimes find serious discrepancies between his stated principles and what he actually did. This is certainly the case with his translation of the Bible, but in his translation of other theological literature, he seems to be more faithful to his principles, because his theory of translating in this respect was much easier to put into practice than in respect of the Bible.

In his *Apology*, Rufinus castigates Jerome generally for his principles of translation.[98] More than this, Rufinus mentions many specific passages in several works where Jerome has perpetrated the very errors of translation of which he (Jerome) has accused Rufinus. Rufinus says:

> 'I said that I had followed or imitated you in your method of translating, in that alone and nothing else... I followed you in the things I saw you had done in the Homilies on St. Luke's Gospel.'[99]

He cites several examples from Jerome's translation of these Homilies of Origen, and also from his translation of Origen's Homilies on Isaiah, Jeremiah, and Ezekiel, where Jerome has made doctrinal additions to Origen's text, or abridged the original text. The most recent editor of Origen's Homilies on St. Luke, M. Rauer,[100] confirms Rufinus' charges but adds that, where a direct comparison can be made, Jerome's is generally quite a faithful translation and that Rufinus' charges are of a

---

[98] See, e.g., *Apol.c.Hier.* 1, 16; 1, 21; 2, 8 (*CCL* 20, 49; 56; 89).
[99] *Apol.c.Hier.* 2, 27 (*CCL* 20, 103).
[100] *GCS* IX, p. xvii.

trivial nature.¹⁰¹ E. Klostermann, the editor of Origen's homilies on Ezekiel,¹⁰² found that, with regard to Jerome's translations of these homilies, Rufinus' charges are substantiated. Klostermann finds evidence of circumlocutions, additions to and abridgements of Origen's text, along with rhetorical glosses. As for the homilies on Isaiah, W. Baehrens notes that, on a comparison with the extant Greek fragments, Rufinus' charge of dogmatic alterations are substantiated.¹⁰³

In connection with the translation of Origen's *De Princ.*, which sparked off the bitter feud between Jerome and Rufinus, there is a scholarly consensus in favour of Jerome's translation being the more accurate rendering. G. Grützmacher and J. Brochet¹⁰⁴ overstate the facts when they contrast Jerome's literal translation with Rufinus' 'free' one. P. Koetschau is closer to the reality of the matter when he denies that Jerome's revision shows any great degree of verbal faithfulness to Origen's original.¹⁰⁵ In his extensive study of the Latin versions of the *De Princ.*, G. Bardy concluded that Jerome's translation was more literal than Rufinus' in the sense that it contained passages which Rufinus had omitted, although Jerome was guilty of changing tentative suggestions in Origen's original into categorical statements, and of making alterations for the sake of clarity and stylistic elegance.¹⁰⁶ Bardy is also of the opinion that, although Jerome has translated Origen's work more faithfully, he does not understand the Alexandrian theologian as well as did Rufinus.¹⁰⁷

In the preface to his translation of Eusebius' *Chronicle*, Jerome stated that he had rendered the Greek 'most faithfully',¹⁰⁸ although he did admit to having made certain additions, especially as regards Roman history and literature. Probably because of the haste with which he made the translation, more than a few errors of translation may be found,¹⁰⁹ as well as a certain cavalier indifference to questions of exact

---

101 For example, Rufinus writes: 'So in the note on the words, "Behold when the voice of your greeting came to my ears, the baby leaped in my womb", you render: "Because this was not the beginning of his substance", and you add on your own the words "and nature".' (*Apol.c.Hier.* 2, 27 [*CCL* 20, 102]).
102 *GCS* VIII, p. xix.
103 *GCS* VIII, p. xlii... See Rufinus: *Apol.c.Hier.* 2, 27.
104 G. Grützmacher: *Hieronymus* I, 18; J. Brochet: *Saint Jérôme et ses ennemis*, p. 232.
105 P. Koetschau: *De principiis* (*GCS* V, p. lxxxviii; xci).
106 G. Bardy: *Recherches sur l'histoire du texte et des versions latines du De Principiis d'Origène*, Paris 1923, p. 176.
107 *Ibid.*, p. 206.
108 *GCS* 47, 2.
109 For these, see A. Sundermeier: *Quaestiones chronographicae ad Eusebii et Hieronymi chronica spectantes*, Bremen 1896; Kelly: p. 74.

dating.[110] We must remember, though, that Jerome did not set out to give merely a translation of Eusebius' work, but to change the original into quite a different work, so that it would be acceptable to Western readers, and, in addition, to bring the original up to date. It is then partly a translation and partly a new work by Jerome.

When we move on to consider Jerome's practice in translating the Bible, especially the O.T., we find that, in many cases he disregards his stated principles about translating holy scripture word for word. The main reasons for this appear to be three-fold. First, the nature of the language from which, and into which he translated did not allow of a strict word for word translation. Second, Jerome's personality, and especially his rhetorical education, inclined him against this kind of literal translation. Third, various influences on Jerome, notably theological considerations, made it impossible for him to adhere totally to his own principles concerning Bible translation. It will be illuminating to look at a few of these influencing factors.

Jerome often changes the word order of the original text. At many places, this can be because of the natural differences between the original Hebrew or Greek and Latin languages. In Greek, for example, the possessive pronoun comes before the noun, but in Latin, it is placed after it:

A. Matt. 9:1 ἦλθεν εἰς τὴν ἰδίαν πόλιν
    Vulg. : *et venit in civitatem suam*
    O.L. : *et venit in civitatem suam*
    (Hilary : *In Matt.*: ad loc.: *in civitatem suam revertitur.*)
B. Lk. 12:18 καθελῶ μου τὰς ἀποθήκας
    Vulg. : *destruam horrea mea*
    O.L. : *destruam horrea... mea*

Again, the Greek demonstrative pronoun is placed after the noun to which it refers, while in Latin it comes before:

A. Lk. 1:29 διελογίζετο ποταπὸς εἴη ὁ ἀσπασμὸς οὗτος
    Vulg. : *cogitabat qualis esset ista salutatio*
    O.L. : *cogitabat qualis esset ista salutatio*
B. Lk. 4:23 πάντως ἐρεῖτέ μοι τὴν παραβολὴν ταύτην
    Vulg. : *utique dicetis mihi hanc similitudinem*
    O.L. : *utique dicetis mihi hanc similitudinem*

---

110 See R. Helm: 'Hieronymus' Zusätze in Eusebius' Chronik und ihre Wert für die Literaturgeschichte', in *Philologus* Supplementum 21 (1929) p. 92f.

C. Lk. 10:38 αὐτὸς εἰσῆλθεν εἰς κώμην τινά
   Vulg. : *ipse intrauit in quoddam castellum*
   O.L.   : *ipse introiuit in quoddam castellum*

Among the examples of changed word order in the Vulgate O.T. is the following:

Prov. 26:20 בְּאֶפֶס עֵצִים תִּכְבֶּה־אֵשׁ וּבְאֵין נִרְגָּן יִשְׁתֹּק מָדוֹן
   Vulg. : *cum defecerint ligna extinguetur ignis et susurrone subtracto iurgia conquiescunt.*
   O.L.   : *in multis lignis uiget ignis...*

In this example, however, Jerome has altered the order of the words in the second half of the verse for stylistic reasons, and has also corrected O.L.'s mistranslation, replacing *uiget* with *extinguetur*, in harmony with the Hebrew text.

One of the characteristics of the Hebrew language is its repetitious style. At several places in the Vulgate, Jerome omits these repetitious elements of Hebrew in order to achieve a more smoothly flowing Latin style:

A. Josh. 2:4 הָאִשָּׁה אֶת־שְׁנֵי הָאֲנָשִׁים ... בָּאוּ אֵלַי הָאֲנָשִׁים
   Vulg. : *mulier viros abscondit et ait fateor venerunt ad me sed nesciebam unde essent*
B. Josh. 2:5 וְהָאֲנָשִׁים יָצָאוּ לֹא יָדַעְתִּי אָנָה הָלְכוּ הָאֲנָשִׁים
   Vulg. : *et illi pariter exierunt nescio quo abierunt*
C. Ruth 1:6 וַתָּשָׁב מִשְּׂדֵי מוֹאָב כִּי שָׁמְעָה בִּשְׂדֵה מוֹאָב
   Vulg. : *...de regione moabitide audierat enim quod...*

As well as omitting words from the original text, Jerome also adds words or even whole phrases, in order either to 'improve' the style or to make the original more easily understood. Among the former words are *ante, autem, ergo, ibi, potius, prius* and *statim*. Of explanatory clauses which Jerome has added, we cite the following examples:

A. Num. 17:8 וַיֹּצֵא פֶרַח
   Vulg. : *et turgentibus gemmis eruperant flores*
B. Judges 8:25 וַיִּפְרְשׂוּ אֶת־הַשִּׂמְלָה
   Vulg. : *expandentesque super terram pallium*

Several scholars have commented on what B. Keder-Kopfstein has called Jerome's 'remarkable stylistic tendency'[111] to translate the same Hebrew word or Greek word in a similar context by a variety of Latin equivalents. In fact, knowing the importance of Jerome's rhetorical education in this context, the fact that he should attempt to vary his vocabulary is not really 'remarkable', but should be expected from this master of the rhetorical art. Jerome practises his rhetorical flair both in formulaic expressions and in other places. Suffice it here to cite a few examples of Jerome's practice in this context. The first example is a formulaic expression.

A. Matt. 3:7   γεννήματα ἐχιδνῶν
   Vulg.   : *progenies uiperarum*
   O.L.   : *progenies uiperarum*

   Matt. 12:34   γεννήματα ἐχιδνῶν
   Vulg.   : *progenies uiperarum*
   O.L.   : *progenies uiperarum*

   Matt. 23:33   γεννήματα ἐχιδνῶν
   Vulg.   : *genimina uiperarum*
   O.L.   : *progenies uiperarum*

   Lk. 3:7   γεννήματα ἐχιδνῶν
   Vulg.   : *genimina uiperarum*
   O.L.   : *progenies uiperarum*

B. In Isa. 24:8, the phrase שְׁבַת מְשׂוֹשׂ occurs twice. In the Vulgate, Jerome translated it differently the second time: *cessavit gaudium, conticuit dulcedo*. The O.L. has *cessabit jocunditas* and *cessabit impudicitia*.

C. At Isa. 2:10, we read מִפְּנֵי פַּחַד יְהוָה, and this is repeated at 2:19. Once again, Jerome renders the same phrase in different ways:

Vulg. (2:10)   : *a facie timoris domini*
O.L.   : *a facie timoris domini*

Vulg. (2:19)   : *a facie formidinis domini*
O.L.   : *a facie timoris domini*

---

111 B. Keder-Kopfstein: *The Vulgate as a translation*, Ph.D. thesis, Hebrew University of Jerusalem 1968, p. 70. I am indebted to Prof. J. Barr for the extended loan of his personal copy of this excellent and detailed thesis.

Jerome occasionally translated the different senses of a Greek or Hebrew word, although it must be said that he did this more often with Greek words than with Hebrew ones, perhaps because his knowledge of and familiarity with Greek was so much better than his knowledge of Hebrew. He translates the word ἱκανός variously as *dignus* (Lk. 7:6), *copiosus* (Matt. 28:12), *multis* (Lk. 23:9), and *plurimus* (Mk. 10:46). The O.L. translates ἱκανός as *dignus* (Lk. 7:6), *copiosus* (Matt. 28:12), *multis* (Lk. 23:9), and *multa turba* (Mk. 10:46).

Again, the Greek word ὀλιγοπίστος is translated by Jerome as *minimus fidei* (Matt. 6:30), *modicus fidei* (Matt. 8:26; 14:31; 16:8), and *pusillus fidei* (Lk. 12:28). The O.L. translates it as *modicus fidei* (Matt. 6:30; 8:26; 14:31; 16:8) and *pusillus fidei* (Lk. 12:28).

With regard to the Hebrew word בַּיִת, Jerome attempted to convey many of its different nuances by translating it differently according to the context in which it was found. Although it is usually translated as *domus* in the Vulgate, he sometimes translates it variously as *aedes* (Amos 3:15), *armamentarium* (Isa. 22:8), *templum* (Mic. 3:12), *cella* and *apotheca* (both in Isa. 39:2). The O.L. has *domus* (Amos 3:15; Isa. 22:8; 39:2), and *mons domini* (Mic. 3:12).

Again, with these and other examples, one does not get the impression that Jerome was attempting to 'show off' his linguistic achievements, but rather that he was making a genuine attempt to grasp what he saw as the 'real' meaning of the scriptures. His use of different Latin words to translate a particular Greek or Hebrew word may be ascribed to his rhetorical flair in using language and his fervent desire to extract the true meaning of the original text.

There were times, however, when Jerome realised that it was not feasible to translate the exact meaning of a Hebrew or Greek word into Latin. Regardless of what he said about even the original order of the words being a mystery, Jerome realised and admitted that the attempt to make a literal translation of the Bible was a futile and impossible undertaking. He writes to Sunnia and Fretela,[112] who questioned him about his translation of Ps. 49:20, where he had translated κατὰ τοῦ ἀδελφοῦ σου κατελάλεις (Heb. תֵּשֵׁב בְּאָחִיךָ תְדַבֵּר) by '*adversus fratrem tuum loquebaris*'. Jerome knew that the exact equivalent of the Greek verb was *detrahere*. But, he says, it would not have been Latin to translate: *adversus fratrem tuum detrahebas*. Must he then put: *de fratre tuo detrahebas*? But if he did this, κατὰ would not be translated. Good Latin usage required him to translate as he did at this point. What is most important to him is that the *meaning* of the text, rather than the exact

---

112 *Ep.* 106, 30 (*CSEL* 55, 261).

wording, is brought out in the translation, and also that the language into which the translation is made is respected:

> 'However, we should always follow the rule which I have repeated so often; viz. that where there is no difference in the sense, we should translate idiomatically and use euphonious language.'[113]

This technique of sacrificing the exact wording of the original text in order to extract its meaning and also to create good Latinity is seen at many points in the Vulgate. It is interesting to see that Jerome is often at pains to justify his translation, to those who criticise him when at variance with the LXX or O.L. It is in the commentaries and epistles that we can see Jerome's earnestness in weighing up the pros and cons of the sense of each word. The following excerpt from *Ep.* 106 illustrates this point very well, and needs no comment.

A.   *Ep.* 106, 6: 'In Ps. 7 (v 9): "*iudica me, Domine, secundum iustitiam meam*", for which the Greek has κατὰ τῆν δικαιοσύνην σου, that is *iuxta iustitiam tuam*. But that is wrong, for the Hebrew has *sedechi*, which is "*iustitia mea*", and not *sedecach*, which means "*iustitiam tuam*". But all translators have rendered "*iustitiam meam*", a similar expression. And nobody should think it presumptuous that the psalmist asks to be judged according to his own justice, since the following verse means the same thing...' (Jerome goes on to quote from Pss. 16, 17, 25, 4 and 85 where the same first person use is found).[114]

Another method of studying how Jerome's theory of translation manifests itself in praxis is by looking at his treatment of proper names. In ancient times, a person's name was understood as being an inseparable part of the person – the name was a publicly affirmed identification mark, characteristic of that person. The proper name may have an easily identifiable meaning which is capable of translation or not, but it is generally not translated.[115]

---

113 *Ep.* 106, 55 (*CSEL* 55, 275): Eadem igitur interpretandi sequenda est regula, quam saepe diximus, ut, ubi non fit damnum in sensu, linguae, in quam transferimus, εὐφωνία et proprietas conseruetur.

114 *Ep.* 106, 6 (*CSEL* 55, 251): De septimo psalmo: 'Iudica me, Domine, secundum iustitiam meam.' Pro quo habetur in Graeco, κατὰ τῆν δικαιοσύνην σου, id est, 'iuxta iustitiam tuam'. Sed et in hoc male, in Hebraeo enim 'sedechi' habet, quod interpretatur, 'iustitia mea'; et non 'sedecach' quod 'iustitiam tuam' sonat. Sed omnes interpretes, 'iustitiam meam', uoce simili transtulerunt. Nec cuiquam uideatur temerarium, quod iudicari secundum iustitiam suam postulet, cum et sequens uersiculus hoc ipsum significet... For other examples of this, see *Ep.* 106, 18, 25 (*CSEL* 55, 256f, 258f).

115 See F. Kaulen: *Sprachliches Handbuch zur biblischen Vulgata*, Freiburg 1904, pp. 110-113; S. Ullmann: *Semantics*, Oxford 1962, pp. 71-79; B. Keder-Kopfstein: *op.cit.*, p. 80f.

When making a translation, the translator is faced with the choice of merely transliterating the proper name, or of attempting to translate it. Within the context of the translation of the Hebrew Bible, Jerome is faced with many such choices. In fact, a general pattern in his actions can be perceived, although, as in every aspect of his work, there are exceptions to this pattern.

When Jerome is faced with a proper name, he does not usually translate it, but instead transliterates it, as was the custom of his predecessors. Examples of this practice can be seen on almost every page of Jerome's translation and need not be cited here. Sometimes, however, when Jerome transliterates a proper name, he feels compelled to add an interpretative gloss as an aid to the reader's understanding of the passage. So, at Judges 12:6, Jerome has: *Sebboleth, quod interpretatur spica*; at Gen. 35:18: *Benoni, id est filius doloris mei... Benjamin, id est filius dexterae*; at Ruth 1:20: *ne uocetis me noemi, id est pulchram, sed uocate me mara, id est amaram.*

There is no apparent systematic reason for the inclusion of these interpretative glosses, and we must conjecture that Jerome felt them necessary as an aid to understanding the text.

With some place names, Jerome is inconsistent. In Ezek. 32:26, for instance, Jerome transliterates תובל as '*thubal*', (LXX θοβελ), but in Isa. 66:19, he interprets the same word as '*Italia*' (LXX θοβελ). In 1 Sam. 6:12, בית שמש is transliterated as '*bethsames*' (LXX βαιθσαμυς), while at Jer. 43:13, it becomes '*domus solis*' (LXX [50:13] Ἡλίου πόλεως).

In connection with Jerome's translation of the Bible, we have already seen some of the major influences on him – differences between the language of the translation and the language being translated; and the influence of Jerome's own personality, especially his rhetorical fervour, making it impossible for him to see a translation made which did damage to good Latin usage. We mentioned above[116] that a third set of influences guided Jerome's translation of the Bible. These may be described as 'ecclesiastical' influences. The term 'ecclesiastical' however, is used in two senses here: first, the influence of various of the already existing translations – the LXX, O.L. especially – can be seen in Jerome's translation. This can be termed 'ecclesiastical' in that Jerome consciously made a conservative translation because he was making it for the Church, and his avowed intention was to alter the existing translations as little as possible. Second, the term 'ecclesiastical' may be used, for in several places in Jerome's translation of the O.T., the in-

---

116 P. 111.

fluence of the N.T. or Christianity can clearly be seen. We will look briefly at several examples of the influence on Jerome of the LXX, the O.L. and the N.T.

The influence of the LXX on Jerome's translation of the O.T. can be seen in the details of grammatical usage. Jerome sometimes follows the LXX's harmonisations of the changes in the grammatical person and number of the Hebrew. For instance, at Isa. 10:34, the Hebrew reads: וְהַלְּבָנוֹן בְּאַדִּיר יִפּוֹל, while Jerome has *cum excelsis*, following the LXX's σὺν τοῖς ὑψηλοῖς. Both Symmachus and Theodotion have ἰσχυρός at this point.

The particular rendering of a word in the LXX is occasionally found in the Vulgate. One example of this is found at Isa. 1:9, where the Hebrew reads: הוֹתִיר לָנוּ שָׂרִיד. Jerome renders this as *reliquisset nobis semen*, which echoes the LXX's ἐγκατέλιπεν ἡμῖν σπέρμα. At Isa. 6:5, the Hebrew has: רָאוּ עֵינָי, while Jerome reads *vidi oculis meis*, obviously following the LXX's εἶδον τοῖς ὀφθαλμοῖς μου. Again, at Isa. 7:20, where the Hebrew reads: בְּעֶבְרֵי נָהָר, Jerome has *in his qui trans flumen sunt*, following the LXX's ὅ ἐστιν πέραν τοῦ ποταμοῦ. These examples show that Jerome was prepared to allow himself to be influenced by the LXX in his own translation of the Hebrew Bible. However, it is wise to heed the caveat of Keder-Kopfstein that Jerome was influenced by the LXX, 'but only as long as this was philologically permissible. The very moment (LXX) introduces paraphrastic extensions, Jerome ceases to follow the Greek version.'[117]

The O.L. is the one already existing version of the scriptures by which we would expect Jerome to be influenced.[118] Not only was it in Jerome's own language, but it was also his avowed intention not to deviate from this version unless it was absolutely necessary.[119] Amos 7:14f provides an example of how Jerome used the O.L. as the basis of his own translation.

Hebrew : וַיַּעַן עָמוֹס וַיֹּאמֶר אֶל אֲמַצְיָה לֹא־נָבִיא אָנֹכִי וְלֹא בֶן־נָבִיא אָנֹכִי כִּי־בוֹקֵר אָנֹכִי וּבוֹלֵס שִׁקְמִים

O.L. : Et respondit Amos, et dixit ad Amasiam: non eram propheta ego, neque filius prophetae: sed pastor vellicans sycamina. Et tulit me Dominus ex ovibus: et dixit Dominus ad me: vade, et prophetiza super populum meum Israel.

---

117 B. Keder-Kopfstein: *op.cit.*, p. 58.
118 For a fuller treatment of the dependence of Jerome on the already existing Latin versions, see A. Condamin: 'Les caractères de la traduction de la Bible par saint Jérôme', in *RSR* 3 (1912) 105-138.
119 *Ep.* 106, 2 (*CSEL* 55, 249).

Vulgate : Et respondit Amos, et dixit ad Amasiam: non sum propheta, et non sum filius prophetae; sed armamentarius ego sum vellicans sycomoros, et tulit me Dominus cum sequerer gregem, et dixit ad me Dominus: vade propheta ad populum meum Israhel.

It is noted in this example that the Vulgate is quite close to the O.L., except where it makes a few small corrections required by the Hebrew. However, as Keder-Kopfstein notes,[120] 'this situation changes radically in the translations of biblical books other than the prophets'. We demonstrate this by citing the example of 2 Chron. 6:15f.

Hebrew : אֲשֶׁר שָׁמַרְתָּ לְעַבְדְּךָ דָּוִיד אָבִי אֵת אֲשֶׁר־דִּבַּרְתָּ לּוֹ
וַתְּדַבֵּר בְּפִיךָ וּבְיָדְךָ מִלֵּאתָ כַּיּוֹם הַזֶּה: וְעַתָּה יְהֹוָה אֱלֹהֵי יִשְׂרָאֵל
שְׁמֹר לְעַבְדְּךָ דָוִיד אָבִי אֵת אֲשֶׁר דִּבַּרְתָּ לּוֹ לֵאמֹר לֹא־יִכָּרֵת לְךָ
אִישׁ מִלְּפָנַי יוֹשֵׁב עַל־כִּסֵּא יִשְׂרָאֵל רַק אִם־יִשְׁמְרוּ בָנֶיךָ אֶת־
דַּרְכָּם לָלֶכֶת בְּתוֹרָתִי כַּאֲשֶׁר הָלַכְתָּ לְפָנָי;

O.L. : Servans puero tuo Dauid quae locutus es illi: et locutus es in ore tuo, et in manu tua implesti, quasi dies iste. Et nunc Domine Deus Israel, custodi puero tuo Dauid patri meo quaecumque locutus es illi, dicens: Non deerit tibi vir a facie mea, sedens in throno Israel: veruntamen si custodierint filii tui legem meam, ut in praeceptis meis ambulent, sicut ambulaverunt in conspectu meo fideles.

Vulg. : Qui praestitisti servo tuo David patri meo quaecumque locutus fueras ei: et quae ore promiseras, opere conplesti, sicut et praesens tempus probat. nunc ergo, Domine Deus Israhel, imple servo tuo patri meo David quaecumque locutus es dicens: Non deficiet ex te vir coram me, qui sedeat super thronum Israhel: ita tamen si custodierint filii tui vias suas, et ambulaverint in lege mea, sicut et tu ambulasti coram me.

The influence of the N.T. may be seen at a very few places in Jerome's translation of the O.T., principally in the messianic passages in the O.T., or those passages which were interpreted by Christians as messianic. We list three examples of this 'christianising' tendency below.

In Hab. 3:13 the Hebrew reads:

יָצָאתָ לְיֵשַׁע עַמֶּךָ לְיֵשַׁע אֶת־מְשִׁיחֶךָ מָחַצְתָּ רֹּאשׁ מִבֵּית
רָשָׁע עָרוֹת יְסוֹד עַד־צַוָּאר:

---

120 B. Keder-Kopfstein: *op.cit.*, p. 45.

But Jerome translates this as:
> Egressus es in salutem populi tui, in salutem *cum christo tuo*. percussisti caput de domo impii, denudasti fundamentum eius usque ad collum.

A few verses later, Hab. 3:18, the Hebrew text reads:
וַאֲנִי בַּיהוָה אֶעְלוֹזָה אָגִילָה בֵּאלֹהֵי יִשְׁעִי׃

But Jerome translates this as follows:
> Ego autem in domino gaudebo, exultabo in *Deo Iesu meo*.

This christological translation of the passage may well be influenced by Luke 1:47, the Magnificat, where Mary says: καὶ ἠγαλλίασεν τὸ πνεῦμά μου ἐπὶ τῷ θεῷ τῷ σωτῆρί μου. Jerome himself translates this passage as:
> et exultavit spiritus meus in Deo salutari meo.

The O.L. at Hab. 3:18 reads 'in Deo salutari meo'.

Another explicitly Christian interpolation into the O.T. translation is found at Dan. 9:26, where the Hebrew text reads:
וְאַחֲרֵי הַשָּׁבֻעִים שִׁשִּׁים וּשְׁנַיִם יִכָּרֵת מָשִׁיחַ וְאֵין לוֹ
וְהָעִיר וְהַקֹּדֶשׁ יַשְׁחִית עַם נָגִיד הַבָּא וְקִצּוֹ בַשֶּׁטֶף
וְעַד קֵץ מִלְחָמָה נֶחֱרֶצֶת שֹׁמֵמוֹת׃

Jerome translates this as follows:
> Et post ebdomades sexaginta duas occidetur *christus*; et non erit eius populus qui eum negaturus est. et civitatem et sanctuarium dissipabit populus cum duce venturo; et finis eius vastitas, et post finem belli statuta desolatio.

The explicit 'christianising' of O.T. texts by Jerome is very rare, but worthy of mention as an influence on his translation of the Bible. There are several other instances in his translation of the O.T. where Jerome may have made an explicitly Christian translation, where he justifies his translation in his Commentary on that book. An example of this is seen at Hos. 13:14b, which Jerome translates as *ero mors tua o mors*. (The O.L. has *ubi est causa tua mors*.) In *Comm.Osee* ad loc., he justifies this translation against the LXX (*ubi est causa tua, mors*), against Aquila and Quinta (*ubi sunt sermones tui*), and against Symmachus (*ero plaga tua*). Jerome explains why he reads *deber* rather than *dabar*, but the real motive behind the translation is seen when he asserts:
> Itaque quod ille (i.e. Paul in 1 Cor. 15:54) in resurrectionem interpretatus est Domini, nos aliter interpretari nec possumus nec audemus.[121]

The influence of the N.T. passage (and perhaps also Rev. 20:14) on Jerome's translation of Hos. 13:14 is quite clear.

---

121 *Comm.Osee* 13, 14 (*CCL* 76, 150).

In concluding this chapter on Jerome's theory and practice of translating, we hope to have given the impression that Jerome's statements vis-à-vis his translation procedure are generally correct and reliable. In the preface to the *Comm.Eccles.*,[122] Jerome states that he first turned to the Hebrew text and ascertained its meaning. Then he compared his results with the Jewish interpretation. After this, he used the LXX whenever it did not differ from the original Hebrew, consulted the other Greek translations (Aquila, Theodotion and Symmachus), especially Symmachus, and finally attempted to leave intact as much of the O.L. version as possible. Jerome's achievement was to blend this enormous amount of information into a single, uniform, smooth Latin version.

Certainly, as we have seen, there are errors and inconsistencies in his translations, both of the Bible and of other works. Some of the causes of these errors and inconsistencies have also been noticed – Jerome's grasp of Hebrew; intrinsic differences between the languages being translated and the Latin language; Jerome's classical rhetorical background; various 'ecclesiastical' considerations. These, however, should not detract from the enormity of Jerome's achievement as a translator. As J.A.O. Preus[123] concludes: 'Jerome was really the first Latin writer to approach the subject of translation in the modern manner. Naturally he made errors and was not perfect at his art; but he did much to bring the practice of translation up to the level of a science.' In relation to his study of the Vulgate version, we may agree with B. Keder-Kopfstein's conclusion:

> '...the more profound one's preoccupation with the Vulgate becomes, the more respectful one is bound to be of this masterpiece produced by one man... the result is a most fortunate blending of a strict adherence to the Hebrew structure in texts where the single words and verses are loaded with profound meaning and a fine literary version of biblical narrative. The Vulgate's impact on later versions into modern European vernaculars is enormous. That this influence was beneficial may be due in the final analysis, to the fact that the Vulgate constitutes, from the point of view of the translation technique employed, a most gratifying compromise.'[124]

---

122 *CCL* 72, 249.
123 J.A.O. Preus: *Saint Jerome's Translation Terminology*, Ph.D. dissertation, University of Minnesota 1951, p. 165.
124 B. Keder-Kopfstein: *op.cit.*, pp. 284-5.

5. Jerome and the Literal Sense

Alexandria and the literal sense

For Clement of Alexandria, the literal sense of scripture was of little importance. He held the view that almost the whole of scripture was expressed in enigmas and figures,[1] which meant the 'real' and important meaning of the Bible was not expressed literally, but was 'hidden' deep in the text. This deeper meaning was only accessible to those believers who had received the γνῶσις from the resurrected Lord. The truth of the Bible was contained in symbols, which it was the task of the interpreter to understand and explain.[2]

Clement's successor, Origen, makes a clear statement on the different senses of scripture in *De Princ.* IV. There are three senses – the literal, the moral and the spiritual. Origen found support for this view in various scriptural passages, notably Prov. 22:20 (LXX): 'Describe these things in a three-fold way'. The three senses must be used to explain scripture to the varying (intellectual) capacities of Christians; the literal sense for simple or new Christians; the moral sense for those who are more mature in the faith; and the spiritual sense for the perfect.[3] However, in almost all of Origen's exegesis, the distinction between the moral and spiritual senses becomes blurred, and, in effect, he practises a two-fold exegesis.[4]

According to Origen, the literal sense does not always have a meaning. It has been shown that Origen understands this in two ways;[5] first, in a weak sense, that some passages in scripture simply do not make sense if taken literally;[6] and second, in a stronger sense, that some

---

[1] *Strom.* VI, 124, 5ff. On the idea of αἴνιγμα in Clement, see R. Mortley: *Connaissance religieuse et hermeneutique chez Clement d'Alexandrie*, Leiden 1973, pp. 229-232.
[2] See Mortley: *op.cit.*, pp. 39-49; 126-149.
[3] *De Princ.* IV, 2, 4.
[4] Cf M.F. Wiles: 'Origen as Biblical Scholar', in *CHB* I, 454-489, especially p. 467f.
[5] *Art.cit.*, p. 470f.
[6] E.g. his interpretation of Zech. 4:10, which, if taken literally, would imply, Origen says, that God had seven bodily eyes.

apparently factual statements are untrue. The dimensions of Noah's Ark, for instance, would simply not be large enough to accommodate all the animals. Instead of dispensing with the literal sense in this case, Origen cites a Jewish authority, who states that, as they were all geometric measurements, the figures must all be squared.[7] When, therefore, Origen thinks of the literal sense in this second, stronger sense, he is usually inclined to defend its meaning. He does not appear, however, to ascribe any real value to the literal sense.[8] Origen holds the facts of the crucifixion to be true, for example, but for him their essential meaning is to be found elsewhere, in their allegorical or spiritual meaning.

In his discussion of Judaism, Origen is always antipathetic towards the literal meaning. This is because he operates (as did all the early Fathers) with the Pauline dichotomy between letter and spirit, law and grace (2 Cor. 3:6). The Jews, he says, understand only the letter of the Law, while Christians understand the better and more important spirit (revealed to them by God, in the person of Jesus Christ). The literal sense is, then, the way of death, and to follow it is to act as a Jew, and not as a Christian.[9]

Antioch and the literal sense

According to Diodore of Tarsus, allegory is foolish and unnecessary: those who use allegorical interpretation are following their own imagination, and are careless and abusive of the historical, literal sense.[10] For Diodore, the literal sense is the primary one for understanding scripture. He explains it in terms of θεωρία:

> 'We will not shrink from the truth, but will expound it according to the historical substance (ἱστορία) and the plain literal sense (λέξις). At the same time, we will not disparage anagogy and the higher θεωρία. For history is not opposed to θεωρία. On the contrary, it proves to be the foundation and basis of the higher senses. One thing is to be watched, however; θεωρία must never

---

[7] *Hom. II, 2 in Gen.*

[8] Cf Wiles: *art.cit.*, p. 472: 'Very often when Origen explicitly defends the historical truth of a passage it appears to be quite unrelated to what he regards as its real meaning.'

[9] For Origen's attitude to the Jews, see the excellent study of N.R.M. de Lange: *Origen and the Jews*, Cambridge 1976.

[10] Diodore: *Comm.Ps.*: Prol.

be understood as doing away with the underlying sense; it would then be no longer θεωρία but ἀλληγορία.'[11]

For Diodore, then, θεωρία complements the literal, historical understanding of scripture. The Psalms adapt to all times and situations. They are truly prophetic, conforming primarily to their original historical setting, but in a deeper sense, conforming also to 'every moment in time, down to the final perfection of humans'.[12] Historical understanding and θεωρία go hand in hand in the interpretation of scripture.

Diodore's pupil, Theodore of Mopsuestia, set down what he believed to be the exegete's task:

'I judge the exegete's task to be to explain words which most people find difficult... (he) must give the meaning and do it concisely.'[13]

Theodore's most interesting work is the *Commentary on Psalms*, written early in his career.[14] Considerable attention is paid to matters of textual criticism, and Theodore, although he did not know Hebrew himself, was convinced that a knowledge of 'the language the prophet actually spoke' was essential for a correct interpretation. In general he depended on the LXX, but, realising that no one translation could perfectly convey the force of the original, he also used other Greek translations, notably that of Symmachus.[15]

One of Theodore's original contributions to exegesis, and which is characteristic of later Antiochenes, is his emphasis on the historical setting of the Psalms. He disregards the traditional headings or titles as being unauthoritative, but ascribes all the Psalms to David. He is also aware, however, that the historical setting of many of the Psalms is not consistent with Davidic authorship.[16] Theodore's solution is to see David as the archetypal prophet, given a vision by the Spirit of future gracious acts of God for his people. Thus, he classifies the Psalms chro-

---

[11] *Ibid.*, transl. K. Froelich: *Biblical Interpretation* 86 (altered).
[12] Diodore: *Comm.Ps. 118*: Pref. For a systematic study of Diodore as an exegete, see E. Schweizer: 'Diodor von Tarsus als Exeget', in *ZNTW* 40 (1941) 33-75.
[13] *Comm.John*: Prol. This is very similar to Jerome's statement on the exegete's task: 'To explain what has been said by others and make clear in plain language what has been written obscurely' (*Ep.* 57, 9; *CSEL* 54, 518); cf *Comm. Isa.* 64, 4-5; *Apol.c.Ruf.* I, 16 (*CCL* 73A, 735; 79, 15).
[14] The original Greek text of much of the *Comm.* was recovered by R. Devreesse: *La Commentaire de Théodore de Mopsueste sur les Psaumes (1-80)*, Rome 1939.
[15] M.F. Wiles: 'Theodore of Mopsuestia as Representative of the Antiochene School', in *CHB* I, 497.
[16] E.g. Pss. 35; 51; 72.

nologically from David's time to that of the Maccabees. David's vision did not go further than the Maccabean period, and this has the consequence that the Psalms are not directly messianic. Theodore believed that only four Psalms were messianic,[17] and rejects the allegorical (messianic) interpretation of Alexandrian exegetes as violating the principle that each Psalm should be treated as a literary unit and that a verse cannot be divorced from the context in which it is found.

The hermeneutical method used by John Chrysostom was similar to that of his teacher, Diodore. In his homilies, Chrysostom's primary aim was to expound the literal sense of scripture. He was concerned with textual matters, for he often cited readings from several versions – those of Theodotion, Symmachus and Aquila – alongside those of the LXX.[18] Chrysostom discussed the difference between θεωρία and ἀλληγορία in a homily on Ps. 9, where he divided biblical statements into those which have only a literal sense, those which have a higher sense as well as a literal one and those which have only a higher sense.[19] As regards the use of the word 'allegory' (ἀλληγορία) in the Bible, Chrysostom stated that Paul's use of the word in Gal. 4:24 was unusual, since what he had called an allegory was, in fact, a 'type' (τύπος).[20] Elsewhere, Chrysostom told students of the Bible that their task was not to adapt passages such as Isa. 5:1-7 to suit their own preconceived ideas of what the allegory meant, but rather to follow the guidance of the context, and to accept the interpretation given in the text itself. Wherever allegories occurred in the Bible, they were always accompanied by their interpretations.[21]

Jerome's terminology for the literal sense

Jerome uses many different terms and phrases to delineate the literal sense of scripture. Among the terminology used by Jerome are the following expressions: *secundum intellegentiam corporalem*;[22] *carnaliter interpretari*;[23] *carnaliter accipere*;[24] *carnaliter intellegere*;[25] *corporea in-*

---

[17] Pss. 2, 8, 45, 110. These Psalms are justified as messianic because of their use in the N.T., where they are used, Theodore says, to describe the incarnation of the Christ.
[18] See, for instance, *In Ps.* 4, 9; 55, 53.
[19] *In Ps.* 9, 4.
[20] *Comm.Gal.* 4, 23f.
[21] *Isa.Interp.* 5, 3.
[22] E.g. *Comm.Isa.* 66, 15 (*CCL* 73A, 782).
[23] *Comm.Isa.* 14, 2 (*CCL* 73, 166-167).
[24] *Comm.Isa.* 65, 21 (*CCL* 73A, 763).

tellegentia;[26] *carnaliter;*[27] *corporaliter;*[28] *simplex historia;*[29] *historia veritas;*[30] *historia accipere;*[31] *historia fundamentum;*[32] *historia humilior;*[33] *humilitatem sequi litterae;*[34] *iuxta litteram;*[35] *secundum litteram intellegere;*[36] *carnaliter Iudaei;*[37] *dimittamus ergo litteram cum Iudaeis;*[38] *si carnalem interpretationem sequimur, Iudaicis fabulis adquiescendum sit;*[39] *si secundum litteram intellegimus, non stat;*[40] *quod iuxta litteram penitus stare non potest;*[41] *quod iuxta litteram impossibile est.*[42]

No one term suffices for Jerome in his discussions of the literal sense of scripture. This observation is not surprising if we bear in mind his early rhetorical training and natural eloquence. The term *historia*, however, is one which he uses frequently[43] to designate the literal sense and which would appear to have a greater depth of meaning for Jerome than some of his other vocabulary. He uses it in two senses. First, he uses it to describe biblical narratives or other past events, as, when discussing Luke, author of one of the Gospels and the Acts of the Apostles, he refers to the latter work as 'history, extending to the second year of Paul's stay at Rome'.[44] Again, Jerome's comment on Hab. 2:11 ('For the stone will cry out from the wall, and the beam from the woodwork respond') is that the words refer back to the historical rapacity of the Assyrian raiders:

'Prophetic speech shows that in history (*historia*), this is close; the stories of the walls have been destroyed because of you, and

---

25 *Ep.* 121, 10 (*CSEL* 56, 43).
26 *C. Gal.* 5, 24 (*PL* 26, 514).
27 *C. Ioel.* 2, 28 (*CCL* 76, 194); *C. Isa.* 11, 16; 60, 3 (*CCL* 73, 157; 73A, 694).
28 *C. Osee* 9, 14 (*CCL* 76, 102); *C. Isa.* 2, 15 (*CCL* 73, 36).
29 *Hom.Orig. in Lucam* 37 (*GCS* 35, 217, 11).
30 *Comm.Ezek.* 21, 19 (*CCL* 75, 289).
31 *Comm.Isa.* 19, 5ff (*CCL* 73, 194-5).
32 *Comm.Ezek.* 26, 15f (*CCL* 75, 353).
33 *Comm.Ezek.* 40, 24f (*CCL* 75, 576).
34 *Comm.Amos* 8, 11 (*CCL* 76, 333); *Ep.* 121, 10 (*CSEL* 56, 43).
35 *Comm.Ezek.* 19, 9 (*CCL* 75, 251); *Comm.Amos* 4, 1 (*CCL* 76, 259).
36 *Tract. de Psalm.* 75, 13 (*CCL* 78, 54); *Comm.Isa.* 58, 11 (*CCL* 73A, 672).
37 *Comm.Isa.* 65, 21 (*CCL* 73A, 763); cf 29, 17 (*CCL* 73, 378).
38 *Tract. in Marc.* 1, 13f (*CCL* 78, 461).
39 *Ep.* 59, 3 (*CSEL* 54, 544).
40 *Tract. in Psalm.* 140, 7 (*CCL* 78, 307).
41 *Comm.Isa.* 58, 14 (*CCL* 73A, 676); *Comm.Zach.* 13, 7f (*CCL* 76A, 875).
42 *Comm.Isa.* 58, 13 (*CCL* 73A, 675).
43 See the references just given, and P. Jay: *L'Exégèse de saint Jérôme*, Paris 1985, pp. 135-140.
44 *De Vir.Illus.* 7 (*PL* 23, 651).

the charred remains of the wall's wood will sound out your harshness.'⁴⁵

The second use of *historia* denotes material which Jerome believes can be understood without recourse to the tropological sense. This second sense has clearly a somewhat wider meaning than the first sense. He remarks at *Comm.Zach.* 11, 4f that 'when prophecy is most evident, and the time unfolding of history (*historia*) is told in translation, then a figurative interpretation (*tropologiae interpretatio*) is superfluous'.⁴⁶ This principle, along with the practical aim of explaining scripture for his own day, allows Jerome to apply historical events to analogous events in more recent times. Zephaniah, according to Jerome, foresaw the sack of Jerusalem, whether by Nebuchadnezzar in the sixth century B.C., or by the Romans in the first century A.D., a disaster it deserved, Jerome cannot refrain from adding, because it killed the servants of God, and finally God's own Son. The terrible imagery in his prophecy, Jerome says, finds its fulfilment in the plight of the Jewish people of Jerome's own day, for they were forbidden to enter the city of Jerusalem, except for one day a year, on the anniversary of its capture and destruction, where they could only lament the ruined Temple. In the midst of their calamity and shame, the Church of the Resurrection shines resplendent, and the cross rises triumphant on the Mount of Olives.⁴⁷

It needs to be noted, however, in connection with Jerome's use of the term *historia*, that, although, as Kelly says,⁴⁸ it was a technical term in the exegetical school at Antioch, it was also in widespread use by Alexandrian writers and other Latin exegetes. Of Antiochene authors, ἱστορία⁴⁹ is used frequently by Diodore of Tarsus,⁵⁰ Theodore of Mopsuestia,⁵¹ and John Chrysostom.⁵² Kelly does not mention its use by the

---

45 *Comm.Hab.* 2, 11 (*CCL* 76A, 605).
46 *Comm.Zach.* 11, 4f (*CCL* 76A, 850).
47 *Comm.Soph.* 1, 15f (*CCL* 76A, 673-4). Jerome mentions (*Comm.Ezek.* 11, 23) that in his day, the Church of the Resurrection (built on the spot from which Jesus was thought to have ascended to heaven) was in full view of the ruined Temple.
48 Kelly: p. 165.
49 There seems no reason to suspect that *historia* and ἱστορία had different meanings.
50 Cf Fragment 59 in Gen. 49, 27 (in J. Deconinck: *Essay sur la Chaine de l'Octateuque*, Paris 1912, p. 133); Prol. to *Expos. in Ps.* (in L. Mariès: 'Extraits du Commentaire de Diodore de Tarse', in *RSR* 9 [1919] p. 88).
51 Cf *In Ps.* 1 (in R. Devreesse: *Le Commentaire de Théodore de Mopsueste sur les Psaumes [I-LXXX]*, Vatican City 1939, p. 3); 25f; *In Ps.* 35; (*ibid.*, p. 194).
52 Cf *In Ps.* 43; *Ps.* 117, 22; *Ps.* 149.

Alexandrians Origen,[53] and Didymus the Blind,[54] or by the Latin exegetes Hilary of Poitiers[55] and Augustine.[56] This means that, although as we shall see, he was probably influenced by the Antiochene school in his respect for the literal sense of scripture, Jerome's use of the term *historia* cannot be utilised to prove this influence, as it was in such general use.

One of the most interesting features of the terminology Jerome uses for the literal sense is the phrase *carnaliter Iudaei* and similar phrases.[57] Sometimes Jerome equates the literal sense of scripture with the Jewish understanding. Generally speaking, he uses this in a favourable sense and not in polemical contexts. When commenting on Isa. 65:21f, ('And they shall build houses and inhabit them; they shall plant vineyards and eat the fruit of them. They shall not build and another inhabit; they shall not plant and another eat'), for example, Jerome quotes Ps. 69: 35f, and accepts at face value the well-known Jewish tradition that Jerusalem would be re-built and be restored to its former glory:

> 'The Jews receive all these things in a wordly manner (*carnaliter*), so that Jerusalem and the cities of Judea may be, once again, set up to its original position.'

On the other hand, there are occasions when Jerome does use this phrase polemically, as at *Ep.* 59, 3 to Marcella, where he discusses Paul's statement (1 Thess. 4, 15f) that 'some shall be alive and remain until the Lord's coming', and that they will be 'caught up to meet the Lord in the air'. Are we going to believe that this refers to a corporeal assumption, and that those assumed will not die? Jerome answers in the affirmative, with the clarification that the bodies of those assumed will be glorified. In effect, Jerome says, the passage must be taken spiritually, for

> 'if we follow the fleshly sense, we will have to be satisfied with the Jewish accounts, that once again Jerusalem be built and sacrificial victims offered in the Temple, and with diminished spiritual worship, wordly ceremonies prevail.'[58]

---

53 Cf *Hom. 19 in Ierem.* 14; *Hom. in 1 Sam.* 28, 3-25; *Comm.Iohan.* 2, 1; 10, 5; *Hom. in Cant.Cantic.* 3, 54.
54 Cf *Frag. in Prov.* 1, 6; *In Ps.* 21, 18f; *In Ps.* 112, 9.
55 Cf *In Ps.* 53, 2.
56 Cf *De Genesi ad litteram imperfectus liber*; *De Genesi contra Manich.* 2, 3; *De Civ. Dei* 15, 27.
57 *Comm.Isa.* 65, 21 (*CCL* 73A, 763).
58 *Ep.* 59, 3 (*CSEL* 54, 544).

Jerome's respect for the literal sense

That Jerome held the literal sense of scripture was very important and that he had a great respect for it is plainly evident. This respect can be seen not only in his mature works, but right through his exegetical career, and can even be traced in his very first piece of exegesis, *Ep.* 18, written in A.D. 381 to Pope Damasus.

In *Ep.* 18A,[59] we have a straightforward piece of exegesis on the call of Isaiah (Isa. 6:1-9), while *Ep.* 18B is more technical exegesis of Isa. 6: 6-9. In *Ep.* 18A, Jerome employs both literal and tropological exegesis, and although he categorically states that the literal sense is subordinate to the tropological sense,[60] yet he does afford the literal sense real significance. The letter begins with a strictly historical exposition of 'who this Uzziah was, how many years he had reigned, and who among the other kings were his contemporaries'[61] as well as the dating of the passage. Following this is what Jerome understands as the spiritual significance of the passage, but the whole letter is interspersed with quotations from other biblical books (both O.T. and N.T.), which Jerome considers to be analogous to both the literal and the spiritual understanding of the passage. In this letter also, Jerome disagrees with an allegorical interpretation put forward by Origen, that the 'Lord sitting upon a throne...' of 6:1 was God the Father, and that the two Seraphim on either side were the Lord Jesus Christ and the Holy Spirit. Jerome disagreed with Origen's interpretation because it implied the subordination of the Son and Spirit to the Father. Although Jerome was not content to understand this verse literally, he shows considerable independence of mind, and expounds his own spiritual interpretation.[62]

---

59 The language of paragraph 16 of *Ep.* 18A implies that a break occurs at this point, and the phrase *in alio loco disputavimus* in paragraph 4 of *Ep.* 18B is seen as a reference back to paragraph 15 of *Ep.* 18A. T.C. Lawlor (in *The Letters of St. Jerome*, Vol. 1, London 1963, p. 214) has argued that *Ep.* 18B reads like a supplement to *Ep.* 18A and conjectures that *Ep.* 18B may have been written in response to a request for further information on the same verses, or perhaps as a response to criticism that Jerome had not fully treated the last few verses of the passage in *Ep.* 18A.

60 *Ep.* 18A, 2 (*CSEL* 54, 76): Praemissa historia spiritalis sequitur intellectus, cuius causa historia ipsa replicata est.

61 *Ep.* 18A, 1 (*CSEL* 54, 74).

62 For Jerome, it was Christ who sat on the throne, and the two Seraphim represented the O.T. and the N.T. His disagreement here with Origen was to prove very useful later, in the Origenist controversy (cf *Ep.* 84, 3 where he refers to Origen's 'detestable exegesis').

The first proper attempt[63] Jerome made at writing in commentary form came in 387-8, shortly after he had taken up residence in Bethlehem. This took the form of four commentaries on Philemon, Galatians, Ephesians and Titus, which he undertook because Paula and Eustochium asked persistently for answers to their many questions about these letters.[64] Jerome wrote them very quickly[65] and derived most of his comments from previous commentaries, especially Origen.[66]

The commentaries on Philemon and Titus are primarily taken up with practical information and straight-forward verse by verse exposition, whereas the *Comm.Eph.* contains more tropological exegesis, although, as Kelly judges, 'in the main... Jerome struggles valiantly to establish the literal sense'.[67] At 5, 14, for example, Jerome says that he heard a certain person discussing this passage in church, explaining that the words were spoken to Adam, who was buried at Calvary, where Christ was crucified. The place was called Calvary because the head of some ancient man had been buried there, and because, when Christ was crucified, he was hanging directly above the place where it was buried.[68] Grützmacher argued that in this commentary, Jerome was mainly dependent on the work of Apollinarius of Laodicea.[69]

Most important of this group of commentaries on the Pauline epistles is *Comm.Gal.*, of which Harnack said: '*in dieser Gestalt ist es der inter-*

---

[63] Many years before, while at Antioch, Jerome wrote a short commentary on Obadiah (now lost), which was to cause him embarrassment, and which he referred to as: 'this brash initial effort of my youthful talent' (*Comm.Abd.*: Prol. [*CCL* 76, 349]). Before he had been forced to leave Rome, he had also begun a commentary on Ecclesiastes, but this was not completed until several years later (*Comm. Eccles.*: Pref. [*CCL* 72, 249]).

[64] Cf *Comm.Philem.* 1 (*PL* 26, 639).

[65] Cf *Comm.Eph. II*: Prol. (*PL* 26, 507).

[66] A. Souter: *The Earliest Latin Commentaries on the Epistles of St. Paul*, Oxford 1927, pp. 107-133; A. von Harnack: 'Origenistisches Gut... in den Kommentaren des Hieronymus zum Philemon-, Galater-, Epheser-, und Titusbrief', in *Der kirchengeschichtliche Ertrag des exegetischen Arbeiten des Origines*, Vol. 2 (TU 42,4), Leipzig 1919, 141-168). That Jerome used other commentaries widely should not necessarily be taken as a castigation of his own scholarship, for he himself states this as his aim in writing commentaries – cf *Comm.Gal.*: Prol. (*PL* 26, 332-4); *Comm. Eph.*: Prol. (*PL* 26, 472) also *Apol.c.Rufin.* 3, 11, where he says that it is the accepted practice of commentators, whether of the bible or secular literature, to set out the interpretations of other men alongside their own. Besides this, Jerome has preserved many passages, especially of Origen, which would otherwise be lost.

[67] Kelly: p. 147.

[68] *Comm.Eph.* 5, 14 (*PL* 26, 559).

[69] Grützmacher II, p. 40. Cf also A. Souter: *op.cit.*, p. 110.

essanteste lateinische Kommentar, den wir besitzen'.[70] Jerome's primary concern in this commentary was to establish the meaning of the author, and for this reason there is little evidence of spiritual exegesis. One of the most interesting sections in the commentary is the discussion of Gal. 2:11-14, where Paul says that he chastised Peter at Antioch 'because he was in the wrong'. That one apostle should chastise another, and that Peter, the most important of the apostles, should have appeared to revert to Judaism seemed very problematic for Jerome, and so he felt obliged to discuss at length what he understood to be the true meaning of the passage. Jerome puts forward the theory that there was no real difference of opinion between the two apostles. Both Peter and Paul knew that the Jewish Law was no longer obligatory for them, since the advent of Christ, but Peter seemed to revert to Jewish practices temporarily in order to convert the Jews to Christianity. Paul knew what Peter was doing (he had himself complied with the Jewish Law on several occasions in the past for the same reason), and so his chastisement was not intended, and was not taken by Peter, seriously. Peter, therefore, was not 'in the wrong' in the eyes of Paul, Jerome argues, but only in the eyes of the Gentile Christians with whom Peter had previously eaten. Jerome thought that Paul wished to assert the primacy (chronologically, not theologically) of the Mosaic Law, and therefore pretended to be angry with Peter, 'to correct St. Peter's pretence of observing the Law... by himself pretending to censure him'.[71] Jerome, in a much later letter to Augustine (who instigated a protracted correspondence with Jerome over this interpretation of Gal. 2:11-14) explicitly says that he had emulated Origen's commentaries on Galatians, as well as various other works, by Didymus, Apollinarius, Eusebius of Emesa, Theodore of Heraclea and John Chrysostom.[72]

Many of Jerome's commentaries were written because various friends had asked him to give explanations of the biblical books. One such friend was Eusebius of Cremona, who, in March 398, asked Jerome to compose a strictly historical commentary on the gospel of Matthew. The *Comm.Matt.* fulfils this request, but on several occasions[73] he includes spiritual interpretations.

The fact that Jerome undertook to write a commentary on Matthew

---

70 A. von Harnack: *op.cit.*, p. 147.
71 *Comm.Gal.* 2, 11-14 (*PL* 26, 363-7).
72 *Ep.* 112, 4 and 6 (*CSEL* 55, 371, 373).
73 Notably in the parables (e.g. Matt. 13, 44; 13, 47; 20, 1ff), and also the story of the entry into Jerusalem (21, 5-7); the feeding of the multitude (14, 19); and the burial of Jesus (27, 59).

according to the historical sense shows clearly that he had a great respect for the literal sense of scripture, and the commentary itself confirms this. His discussion of the story of the birth of Jesus, for example, is written in a measured and concise style, giving a strictly controlled and historical interpretation, being little more on occasion than a paraphrase.

Jerome occasionally made historical errors. At *Comm.Matt.* 2, 22 for instance, he says that Herod Antipas was the successor of Archelaus, and that Lyons, and not Vienne, was the place of his exile.[74] At *Comm. Matt.* 24, 15 he also states incorrectly that Pontius Pilate installed a statue of Caesar in the Temple.

In the latter part of 406, Jerome finished a group of five commentaries on Zechariah, Malachi, Hosea, Joel and Amos, thus bringing to completion his work on all twelve Minor Prophets, begun some fifteen years previously. One or two statements in these commentaries are very interesting for the purpose of showing Jerome's respect for the literal sense of scripture. After the end of the Origenist controversy, in which Jerome had played a leading part, he became rather more critical of the famous Alexandrian theologian than he had been previously. In the *Comm. Mal.*, Jerome criticises Origen's almost total neglect of the literal sense:

'But he foolishly does not touch entirely on history (*historia*), for he is very skilled in his own allegorical interpretation.'[75]

Also in *Comm.Mal.*, Jerome repeats a statement he had already made about the literal sense in *Comm.Zach.* 11, 4f:

'There is a rule of writing: where it [*historia*] is intertwined by the clearest prophecy concerning the future, the things which have been written do not diminish because of a cloudy allegory.'[76]

This same respect for the literal sense can be seen in Jerome's last commentary, on Jeremiah, begun in 414 or 415,[77] but unfinished at the time of his death in 420. This commentary has two noticeable characteristics: first, his criticisms of Origen's excessive allegorical interpretations are more vicious than in any previous commentary (he refers to Origen as 'that allegorist'[78]); and second, his own interpretation is mainly historical, partly because he was writing once again for his friend Eusebius of Cremona (who had commissioned the *Comm.Matt.*) and partly because of the nature of the material he was commenting on.[79]

---

74 Cf Josephus: *Antiq.* XVII, 13, 2.
75 *Comm.Mal*: Prol. (*CCL* 76A, 902).
76 *Comm.Mal.* 1, 11 (*CCL* 76A, 911).
77 Cf Kelly: p. 316, for a discussion of the date of this commentary.
78 Delirat in hoc loco allegoricus interpres, *Comm.Hier.* 24, 1-10 (*CCL* 74, 236); 27, 9-11 (74, 265); 28, 12-14 (74, 273); cf 25, 26 (74, 246).
79 Cf. Kelly: p. 316.

We have seen that Jerome had a great deal of respect for the literal sense of scripture, and that this extended right through his exegetical career, from *Ep.* 18A, his earliest exegetical piece, to the unfinished *Comm.Hier.* It still remains to ask whether we can discover the origins of this respect, for which it will be necessary to go back to Jerome's first few years as a student of Christianity.

Jerome mentions the name of Apollinarius of Laodicea in his writings several times.[80] During one of Jerome's stays in Antioch,[81] he attended Apollinarius' lectures on holy scripture, for he recalled twenty years later that 'at Antioch I frequently listened to Apollinarius of Laodicea and held him in high regard'.[82] Apollinarius was widely admired for his strongly anti-Arian stance, with his emphasis on the full divinity of Jesus Christ, as well as for his influential refutation of the Neo-Platonist, Porphyry's attack on the Christian faith.[83] He wrote many commentaries on scripture (both O.T. and N.T.), as well as directly theological works, but because he was deemed to hold unorthodox christological views, he was condemned and almost all his works were destroyed.[84] Jerome claimed that 'although he taught me in scripture, I never accepted his disputable doctrine on Christ's human mind'.[85]

The only substantial fragments of any of Apollinarius' commentaries which are extant are those on Paul's letter to the Romans.[86] On the strength of these fragments, Kelly has asserted that 'Apollinarius was one of the most accomplished and keen-sighted Greek exegetes of his time'.[87] His exegetical method stresses the theological and dogmatic importance of the letter. Jerome opines that Apollinarius' explanations were too brief, sometimes consisting of little more than a table of contents.[88]

Unfortunately, we have no knowledge about the lectures on scripture

---

80 E.g. *Ep.* 84, 3 (*CSEL* 55, 123); *De Vir.Illus.* 104 (*PL* 23, 742); *C.Osee*: Prol. (*CCL* 76, 4); *Comm.Mal.*: Prol. (*CCL* 76A, 902); *Comm.Isa.*: Prol. (*CCL* 73, 4).
81 For the problems of dating, see Kelly: p. 59.
82 *Ep.* 84, 3, dated A.D. 398 (*CSEL* 55, 123).
83 Jerome reports (*De Vir.Illus.* 104) [*PL* 23, 742] that Apollinarius' *Against Porphyry* in thirty books are generally regarded to be among the best of his books.
84 Only fragments remain; cf Altaner: *Patrology*, p. 354-5, and the literature cited there.
85 *Ep.* 84, 3.
86 Collected by K. Staab: *Pauluskommentare aus der Griechischen Kirche*, Münster i.W. 1933, pp. xxiii-xxv; 57-82.
87 Kelly: p. 59.
88 *Comm.Isa.*: Prol. (*CCL* 73, 4).

given by Apollinarius and attended by Jerome, but we can be reasonably sure that Jerome was influenced in his exegetical method by this famous exegete and theologian. Although Apollinarius' exegetical method does not seem to have been the same as the other leading Antiochene exegetes we have seen, he is normally classed as an Antiochene.[89] He certainly appears to have concerned himself with finding the meaning of what Paul had to say, which implies the use of at least some of the historical methods of the Antiochene school, and a rejection of allegorical method. We may therefore echo Kelly's words and say that it was at Antioch, from Apollinarius, that Jerome learned his respect for the historical or literal approach to exegesis.[90]

Jerome's use of biblical history

Jerome makes many references, although usually only in passing, to the date of composition of a biblical book, or the historical situation envisaged in a particular book. He makes use of this information in his explanation of the literal sense of scripture, as the following examples will show.

The prologue of the *Comm.Amos*[91] gives a description of Tekoa, the birth-place of the prophet. It is *sex millibus ad meridianam plagam abest a sancta Bethleem, quae mundi genuit Saluatorem.* In 1, 1,[92] Jerome discusses the genealogy of king Uzziah:

> 'This, then, is Uzziah, whose cognomen is Azariah, king of Judah, who attempted to claim a priesthood not due to him, and was struck on the forehead with leprosy. The anger of the Lord was shown not only by his punishment for committing sacrilege, but also by the earthquake, which the Hebrews recall as occurring at that time. However, Jeroboam is not the son of Nebat who made Israel sin, but is the son of Joash, son of Jothan, son of Jehu, and hence great-grandson of this same Jehu under whom Hosea, Joel and Amos prophesied.'

In the prologue to the *Comm.Ioelem*, Jerome gives the order of the twelve Minor Prophets in the LXX and in the Hebrew Bible. He also gives the etymological meaning of the names of each of the prophets.[93]

---

[89] E.g. by Altaner and Quasten in their Patrologies.
[90] Kelly: p. 60.
[91] *CCL* 76, 211.
[92] *CCL* 76, 213f.
[93] *CCL* 76, 159-160.

Jerome refers to a Jewish tradition in the *Comm.Ionam*[94] for evidence that Hosea, Amos, Isaiah and Jonah all lived at the same time. He also opines that the author of this prophecy is the same person referred to as 'Jonah, son of Amittai, the prophet from Gath Hepher' in 2 Kings 14: 25.[95]

In the *Comm.Aggaeum*, Jerome believes that this prophet was contemporary with the reign of Tarquinius Superbus (535-510 B.C.).[96] Jerome identifies the prophet Malachi with Esdras, rejecting the view that Malachi was an angel who assumed a human body and appeared to humans, rightly noting that Malachi prophesied at the same time as Haggai and Zachariah.[97]

In the *Comm.Isa.* 7, 8,[98] Jerome reviews events recorded at 2 Kings 16:9; 17:1, 6, and states that the prophecy ('Within 65 years Ephraim will be too shattered to be a people') predicts the destruction of the kingdoms of Syria by Tiglath-Pileser and Ephraim by Salmanasar.

Many more examples could be cited to emphasise the fact that Jerome refers to events in biblical history when he is expounding the literal sense of scripture. He does not normally dwell on these historical facts, but often considers it necessary to recall the historical situation of individual books or passages in order to make a satisfactory exegesis of that book or passage.

Jerome's interest in biblical topography

As an aid to his interpretation of the Bible, Jerome developed an interest in topography, especially the topography of the Holy Land and those other lands which had some connection with the Bible, namely Syria, Assyria and Egypt. In this respect, Jerome was one of a growing number of Christians in the 4th century who travelled to the Bible lands on pilgrimage. After he was forced to leave Rome in A.D. 385,[99] following the death of his patron, Pope Damasus, in December A.D. 384, Jerome de-

---

[94] *CCL* 76, 379: Traduntque Hebraei, Osee et Amos et Isaiam ac Ionam iisdem prophetasse temporibus.
[95] *CCL* 76, 378.
[96] *CCL* 76A, 713.
[97] *CCL* 76A, 901.
[98] *CCL* 73, 98f.
[99] On the background to this topic, see J. Wilkinson: *Egeria's Travels*, rev. ed., Warminster 1981, pp. 10-26; E.D. Hunt: *Holy Land Pilgrimages* Oxford 1982; C. Kopp: *The Holy Places of the Gospels*, London 1963.

cided to travel round the Holy Land. This he did from summer A.D. 385 to summer A.D. 386, accompanied for most of the time by Paula, Eustochium and several other Christian women. The route taken by the group is described by Jerome in his *Apol. contra Rufin.* and in *Ep.* 108, written to Eustochium.[100]

In these travels, Jerome learned much about the topographical sites important to his exegesis of both Testaments, and this information was of great benefit in his explanations of the literal sense of scripture.

Jerome settled at Bethlehem in A.D. 386.[101] After completing his commentaries on Ecclesiastes and on Galatians, Ephesians, Philemon and Titus, he began work, between A.D. 389 and 392, on a trilogy of books designed to be of great importance to him in his exegetical labours. These were the *Liber Interpretationis Hebraicorum Nominum*; the *De Situ et Nominibus Locorum Hebraicorum* and the *Quaestiones Hebraicae in Libro Geneseos*.

This kind of etymological work had had a long history, not only in Christianity, but in paganism and also in Judaism. Jerome himself believed that he was restoring and improving upon a previous work by Origen, who had, in fact, revised and Christianised an earlier work by Philo. This belief, however, has been shown to be false.[102] The *Liber Locorum* is a gazetteer of biblical places, which is a rendering of Eusebius of Caesarea's *Onomasticon*, first published in A.D. 330. Jerome claims that another Latin version already existed but that it was a slovenly one.[103] Eusebius had listed place-names alphabetically, and appended brief notes; he had also included the names of some rivers and a few heathen deities; for the N.T., Eusebius' work left a great deal to be desired, for he omitted many place-names in Acts and in the Epistles.

The cave of the Nativity in Bethlehem was a greatly venerated place for Christians in Jerome's day. In a letter written to the deacon Sabianus, Jerome reproaches him for having seduced a virgin and, in the cave of the Nativity, for having left love-letters in the opening in which once was the cradle of the Lord. The sin of Sabianus is made much greater because it had taken place in such a holy location. Jerome says:

> 'How great must be the sin beside which seduction and adultery are insignificant? Miserable wretch that you are; when you enter the cave in which the Son of God was born... it is to make an assignation. Have you no fear that the baby will cry from the man-

---

100 On this, see Kelly: pp. 104-123; *Apol.* 3, 22; *Ep.* 108, 7-14.
101 Cavallera: I, pp. 127-9; 151-3.
102 F. Wutz: *Onomastica Sacra* (TU 41, Berlin 1914).
103 *Lib.Loc.*: Prol. (*GCS*: Eus.Werke III) p. 3.

ger, that the newly delivered virgin will see you, that the mother of the Lord will behold you? The angels cry aloud, the shepherds run, the star shines down from heaven, the wise men worship, Herod is terrified, Jerusalem is in confusion, and meanwhile you creep into a virgin's cell to seduce the virgin to whom it belongs. I am filled with consternation and a shiver runs through me, body and soul, when I try to set before my eyes the deed you have done. The whole church was keeping vigil by night and proclaiming Christ as its Lord; in one spirit though in different tongues the praises of God were being sung. Yet you were securing your love-notes in the openings of what is now the altar, as it was once the manger of the Lord, choosing this place in order that your unhappy victim might find and read them when she came to kneel and worship there.'[104]

Among the details of this impassioned piece by Jerome, we may glean some information about the cave of the Nativity and something of the veneration and worship which took place there. When Paula visited this cave, she was happy 'to kiss the manger in which the Lord cried as a baby', and to find 'the lodging (*diversorium*) of the virgin and the stall (*stabulum*)'.[105]

Jerome records a little information about the traditional topography of the field where the shepherds were addressed by the angel at the birth of Jesus. In an addition he made to Eusebius' *Onomasticon*, Jerome says:

'...and about 1,000 yards from Bethlehem is the tower of Ader, which means "the tower of the flock", by a sort of prophecy pointing in advance to the shepherds who there learned of the Lord's birth.'[106]

---

104 *Ep.* 147, 4 (*CSEL* 56, 319f): Rogo, quantum crimen est, ubi stuprum et adulterium parum est? Infelicissime mortalium, tu speluncam illam, in qua dei filius natus est et ueritas de terra orta est et terra dedit fructum suum, de stupro condicturus ingredieris? non times, ne de praesepe infans uagiat, ne puerpera uirgo te uideat, ne mater domini contempletur? angeli clamant, pastores currunt, stella desuper rutilat, magi adorant, Herodes terretur, Hierosolyma conturbantur et tu cubiculum uirginis uirginem decepturus inrepis? paueo, miser, et tam mente quam corpore perhorresco ponere tibi uolens ante oculos tuos opus tuum. tota ecclesia nocturnis uigiliis Christum dominum personabat et in diuersarum gentium linguis unus in laudem dei spiritus concinebat; tu inter ostia quondam praesepis domini, nunc altaris amatorias epistulas fulciebas, quas postea illa miserabilis quasi flexo adoratura genu inueniret et legeret...
105 *Ep.* 108, 10 (*CSEL* 55, 318); cf also *Ep.* 46, 11 (*CSEL* 54, 341), where Jerome again describes the cave. On this, see Kopp: *op.cit.*, pp. 11-13.
106 *Onom.* 43f (*GCS* Eus. III, 1, 43, 45): et mille circiter passibus procul turris Ader, quae interpretatur turris gregis, quodam uaticinio pastores natiuitatis dominicae conscios ante significans.

The prophecy of which Jerome speaks, is, in fact, a Jewish tradition, linking the *Migdal 'eder* (tower of the flock) with Jacob's first stop on the way to Hebron after the funeral of Rachel (Gen. 35:21). The same word is also used in Micah 4:8. Jerusalem's glory had departed, like a wasteland which supports only a solitary shepherd's tower, which served the purpose of allowing the shepherd to watch and guard his flock. This verse was given a messianic understanding in Judaism, because it includes the phrase, 'but power shall come back to you as of old'. Micah 5:2 states that the Messiah will come from Bethlehem, and so the prophecy of 4:8 was understood as applying also to Bethlehem. Jerome simply took over the Jewish messianic tradition and believed that the prophecy had been fulfilled when the shepherds received the visitation by the angel, announcing Jesus' birth. He maintains the same tradition again in *Ep.* 108, when he says that Paula

> 'climbed down to the tower of Ader, that is, of the flock, where Jacob grazed his flocks and where the shepherds on their night watch were chosen to hear the *Gloria in excelsis*...'[107]

Elsewhere, he calls the shepherds' field *pastorum caulae*[108] and *pastorum locus*.[109]

This brief example of some of the information which Jerome imparts about Bethlehem shows that his interest in the topography of lands connected with the Bible was useful to him in his exegetical studies as well as in his other writings. This interest in, and knowledge of,[110] the topography of the Bible lands was to assist him in the establishment of a correct understanding of the literal sense of scripture. This understanding was necessary before he could go on to discuss the spiritual sense.

Inadequacy of the literal sense

In this chapter, we have shown that Jerome viewed the literal sense of scripture in a favourable light, and that his respect for it can be traced right through his exegetical career. However, as we shall see in the next chapter, Jerome also had great respect for the spiritual sense of scripture

---

[107] *Ep.* 108, 10 (*CSEL* 55, 318): Haut procul inde descendit ad turrem Ader, id est 'gregis', iuxta quam Iacob pauit greges suos et pastores nocte uigilantes audire meruerunt: gloria in excelsis...

[108] *Ep.* 46, 13 (*CSEL* 54, 343).

[109] *Ep.* 147, 6 (*CSEL* 56, 321). See Kopp: *op.cit.*, pp. 35-7.

[110] For the view that Jerome's knowledge of topography was limited, see J. Wilkinson: 'L'Apport de Saint Jérôme à la Topographie', in *RB* 81 (1974) 245-257.

and was greatly influenced in this by Origen. This means, of course, that for Jerome there were times when the literal sense was not adequate to express the full meaning of the passage. In the *Tract. in Marc.*, Jerome explains that the literal sense of Mk. 1:13 ('After John had been arrested, Jesus came into Galilea') is obvious, but then says:

> 'Therefore let us leave the letter with the Jews, and follow the spirit with Jesus: not because we condemn the literal words of an evangelist – for all that was written actually happened – but because we ascend to greater things by certain steps.'[111]

Jerome's first real piece of O.T. exegesis was the *Comm.Eccles.*, finished in c 389. In it, although he aims at 'not neglecting the matter-of-fact sense (*simplicem sensum*)',[112] most of the commentary is taken up with a spiritual interpretation of the preacher's words. For Jerome, the literal sense of Eccles. 1:4f ('One generation goes, another comes... The sun rises and the sun goes down') is straight-forward and obvious. But there is more in the saying than meets the eye, Jerome believes, and he expounds what he understands to be the fuller sense. The first generation referred to is the synagogue, and the second one is the church, which supersedes Judaism. The rising sun points to Christ, whose righteousness rises for those who fear God, and goes down for false prophets.[113]

---

111 *Tract. in Marc.* 1, 13 (*CCL* 78, 461): Dimittamus ergo litteram cum Iudaeis, et sequamur spiritum cum Iesu: non quod litteram euangelii condemnemus – factum est enim omne quod scriptum est – sed quod quibusdam gradibus ad maiora scandamus.
112 *Comm. Eccles.* 2, 24-26 (*CCL* 72, 272).
113 *Comm. Eccles.* 1, 4 (*CCL* 72, 253f).

6. Jerome and the Spiritual Sense

Alexandria and the spiritual sense

We have seen that Jerome ascribed real value to the literal sense in his interpretation of scripture, but also that he believed that this literal sense was inadequate for unlocking all the truths contained in the biblical writings. In order to arrive at an adequate exegesis of scripture, Jerome utilised another method of interpretation, which had its origins at Alexandria – the allegorical method.

The allegorical method, which attempted to extract a more-than-literal meaning from a passage, was used to great effect by early Christian exegetes, but was not itself a Christian invention. The allegorical method had been used for many centuries by Greek philosophers to interpret the myths and legends about the gods as recorded in Homer and Hesiod. Above all, the Stoa developed the method of finding more-than-literal meanings in specific passages. From the mid-second century B.C., due to the increasing Hellenisation of the East, a Jewish tradition of allegorical interpretation developed, beginning with Aristobulus of Alexandria, continued in the *Letter of Aristeas*, where allegory is used to justify O.T. food laws,[1] and culminating in Philo's widespread application of allegory in his study of the bible.[2]

Philo's allegorical method was taken over enthusiastically by Christianity in Alexandria, and especially by the two great heads of the catechetical school, Clement and Origen. Clement was the first Christian scholar to formulate the doctrine that the text of scripture contains a hidden meaning everywhere. Mysteries have been hidden in the bible for the benefit of intellectual Christians and to disguise some doctrines in scripture which would prove disturbing for simple Christians.[3] Clement frequently uses the word ἐπίκρυψις in connection with his theory of exe-

---

[1] *Letter of Aristeas*, 128-171.
[2] For expositions of Philo's allegorising, see the studies of S. Sandmel: *Philo of Alexandria; An Introduction*, Oxford 1979, and E.R. Goodenough: *By Light, Light*, New Haven 1935, and see above, Ch. 1.
[3] *Strom.* 6, 15, 129. See also *Strom.* 1, 28, where Clement discusses the four senses of Mosaic Law.

gesis: the fifth book of the *Stromateis* is largely an apology for the doctrine of 'concealment'.[4] For Clement, what is written in scripture is only a symbol, parable or image of its 'real' or 'true' meaning, which lies beneath or beyond the actual words. Truth is hidden in the shrine. Poets and philosophers have expressed themselves in symbolic language:

> 'All then, in a word, who have spoken of divine things, both Barbarians and Greeks, have veiled the first principles of things, and delivered the truth in enigmas and symbols and allegories and metaphors and similar tropes.'[5]

The way of knowledge is the way of 'deep sayings'; God intended this, and this is why Jesus likened the kingdom of God to leaven.[6] To fail to read the bible in a spiritual way is to think of the divine writings as merely human, to be like the Jews who believe in the bare word of the Law, and the heretics who understand literally what was spoken in parables.[7] Not all Christians are able to understand the mysteries of scripture, and Clement makes a distinction between the different classes of believer. The plain meaning of scripture is sufficient for simple Christians,[8] but for the true 'Gnostic', only the deeper, spiritual meaning will suffice.

Clement's principles were taken up and developed by his pupil Origen. For Origen, as for all the Fathers, the Holy Spirit was the real author of scripture, the human 'authors' being mere instruments in the process. It followed from this view of inspiration that not only the general meaning of the biblical books was true, but also that every detail had to be true. Not even the smallest particle is empty of meaning.[9]

That, in theory, Origen divided the interpretation of scripture into three senses, corresponding to the tripartite division of the person into body, soul and spirit, and to simple Christians, those who are more advanced in the faith, and those who are τελείοι, is well known. In practice, however, Origen rarely mentions the moral sense, so that he operates, by and large, with a two-fold method of exegesis.[10] In fact, more often than not, Origen castigates or dismisses the literal sense,[11] so

---

[4] See *Strom.* 5, 4, 19.
[5] *Strom.* 5, 4, 21.
[6] *Strom.* 5, 12, 80.
[7] *Strom.* 2, 16, 72.
[8] *Paidagogus* 3, 12, 97.
[9] Origen: *Comm.Matt.* 16, 12.
[10] See R.P.C. Hanson: *Allegory and Event*, London 1959, p. 235.
[11] See, for instance, *Hom. on Num.* 11, 1; *Comm.Rom.* 1, 10; *Comm.Matt.* 15, 2. See also Hanson's comments in *Allegory and Event*, pp. 238-243.

that one is left only with the spiritual meaning. This spiritual sense is equated by Origen with the allegorical sense.[12]

Origen justifies his use of the allegorical sense with reference to 1 Cor. 10:11 ('these things happened to them figuratively, and they were written for our sake'); Gal. 4:21-4 (the allegory of Sarah and Hagar), and Col. 2:16f ('the shadow of things to come').[13] The content of the allegorical sense is defined as 'knowledge of the mysteries concerning the affairs of men',[14] by which Origen means the speculative philosophy of Alexandria.[15] Origen does not, however, allegorise according to an unbreakable set of rules: his allegorical interpretations are often arbitrary and subjective. We may take this treatment of the account of the Feeding of the Five Thousand in Matt. 14, where every detail is allegorised. That the evening was approaching means that the end of time is near; the hour had passed refers to the time of the Law and the Prophets; the five loaves are the five perceptible senses of scripture; the two fish are the προφορικὸν καὶ τὸν ἐνδίαθετον λόγον; the crowd is made to sit on the grass because it is necessary for a Christian to master the flesh; they are put in rows of 100 because this is a holy number, representing the unity of God, in 50's, because this number represents pardon, as it is that of the Jubilee year and also of Pentecost; the twelve baskets of remains are the twelve tribes of Israel.[16]

The influence which Origen had, both in his own day and in later centuries, was very great, and even in recent times scholars have been enthusiastic in their acceptance of Origen's allegorism.[17] His exegetical principles and voluminous works became so widespread that no Christian scholar in the East or in the West, could ignore him. We shall find later in this chapter that Jerome made great use of Origen's exegesis, even after his involvement in the Origenist Controversy, although he was not uncritical of the Alexandrian exegete.

---

[12] See Hanson: *op.cit.*, p. 243. It is not our intention here to enter into the debate over the differences between typology and allegory. It is sufficient to work with Hanson's careful definition of the two terms (*op.cit.*, p. 7). See also J. Barr: *Old and New in Interpretation*, London 1966, Ch. 4; also the bibliography listed in D.L. Baker: 'Typology and the Christian Use of the O.T.', in *SJT* 29 (1976) 137-157.
[13] *De Princ.* 4, 2, 6.
[14] *Ibid.* 4, 2, 7.
[15] Hanson: *op.cit.*, p 244.
[16] *Comm.Matt.* 11, 1f (*CCL* 77, 77-78).
[17] Especially H. de Lubac: *Histoire et Esprit*, Paris 1950, pp. 135, 307, 314f.

Jerome's technical vocabulary

Jerome uses both general and specific (technical) terms to introduce his discussion of and describe the spiritual sense of scripture. As far as the general terms are concerned, the most frequent he uses is *secundum intellegentiam spiritalem*, which is very often found when Jerome, having discussed the literal meaning of the passage in question, goes on to discuss its spiritual meaning. One or two examples of this may be given. After his discussion of the literal sense of Hos. 7:5-7, Jerome mentions a Jewish tradition which he finds helpful for understanding the passage, and then says:

> 'I have said these things, according to the tradition of the Hebrews, in a way which is more daring than wise, relinquishing the fidelity of words to their authors. Now let us cross to the spiritual understanding...'[18]

Again, after having explained Obadiah 2-4 according to the *historia*, he says: *Si didicimus historiam, sequamur intellegentiam spiritalem*, in which he castigates the heretics for condemning the Church, applying Obadiah's phrase 'You shall be utterly despised' to them.[19] This phrase (*sequamur intelligentiam spiritalem*) is very common in Jerome's works.[20]

Another general phrase used by Jerome to introduce his spiritual interpretations is *secundum mysticos intellectum*, found, for example, at *Comm.Matt.* 5, 39f, where, after explaining the literal sense of the dominical saying 'if anyone strikes you on the right cheek, offer to him the other one also', by reference to Ps. 7:4 and Lam. 3:27-30, he continues with the spiritual meaning: *secundum mysticos intellectum*... arguing that when the heretics assail the good Christians with their arguments, these latter must oppose them with scriptural teachings until the heretics grow weary.[21]

A very common term which Jerome uses to indicate the spiritual sense is *tropologia*. It is clear that for him this is a general expression equiva-

---

[18] *Comm.Osee* 7,5-7 (*CCL* 76, 74): Haec iuxta Hebraeorum traditionem audacter magis quam scienter locuti sumus, fidem dictorum auctoribus relinquentes. Nunc ad spiritalem intelligentiam transeamus...
[19] *Comm.Abdiam* 2-4 (*CCL* 76, 357).
[20] See, for example, *Comm.Gal.* 2, 3 (*PL* 26, 359); 3, 3 (26, 375); 5, 25 (26, 451); *Comm.Ezek.* 16, 13 (*CCL* 75, 178); *Comm.Amos* 2, 2 (76, 230); 4, 4 (76, 262); *Comm.Ioelem* 2, 1ff (76, 179); *Ep.* 121, 6 (*CSEL* 56, 24).
[21] *Comm.Matt.* 5, 39f (*CCL* 77, 33). For this phrase, see also *Comm.Matt.* 17, 27 (*CCL* 77, 155); 27, 29 (*CCL* 77, 268); *Comm.Ezek.* 6, 14 (*CCL* 75, 70); *Comm. Amos* 8, 9f (*CCL* 76, 331); *Comm.Ionam* 2, 1 (*CCL* 76, 393).

lent to *intellegentia spiritalis* and *secundum mysticos intellectum*.[22] Two other interesting general terms used by Jerome for the spiritual sense, although occurring less frequently than those already mentioned, are *altior intellegentia*[23] and *sacramenta Spiritus Sancti*.[24]

As well as these general phrases, Jerome uses several technical terms in his spiritual interpretation of scripture. It is important that we look at the history of these terms and Jerome's use of them in order to determine the influences on him and whether he makes any advance on their previous use.

A. Typus
The use of this word in the N.T., where it means 'pattern' or 'model' has been sufficiently charted in other works and need not be recounted here.[25] In the Alexandrian tradition, τύπος does not seem to have been an important term. The term rarely appears in the writings of either Clement or Origen, and when it does it usually has no specific exegetical significance.[26]

Among the Antiochene Fathers, however, τύπος has much more importance. Theodore of Mopsuestia, with whose works Jerome may have been familiar, elucidated a 'theory of typology' in his *Commentary on Jonah*. A type has three characteristics: first, it has a resemblance to the object of which it is the image; second, the persons involved derive profit from it, and this is an indication of the benefits in the future promises; third, it contains the firm belief that the future reality will be of greater importance than the present image.[27] Theodore finds examples of this in O.T. incidents like the smearing of blood on the doorposts at the exodus from Egypt, which was a type of Christian liberation from sin and death by Christ's resurrection, and in Jonah's mission

---

[22] See *Comm.Ezek.* 7, 15f (*CCL* 75, 80); 25, 1-7 (75, 336); *Comm.Amos* 7, 14ff (*CCL* 76, 325); *Comm.Abacuc* 1, 6ff (*CCL* 76A, 589); *Comm.Ioel.* 2, 18 (*CCL* 76, 187); *C.Ioh.Hier.* 7 (*PL* 23, 375); *Comm.Matt.* 9, 15 (*CCL* 77, 57).
[23] See *Comm.Gal.* 1, 16 (*PL* 26, 353); 6, 3 (26, 456); *Comm.Amos* 5, 7-9 (*CCL* 76, 282).
[24] See *Comm.Ezek.* 1, 13f (*CCL* 75, 19); *Comm.Matt.* 14, 19 (*CCL* 77, 122); *Ep.* 52, 3 (*CSEL* 54, 419); cf *Comm.Gal.* 5, 19-21 (*PL* 26, 445). On the word '*Sacramentum*', see C. Mohrmann: '*Sacramentum* dans les plus anciens textes chrétiens', in *HTR* 47 (1954) 141-152.
[25] See K.J. Woollcombe: 'The Biblical Origins and Patristic Development of Typology' in *Essays on Typology* (SBT 22), London 1957, pp. 60-65; L. Goppelt: *Typos*, Gütersloh 1933.
[26] See, for example, Clem.: *Paed.* 1, 5; *Strom.* 4, 25; Origen: *Comm.John* 10, 35.
[27] *Comm.Ion.*: Prol. (*PG* 66, 320B).

which typified Christ's preservation 'during a period of time, and that on rising from the dead to immortality he offered universal salvation to the nations, namely, one rising from repentance...'[28] For Theodore, the types of the N.T. are greatly superior to those of the O.T.[29]

In the Latin Church, the use of *typus* as an exegetical term is not attested before Cyprian. It is found in Tertullian only very rarely,[30] as he prefers to use other terms.[31] Cyprian uses *typus* twelve times in his writings, in the phrase *typus Christi* (in connection with Christ's sacrifice in the eucharist), and in his descriptions of various O.T. characters whom Cyprian regarded as types of the Church.[32]

When Jerome's use of *typus* is examined, we find that it is not used often in the commentaries. He gives a definition of *typus* in *Comm.Osee* 11, 1 ('Out of Egypt have I called my son'):

> 'It remains for us to say that those things which happen previously τυπικῶς in other contexts are referred to Christ in accordance with truth and fulfilment.'[33]

He goes on to mention the apostle Paul's use of the figures of mounts Sinai and Sion, which he saw as types of Sarah and Hagar (Gal. 4:22-4); Isaac as a type of Christ; and Leah and Rachel, who are, Jerome says, types of the synagogue and Church respectively. Jerome then continues:

> 'Typus therefore indicates a part, because if it precedes the whole typically, it must now be known not as *typus*, but as the truth of history.'

This last sentence is reminiscent of one of the characteristics of the Antiochene school, and especially of Theodore of Mopsuestia, who, as we have seen above, stressed that a type must have a clear object or anti-type.[34]

---

28 *Comm.Ion.*: Prol. (*PG* 66, 320-321D).
29 *Ibid.* (*PG* 66, 324A).
30 *De Castit.* 6, 1; *De Idol.* 24, 4 (twice); *De Patient.* 6, 1 (*typicus*). Cf also *De Bapt.* 8, 4.
31 He uses *figura, allegoria, aenigma* and *parabola* among others. See the study of T.O. O'Malley: *Tertullian and the Bible* (Latinitas Christianorum Primaeva 21), Nijmegen 1967, pp. 117-173.
32 See M.A. Fahey: *Cyprian and the Bible*, Tübingen 1971, p. 614.
33 *CCL* 76, 121-2: Superest ut illud dicamus quod ea quae τυπικῶς praecedunt in aliis, iuxta ueritatem et adimpletionem referantur ad Christum... Typus enim partem indicat, quod si totum praecedat in typo, iam non est typus, sed historiae ueritas appellanda est.
34 See *Comm.Ion.*: Prol. (*PG* 66, 320B); *Comm.Mic.* 4, 1-4 ('It is surely obvious that every type has some resemblance to that which it is said to typify') (*PG* 66, 364); cf J. Guillet: 'Les exégèses d'Alexandrie et d'Antioche. Conflit ou malentendu?', in *RSR* 34 (1947) pp. 290 ff. Other examples of Jerome's use of *typus* include *Comm.Isa.* 20, 2; *Comm.Ezek.* 40, 1; *Comm.Amos* 3, 12; *Comm. Osee* 1, 6f (*CCL* 73, 201; 75, 551; 76, 252; 76, 14).

B. Allegoria

Allegory in pre-Christian use had two meanings. It was defined by Quintilian (c A.D. 30-100) as the continuous use of analogy; it was therefore a mode of expression (σχῆμα λέξεως).³⁵ This was its original meaning, but later, from the time of Plutarch (c A.D. 50-120) it was used in the sense of allegorical interpretation. In Patristic Greek both meanings occur, although the second is more common than the original.

H.N. Bate has shown³⁶ that in the Alexandrian school ἀλληγορία is primarily a method of exegesis which is contrasted with the literal interpretation, and which is discernible from the content of the text in question. The examples from Origen's commentaries we shall quote later in this chapter will prove this to be the case.³⁷ For the Antiochenes, however, ἀλληγορία is 'a literal mode of expression i.e. as one in which it was plain from the actual words employed that they were intended to be taken "tropically"'.³⁸ They held to τὸ ῥητὸν (the literal, rational contents), and explained contradictions, anthropomorphisms and other difficulties as arising from the idiosyncrasies of Hebrew speech. Whereas the Alexandrian Fathers often tended to give full vent to their imaginations in their allegorical interpretations, the Antiochenes had a very cautious approach to allegory. John Chrysostom, for example, states that the treatment of scripture as allegorical should not be allowed to depend on the will of the interpreter, but ought to be kept strictly subservient to the meaning of the text.³⁹

In the Latin Church, both Tertullian and Cyprian use the word *allegoria*. Tertullian is the first Latin writer to use the adjectival form *allegoricus*, the adverb *allegorice*, and also the verb *allegorizare*.⁴⁰. He is aware of the pagan use of *allegoria*,⁴¹ and its religious use by Gnostics.⁴² His own use of it, and his attitude towards it, is very different from one work to another. His principle that allegory should be used when the literal sense results in nonsense, has a reverse side: allegory is not present where the scripture is confirmed by actual events.⁴³

---

35 H.N. Bate: 'Some Technical terms of Greek exegesis', in *JTS* 24 (1922) p 60. Cf Quintilian: *Inst.Orat.* 8, 6, 44.
36 *Art.cit.*, pp. 59-66.
37 See also Origen: *C.Celsum* 4, 48; 6, 29; *Comm.Ioan.* 6, 4; 13, 9.
38 Bate: *art.cit.*, p. 61.
39 *In Isa.* 5, 7.
40 See T.P. O'Malley: *op.cit.*, p. 147, where he lists all the occurrences of these forms.
41 *Ad Nat.* 2, 12, 17.
42 *Adv.Val.* I, 3.
43 O'Malley: *op.cit.*, pp. 157-8.

Cyprian also uses *allegoria*, but much less frequently than Tertullian. The kind of allegorical interpretation practised at Alexandria is almost totally absent from Cyprian, although a few examples can be found.[44] It may be said that Cyprian uses *allegoria* as an equivalent term to *typus* and *figura*.[45]

Jerome is aware of the rich background of the word *allegoria* and, as might be expected, his most systematic treatment of the word comes in his comment on Gal. 4:24: 'Now this is an allegory', the only time it appears in the N.T. In fact, Jerome defines *allegoria*:

> 'Allegory is specially to do with the art of philology, and how it differs from metaphor or other figures of speech we learn as little children in school. It puts forward one thing in the words but means another in the sense. The books of the orators and poets are full of allegories.'[46]

Then, after proving to his own satisfaction that the apostle Paul was not ignorant of secular literature (quoting from Titus 1:12; Acts 17:28 and 1 Cor. 15:33), he goes on to say:

> 'Because of these and other points, it is clear that Paul was not ignorant of secular literature, and what he here calls allegory, he elsewhere called the spiritual understanding.'[47]

As far as Jerome is concerned, therefore, allegory is merely another word for the spiritual interpretation of scripture. This can be seen in many of the commentaries. We may cite just one example here, from the *Comm.Amos*, where he says explicitly: *iuxta allegoriam, id est, intellegentiam spiritalem.*[48]

Although Jerome uses the word *allegoria* and its cognates frequently, he does not seem to use it as a technical term, either in the Alexandrian or Antiochene senses. For Jerome, it seems to be merely an equivalent to *spiritalis intellegentia*, that is, a general term which he uses to contrast with the literal sense.[49]

---

44 *Ep.* 63, 5, 6; *Test.* I, 2; II, 2; *De Dom.Orat.* 17.
45 Fahey: *op.cit.*, p. 49; cf p. 612.
46 *Comm.Gal.* 4, 24 (*PL* 26, 416): Allegoria proprie de arte grammatica est, et quo a metaphora, vel caeteris tropis differat, in scholis paruuli discimus. Aliud praetendit in verbis, aliud significat in sensu. Pleni sunt oratorum [Sup.allegoriis] et poetarum libri.
47 *Ibid.* Jerome then quotes from Rom. 7:14; 1 Cor. 10:34; 6:1; 2:25. Ex quibus et aliis, evidens est Paulum non ignorasse litteras saeculares, et quam hic allegoriam dixit, alibi vocasse intellegentiam spiritualem.
48 *Comm.Amos* 4, 4-6 (*CCL* 76, 262).
49 Penna: *op.cit.*, p. 123 also holds this opinion: 'When speaking of *allegoria*, Jerome always intends spiritual exegesis in general.'

C. Aenigma

According to the Greek rhetoricians, an αἴνιγμα is a figure of speech which is obscure both in expression and in meaning. It differs from allegory in that an allegory is obscure *either* in its mode of expression *or* in its meaning, whereas an enigma is obscure in *both*.[50] Tryphon (1st century B.C.) cites as an example Androcydes' interpretation of the Pythagorean maxim: 'a set of scales should not be falsified', meaning 'justice should not be violated'; and 'fire should not be poked with a dagger', meaning 'anger should not be provoked by words'.[51] By the time of Quintilian, however, *aenigma* had come to mean the same as *allegoria*, for he defines *aenigma* as 'dark in a figurative representation, an allegory'.[52]

For Origen, an enigma is to be compared with, and distinguished from, a parable. An enigma is a narrative which reports things as having happened, even though they have not happened, since they are impossible. An enigma signifies something hidden and inexpressible. As examples, Origen refers to Judges 9:7-15 (Jotham's story of the fig-tree), 2 Kings 14:9 (Jehoash's fable), and Ezekiel 17:3 (the story of the eagle). What parables and enigmas have in common is that both describe things as having happened, which did not happen. They differ in that what is described in a parable is capable of historical realisation, whereas what is described in an enigma is not.[53]

A somewhat different view is seen in Diodore of Tarsus, who distinguishes sharply between enigma and allegory. When discussing the nature of the serpent which tempted Eve in Genesis, he claims that the serpent is an enigma and not an allegory. It would have been an allegory if nothing other than the serpent's name had been mentioned, but the serpent was real; the fact that it spoke to Eve proves that it (an irrational animal) was under the power of the devil.[54] Diodore believes that enigmas are real entities and contain hidden meanings: 'An enigma is a reality belonging to the order of visible things which secretly denotes some other thing.'[55]

For John Chrysostom, the importance of αἴνιγμα lies in its literary as-

---

50 Tryphon Περὶ Τρόπων 4 (L. Spengel: *Rhetores Graeci* III, Lipsius 1856, p. 193, 14-18).
51 *Ibid.* III, p. 193, 30ff.
52 Quintilian: *Inst.Orat.* 8, 6, 52. Cf Cicero: *De Orat.* 3, 42.
53 Origen: *Frag. in Prov.* 1, 6 (*PG* 13, 25B).
54 See L. Mariès: 'Extraits du Commentaire de Diodore de Tarse sur les Psaumes', in *RSR* 9 (1919) pp. 94ff.
55 *Ibid.*, p. 95.

pect. He appears to equate αἴνιγμα with παραβολή: both use vivid description in order to impress upon the memory the message contained in them.[56]

In Jerome's writings, *aenigma* is not a common word, but where he does use it, he frequently associates it with *parabola*.[57] In the *Comm. Ezek.*, for instance, he equates *aenigma* with *parabola*, stating that both are obscure and both use figurative language:

> 'When it is said to a prophet: set forth the enigma, narrate the parable, (or, as the Septuagint translated it, narrate the speech and speak the parable), it is shown that what is said is obscure. For nobody is in doubt that both the enigma and the parable put forward one thing in words, but contain a different thing in sense.'[58]

Elsewhere, however, Jerome, while implying that parables give an obscure clue to the truth, classifies them with similies as the rhetoricians do.[59] Thus it is implied, if never explicitly stated, that parables and enigmas are not synonymous terms. Both have common elements, namely their figurative language, but enigmas are more complex than parables and are therefore more difficult to interpret aright. This is quite similar to Origen's comparison of parable and enigma which we saw above.

An interesting passage in his *Apol. contra Rufin.* gives us a clue as to how Jerome thought of the term *aenigma*. In a section dealing with the legitimacy of the works of Pythagoras, Plato, Empedocles and other classical authors and their use by Christians, Jerome refers to the enigmas to which Aristotle referred:

> '...and those enigmas which Aristotle so diligently pursued in his books...'[60]

From this we may infer that Jerome, the great classicist, understood and used the term *aenigma* in his works from the standpoint of a grammarian. He is not concerned with the philosophical question of whether an enigma has any reality of its own. For him, an *aenigma* is a 'dark saying' in the bible, rather like a *parabola*. Both must be interpreted with skill, under the guidance of the Holy Spirit.

---

56 *Hom.Matt.* 44, 2 (*PG* 57, 467).
57 See, for example, *Comm.Isa.* 16, 1; *Comm.Amos* 9, 1; *Comm.Ioel.* 2, 17; *Comm.Abd.* 2-4 (*CCL* 73, 179; 76, 338; 185; 357).
58 *Comm.Ezek.* 17, 1ff (*CCL* 75, 215): Quando prophetae dicitur: Propone aenigma, narra parabolam (siue, ut Septuaginta Transtulerunt: Narra narrationem et dic parabolam), ostenditur obscurum esse quod dicitur; nulli enim dubium est, et aenigma et parabolam aliud proferre in uerbis, aliud tenere in sensibus.
59 *Ep.* 121, 6 (*CSEL* 56, 23).
60 *Apol.c.Ruf.* 3, 39 (*CCL* 79, 109): illaque aenigmata quae diligentissime Aristoteles in suis libris persequitur...

D. Theoria

Scholars believe that the background of this word is Platonic.[61] By the mid third century, it was widely used by Christian scholars as a technical exegetical term. In the Alexandrian school, it referred to a method of reading meanings which go beyond the literal sense. For the Alexandrians, therefore, θεωρία and ἀλληγορία were virtually synonymous terms.[62] Didymus the Blind, for instance, when commenting on Ps. CXIX, 72 ('Dearer to me than gold or silver',), says that κατὰ θεωρίαν, gold means the νοῦς, and silver the λόγος.[63] Origen also used the word in this sense.[64]

In the Antiochene school, the term θεωρία took on greater subtlety of meaning than in Alexandria. Diodore of Tarsus distinguishes θεωρία from ἀλληγορία and at the same time does not equate it with ἱστορία.[65] θεωρία is a *via media* which respects the literal sense and yet does not introduce comments which are not already in the context of the passage.

A. Vaccari, in his important article on θεωρία in the Antiochene school, stated that the term has four characteristics or properties: 1) it always pre-supposes the literal sense; 2) in addition to the literal sense, a second sense is present; 3) the first stands in relation to the second as an image does to the person it represents, or a rough sketch to a finished painting; 4) both senses are attained at the same time, although diversely; the lesser is the means by which the greater is known.[66]

From this it can be seen that θεωρία is primarily a psychological process going on in the mind of the interpreter. For Theodore of Mopsuestia, this was true especially of the O.T. prophets. θεωρία was the perception of things present and future given to the prophet by God.[67] This became, in the Antiochene school, a rule of hermeneutics which enabled them to interpret the messianic prophecies of the O.T. according to Christian tradition, without having to refute the historical contexts and without seeming to impose an interpretation on those passages from the outside.[68]

When Jerome's use of the word is studied, it is seen that he under-

---

61 See H.N. Bate: *art.cit.*, p. 61.
62 *Ibid.*
63 Quoted in Bate: *art.cit.*, p. 61.
64 See, for instance, *De Princ.* 2, 11, 3; *C.Celsum* 2, 6; *In Gen. Hom.* 8, 10; also H. de Lubac's article 'Typologie et Allegorie', in *RSR* 34 (1947) p. 206.
65 Mariès: *art.cit.*, p. 80.
66 A. Vaccari: 'La θεωρία nella scuola esegetica di Antiochia' in *Biblica* 1 (1920) 3-36.
67 Bate: *art.cit.*, p. 60.
68 See Vaccari: *art.cit.*, pp. 24ff; also Guillet: *art.cit.*, p. 283.

stands it in the same way as do the Antiochene Fathers, using it especially of prophecy. He endeavours, that is to say, to understand a passage in its historical context while at the same time attempting to do justice to its inherent spiritual meaning.[69]

A good illustration of Jerome's use of *theoria* is seen in his *Comm. Mal.* 1, 11-13. First of all, Jerome explains the prophecy in its historical context, showing its application to the situation in which the Jewish people found themselves at that time. Then he claims that a prediction concerning Christ is inextricably connected with it:

> 'For he composes the prophecy of the future in such a way that he does not forsake the present time.'[70]

Jerome believes this interpretation to be the direct opposite of allegory, for, before exegeting, he states what he means to be understood as a general rule of interpretation, which is unmistakably like the tenets of the Antiochene school:

> 'There is a rule of scripture: where a most clear prophecy about future events is composed, through the unclearness of allegory one must not diminish what has been written.'[71]

From this brief study of the technical vocabulary used by Jerome to denote the spiritual sense of scripture, two important points emerge. We have seen that the exegetical schools of Antioch and Alexandria often use the same terms in their exegesis – ἀλληγορία, αἴνιγμα and θεωρία for instance – but that there were real differences in the significance and meaning given to each in the two schools. It is legitimate to ask whether Jerome was influenced more by one of these schools than by the other in the meaning he gave to his technical vocabulary.

Scholars are united in asserting that Jerome was influenced by Origen in his exegesis. That this is so with reference to specific interpretations of many passages (even to the point of verbal borrowing) will be shown later in this chapter. But the assumption that Jerome used Origen's technical vocabulary and the meaning Origen attached to it, is manifestly false. We have shown, for instance, that in Jerome's use of *typus* and *theoria* the meaning he attaches to these words is very similar to that of the Antiochene school, and is opposed to that of Origen and the Alexandrian school. We can say, therefore, that in his technical vo-

---

[69] This point has been confirmed by Penna: *op.cit.*, pp. 164-7 with regard to the *Comm.Hier.*; see also Guillet: *art.cit.*, p. 283.

[70] *Comm.Mal.* 1, 11-13 (*CCL* 76A, 912): Sic enim futurorum texit uaticinium, ut praesens tempus non deserat.

[71] *Ibid.* (*CCL* 76A, 911): Regula scripturarum est: ubi manifestissima prophetia de futuris texitur, per incerta allegoriae non extenuare quae scripta sunt.

cabulary and the meaning given to it, Jerome was influenced by the Antiochene exegetical school, not by Origen and not by the Latin tradition of Tertullian and Cyprian.

The second point to note in connection with Jerome's vocabulary for the spiritual sense is that he was not an innovator. This does not mean, however, that he merely took over piecemeal the vocabulary of others. His use of the term *allegoria* and *aenigma* shows that he did not agree with their accepted meaning in either of the exegetical schools, that he gave considerable thought to their meaning, and that, although not interested in (or perhaps not capable of) discussing the philosophical problems connected with them, by and large the meaning he gave them remained consistent throughout his career.

Jerome's esteem for the spiritual sense

That Jerome held the spiritual sense of scripture in great esteem is abundantly clear from his works. It may safely be said that every work of Jerome's on scripture, including those (like the *Comm.Matt.*) where he states explicitly that he wishes primarily to expound the historical or literal sense, shows evidence of spiritual exegesis. The importance which he gave to the spiritual sense of scripture may be seen from two different angles; first, from the scholars with whom Jerome studied, or whose works he read; and second, from the abundant use he made of it in his commentaries.

The first evidence we have of Jerome's Christian reading is his own report[72] that he had transcribed two works of Hilary of Poitiers at Trier shortly after he had come to the end of his (secular) education at Rome. These were the *De Synodis*, in which Hilary had translated various creeds for the Latin bishops and attempted to reconcile supporters of the ὁμοιούσιος and ὁμοούσιος, and the *Tractatus super Psalmos*, where the exegesis is much indebted to Origen,[73] although Hilary had added some original comments.[74] Although Jerome does not mention his first impressions of Hilary's work, it is important to note that in the first Christian book he read (as far as we know), he was exposed to spiritual interpretations of the Psalms, and that he viewed these favourably

---

[72] *Ep.* 5, 2 (*CSEL* 54, 22).
[73] See E. Goffinet: *L'Utilisation d'Origène dans le commentaire des Psaumes de S. Hilaire de Poitiers*, Louvain 1965.
[74] See Jerome: *De Vir.Illus.* 100; 'In this work, he imitated Origen, but also added some additional material' (*PL* 23, 738).

(for we do not hear anything to the contrary, and, if he had not liked Hilary's/Origen's interpretations, he would not have transcribed the work). Jerome left Trier in 379, and travelled to Constantinople, where he stayed until 382. Here, he studied with the Cappadocian Father, Gregory of Nazianzus. It may have been for this reason that Jerome, the eager young scholar, made the journey to Constantinople. Jerome mentions Gregory several times in his writings, referring to him as *praeceptor meus*, recalling the scriptural teaching he received from the Cappadocian, and the discussions they had on difficult passages.[75] Here again we see that Jerome studied with a scholar who had been influenced by Origen, and hence his spiritual interpretations, for Gregory had studied at Caesarea and Alexandria.[76]

Another Alexandrian exegete who emphasised the spiritual interpretation of scripture, and with whom Jerome studied, was Didymus the Blind. Didymus was a faithful disciple of Origen. Jerome several times calls him 'my master'.[77] He says that his primary purpose in visiting Egypt was 'to see Didymus and to ask him about what was doubtful throughout all the scriptures'.[78] Although Jerome spent only a month with Didymus,[79] he boasts more than once that at his request Didymus dictated three volumes on the prophet Hosea, thus filling a gap left by Origen, and also five volumes on Zechariah.[80]

A further point which must be made in relation to Jerome's esteem for the spiritual sense of scripture is that, for him, the spiritual sense is superior to the literal sense. This is a fundamental point for him, and he makes it consistently throughout his exegetical works.

In his first piece of exegesis, *Ep.* 18A, which is a study of the call of Isaiah (Isa. 6:1-9), written for Pope Damasus in 381, Jerome says that first of all it is necessary to set forth the historical sense of the passage – who king Uzziah was, how long he had reigned and who his contemporaries were. Then, 'after the *historia* has been explained, there follows

---

[75] *De Vir.Illus.* 117; *Adv.Iovin.* 1, 13; *Apol.c.Ruf.* 1, 13; 30; *Comm.Eph.* 5, 32; *Comm.Isa.* 6, 1; *Epp.* 50, 1; 52, 8.

[76] See R.R. Ruether: *Gregory of Nazianzus: Rhetor and Philosopher*, Oxford 1969, p. 19: 'Gregory's studies in Palestine and in Alexandria undoubtedly helped to shape his predilection for Platonism and for Origenist theology and exegesis.'

[77] For example *Ep.* 50, 1; 84, 3; *Apol.c.Ruf.* 3, 27; even after the Origenist Controversy, Jerome stresses his friendship with Didymus; *Comm.Isa.*: prol.

[78] *Comm.Eph.*: Prol (*PL* 26, 469).

[79] Rufinus: *Apol.c.Hier.* 2, 12.

[80] *Comm.Hos.*: Prol.; *Comm.Zach.*: Prol.; *De Vir.Illus.* 109 (*CCL* 76, 5; 76A, 748; *PL* 23, 74).

the spiritual interpretation, for the sake of which the *historia* has been unfolded'.[81] Jerome goes on to show, by a comparison with other passages (Ex. 3:15; Ezek. 11:13; Rom. 6:12), that Isaiah could not have had a vision as long as king Uzziah was alive.

Jerome wrote the *Comm.Ezek.* between 411-414, and in his comment on 42:13, he says:

> 'The north and south chambers are, I think, either what they merely were in history, or they symbolise the secrets of spiritual understanding, so that through them the *aquilo* (the dark clouds of the north), we should come to the *meridies* (the high point of the south). For the *littera* is not so to be read nor the foundations of the *historia* so to be laid, that we may not come to the *culmen* (the top of the building, hence the highest sense of scripture). Yet neither is a most beautiful edifice to be built up to the roof, when the foundations beneath are by no means solid.'[82]

Again, in his eulogy of Paula,[83] Jerome describes her love of the scriptures, and especially the spiritual interpretation, in terms with which he himself obviously agrees whole-heartedly:

> 'She knew the holy scriptures by heart. Although she loved their literal meaning (*historia*), and used to say that this was the basis of truth, she was still more concerned with their spiritual understanding (*intellegentiam spiritalem*), and with this high roof (*culmen*) she protected the edifice of her soul.'

Jerome consistently held, therefore, that the spiritual sense was superior, and to be preferred to the literal sense.

Jerome's spiritual interpretations

In the section on Jerome's technical vocabulary for the spiritual sense of scripture, we argued that the influence of Origen is not to be seen in the exegetical vocabulary Jerome uses to describe the spiritual sense. It is quite clear, however, that Jerome held Origen in high regard, and that he continually used the Alexandrian exegete's spiritual interpretations in his own commentaries. It is the purpose of this section a) to show Jerome's high regard for Origen, and b) to show the extent of Jerome's use of Origen's commentaries in his own exegesis.

Jerome often mentions Origen in his works. Generally speaking, most

---

81 *Ep.* 18A, 2 (*CSEL* 54, 76).
82 *Comm.Ezek.* 42, 13f (*CCL*, 75, 615-6).
83 *Ep.* 108, 26 (*CSEL* 55, 344), written in 404.

of Jerome's comments are favourable.[84] We have already seen that Jerome's first contact (with) Origen was indirect, made through the writings of Hilary of Poitiers and Gregory of Nazianzus, among others. The first direct contact of which we know came in 380, when he translated thirty seven homilies of Origen on Jeremiah, Ezekiel and Isaiah. In the preface to the homilies on Ezekiel,[85] he says that, although he would like to translate a great number of Origen's works into Latin, he has been prevented from doing so by an eye complaint which has been brought on by too much reading, and by a shortage of copyists. He was careful, he says, to preserve Origen's simple homiletic style.

A little later (383-4), Jerome translated two of Origen's homilies on the Song of Songs. In the preface to the translation, which is addressed to Pope Damasus, he shows his admiration for Origen when he says:

> 'Origen, who has surpassed everyone in his other books, has surpassed even himself in the Song of Songs.'[86]

The puzzling *Ep.* 33,[87] an incomplete and unsystematic list of the writings of Origen, shows Jerome's complete and, at this time (c 382-3) uncritical enthusiasm for the Alexandrian. After listing Origen's works, Jerome goes on to say:

> 'So you see, the labours of this one man have surpassed those of all previous authors, either Greek or Latin. But he has been condemned by various Church leaders because men could not tolerate the incomparable eloquence and knowledge which, as soon as he opened his lips, made others look dumb.'[88]

In the *De Viris Illustribus*, written in 392, Jerome refers to Origen's 'immortal genius',[89] and admits that, when in the library at Caesarea he found twenty five volumes of Origen's commentary on the Twelve Minor Prophets, written in Origen's own hand, he hugged them and guarded them with such joy that he thought himself the possessor of the wealth of Croesus.[90]

Jerome's prominent part in the Origenist Controversy obviously

---

[84] For Jerome's criticisms of Origen, see below, pp. 157-165.
[85] *GCS* 33, 318.
[86] *GCS* 33, 26. Origenes, cum in ceteris libris omnes vicerit, in Cantico Canticorum ipse se vicit.
[87] On the problems of this letter, see E. Klostermann: 'Die Schriften des Origenes in Hieronymus' Brief an Paula', in *Sitzungsberichte der kön. preuss. Akad. der Wissenschaften*, 1897, pp. 855-870, and P. Courcelle: *Late Latin Writers and their Greek Sources*, Cambridge Mass. 1969, pp. 103-113.
[88] *Ep.* 33, 5 (*CSEL* 54, 259).
[89] *De Vir.Illus.* 54 (*PL* 23, 702).
[90] *De Vir.Illus.* 75 (*PL* 23, 722).

made a difference to his enthusiasm for the Alexandrian. Rufinus accused him of praising Origen and of being an Origenist,[91] but Jerome replied that he had praised Origen as an exegete and not as a theologian. In fact, he said, when he had translated Origen's works, he had changed those parts of the original which diverged from orthodox theology.[92] Jerome, therefore, had a high regard for Origen as an exegete right through his career. It remains now to show how this regard manifested itself in Jerome's commentaries, and we will show that he used many of Origen's spiritual interpretations in his own works.

Early in his literary career, Jerome was asked by Paula and Eustochium to comment on the Pauline epistles. Jerome was reluctant at first, but attempted a commentary on the shortest of the letters, Philemon.[93] A few days after completing this, he started work on a commentary on Galatians,[94] after which came one on Ephesians, working so fast on this that he sometimes dictated as much as 1,000 lines a day,[95] and finally one on Titus. The four works took less than a year to complete,[96] and in 401 Rufinus speaks of the *Comm.Eph.* as having been written about fifteen years previously, so the four commentaries were probably composed in 387-8.[97]

Jerome explicitly mentions that he had 'plucked flowers' from the garden of Origen in the *Comm.Gal.*[98] In the *Comm.Eph.* he says: 'Origen composed three volumes on this epistle and I have partly followed him.'[99]

A striking instance of Jerome's use of Origen is the long quotation from the tenth book of the *Stromateis*[100] which Jerome includes in his interpretation of Gal. 5:13. Jerome justifies the length of the quotation by saying that it is very obscure: *Hunc locum quia valde obscurus est, de*

---

91 *Apol.c.Hier.* 1, 22-44; 2, 13-22; 28.
92 *Apol.c.Ruf.* 1, 11, 14-16, 21-29.
93 *Comm.Phil.* 1 (*PL* 26, 638).
94 *Comm.Gal.*: Prol. (*PL* 26, 331-2).
95 *Comm.Eph.*: Prol. II (*PL* 26, 507).
96 In *Comm.Titus* 1, 11 (*PL* 26, 605), he notes that he had dictated the *Comm. Gal.* 'a few months ago'.
97 Rufinus: *Apol.c.Hier.* 1, 36. Kelly dates it 387-8; Cavallera (II. 27) pp. 389-392; Dom J. Chapman: *JTS* 24 (1922-3) p. 38 n.1 387; Souter: *Earliest Latin Commentaries on the Epistles of St. Paul*, Oxford 1927, p. 100, prefers a date close to 392.
98 *Comm.Gal.*: Prol. (*PL* 26, 332-3). It is interesting to note that St. Augustine discounts Origen's influence in this commentary (*Ep.* 82, 23; *CSEL* 34, 376).
99 *Comm.Eph.*: Prol. (*PL* 26, 472).
100 *Comm.Gal.*: 5, 13 (*PL* 26, 434A-436A).

Stromatum libro transferri placuit ad verbum. At its end, he names Origen, and merely says that he can add nothing more.

Many passages in the *Comm.Gal.* can be traced back to Origen, most with certainty. A. Souter[101] gives a comprehensive list of passages (excluding exegetical passages, and taken from all four commentaries) grouping them under three headings: mention by Jerome of any Greek writer or literary work whose date is prior to Origen; passages referring to Greek philosophy; and references to pagan Greek literature and mythology.

A good example of Jerome's exegetical dependence on Origen in the *Comm.Gal.* is the incident between Peter and Paul at Antioch (Gal. 2: 11-21). Jerome could not believe that two apostles could quarrel and that Peter could revert to Judaism, so he explains the passage by arguing that Paul only reproached Peter for the sake of the Judaizers and Gentiles, and that the disagreement was only a piece of play-acting; Peter and Paul remained friends.[102] In *Ep.* 112, 4-6, written to Augustine in 404, Jerome recalls that he had taken this interpretation from the tenth book of the *Stromateis* of Origen:

> '...this interpretation, which Origen was the first to follow in the tenth book of Stromateis, when he was commentating on Paul's epistle to the Galatians.'[103]

Jerome also notes (correctly) that John Chrysostom had adapted the same interpretation.[104]

To show Jerome's use of Origen in the four commentaries on the Pauline epistles we are dependent on what Jerome himself says, and on the few fragments[105] of Origen's commentary which are extant. For almost all of Jerome's later commentaries, however, direct comparisons can be made to show the extent of Jerome's borrowing, even at the time of the Origenist Controversy.

The Origenist Controversy in which Jerome was involved from 393-402 was not the first time Origen's doctrines had been called into question. During his own lifetime, he was exiled from Alexandria. After his

---

[101] A. Souter: *The Earliest Latin Commentaries on the Epistles of St. Paul*, Oxford 1927, pp. 116-125. See also M.A. Schatkin: 'The Influence of Origen upon Jerome's Commentary on Galatians', in *Vig Chr* 24 (1970) 49-58.
[102] *PL* 26, 364.
[103] *Ep.* 112, 6 (*CSEL* 55, 372): Hanc autem expositionem, quam primus Origenes in decimo Stromatum libro, ubi epistulam Pauli ad Galatas interpretatur (est secutus)...
[104] Cf John Chrysostom: *C.Gal.* 2, 12.
[105] These come primarily from Pamphilus' *Apologia pro Origene*, and were collected by C.H.E. Lommatzsch in *PL* 14, 1293-8.

death, although he had many supporters, there were some, like Methodius of Patara, early in the fourth century, who severely criticised his doctrines of creation, free will, resurrection and the relation between body and soul. Later in the fourth century, Epiphanius, Bishop of Salamis, argued vigorously against Origen, recapitulating many of Methodius' arguments and adding some new ones (*Panarion* 64).[106] When, early in 393, Jerome became involved in the controversy, there had been a long history of theological argument over Origen's doctrines. But after Jerome became involved, and certainly after 398, the controversy became a bitter personal struggle between the two erstwhile friends, Jerome and Rufinus.[107]

Jerome first became directly involved in 393, when, at Epiphanius' instigation, a certain Atarbius travelled to Jerusalem and Bethlehem in order to stamp out any traces of Origenism there (especially in the monasteries), and to demand formal rejections of Origen's heretical doctrines.[108] Jerome acceded with alacrity. Rufinus, on the other hand, objected to Atarbius' demands, refused to see him, barred his gates and threatened to drive him off with violence. Atarbius interpreted Rufinus' actions as an admission of Origenism and began spreading accusations against him in Jerusalem, and persisted 'howling against him' for some time.[109]

Later, Epiphanius and Bishop John of Jerusalem, with whom Rufinus was on friendly terms, engaged in an acrimonious battle of words over Origen.[110] There was an eventual reconciliation in 397 in the Church of the Resurrection in Jerusalem between Epiphanius (with whom Jerome sided) and John (with whom Rufinus sided).[111]

The controversy took a new twist, however, in 398, when Rufinus translated Origen's *De Principiis*, and composed *The Falsification of the Works of Origen*, in which he propounded the thesis that Origen's writings had been interpolated by heretics on a large scale, and this ac-

---

[106] A.W.W. Dale's account of the Origenist Controversy in the *Dictionary of Christian Biography* IV, ed. W. Smith and H. Wace, London 1887, pp. 142-156, is still valuable; see also Kelly: pp. 227-240.

[107] Jerome and Rufinus had been close friends while students together in Rome. See F.X. Murphy: *Rufinus of Aquileia*, Washington D.C. 1945; *Epp.* 48, 1; 49, 1; 66, 9.

[108] Our sole knowledge of this incident comes from Jerome's *Apol.c.Ruf.* 3, 33 (written in 401).

[109] Jerome: *Apol.c.Ruf.* 3, 33.

[110] See Jerome's vivid account in *C.Ioh.Hier.* 11.

[111] *Apol.c.Ruf.* 3, 33; *Ep.* 81, 1; Ruf.: *Apol.c.Hier.* 2, 37.

counted for all the unorthodox passages.¹¹² Jerome was outraged at Rufinus' statements in favour of Origen, and in reply made a literal translation of the *De Princ.*, sending it, along with a letter,¹¹³ in which he declares with characteristic rhetorical flourish, 'I have praised the commentator but not the theologian, the man of intellect but not the believer, the philosopher but not the apostle.'¹¹⁴ This is an important letter for it is primarily concerned with justifying and defining exactly his attitude to Origen, playing down his early enthusiasm for the Alexandrian, appealing to his own commentaries on Ecclesiastes and Ephesians, and claiming that he had admired Origen in the same way that Cyprian had admired Tertullian for some things, but had rejected the latter's Montanist views. Jerome criticises Origen's heretical opinions and Pamphilus' *Vindication of Origen*.

Rufinus retorted at length in his *Apol.adv.Hier.*, published in 401. In this work, Rufinus charges Jerome, in the *Comm.Eph.*, (to which Jerome had appealed as being free from Origen's speculative doctrines¹¹⁵), with adapting and reproducing uncritically some of Origen's worst theses.¹¹⁶ If Jerome was denouncing Origen, Rufinus argues, he was therefore denouncing himself.

Jerome's reply, full of indignation and rage, came immediately and was in two parts, the first being a justification of his own actions, the second a violent castigation of Rufinus. He replies to the accusations of holding Origen's speculations. His fundamental argument is summed up as follows:

> 'Does anyone dare, then, after this statement of my opinion, to accuse me of agreeing with Origen's heresy? It is now about 18 years since I dictated those books (the *Comm.Eph.*) at a time when the name of Origen was famous throughout the world, and when his work the Περὶ Ἀρχῶν had not yet reached the ears of the Latins: and yet I distinctly stated my belief and pointed out what I did not agree with. So, even if my opponent (Rufinus) could have pointed out anything heretical in other places, I should be held guilty only of carelessness, not of the perverse

---

112 Jerome: *Apol.* 2, 20. On the question of literary frauds in antiquity, see G. Bardy's interesting article: 'Faux et fraudes littéraires dans l'antiquité chrétienne', in *RHE* 32 (1936) 5-23; 275-302.
113 *Ep.* 84.
114 *Ep.* 84, 2 (*CSEL* 55, 122).
115 *Ep.* 84, 2 (*CSEL* 55, 122).
116 Ruf. *Apol.c.Hier.* 1, 22-44. Rufinus was later to cite a score of passages in the *Comm.Eph.* which were dependent on Origen (*Apol.* 2, 13-22; 28).

doctrines which both here and in my other works I have often condemned.'[117]

In the following year (402), Jerome wrote a third *Apol.*, which is 'quite extreme in its violence'.[118] This added little to what he had already written, reinforcing the charges of heresy, falsehood and provocative translations. After this, Rufinus made no further reply, and indeed dropped out of the controversy altogether, mentioning the quarrel only once.[119] He may, however, have continued to criticise Jerome in private.[120]

For the duration of the Origenist Controversy, most of Jerome's energies were spent in the production of polemical material against Rufinus and Origen's heresy. But Jerome makes the important point that one can distinguish between Origen the theologian and Origen the exegete. It is perfectly legitimate, he says, to study Origen's exegesis, and much can be learned from it, but this does not mean that his speculative doctrines must be accepted as well. Jerome rejects categorically those doctrines of Origen which diverge from those of the Church.[121]

Jerome did write a few commentaries during the controversy.[122] In these, as in the earlier commentaries, we may still see borrowings from Origen. The *Comm.Matt.* is a good example, for large portions of Origen's commentary on this gospel are extant,[123] and detailed comparisons can therefore be made. Jerome wrote his *Comm.Matt.* in March 398 for his friend, Eusebius of Cremona, who commissioned it to read on a sea journey. In order to have it ready for this journey, Jerome had to compose the work at great speed; he completed it in two weeks.[124] Jerome mentions Origen in the preface as one of the commentators on this gospel he had read:

---

[117] *Apol.* 1, 22 (*CCL* 79, 22).
[118] F.X. Murphy: *op.cit.*, p. 153.
[119] Pref. to his translation of Origen's *Comm.Rom.* (*PG* 14, 1293-4).
[120] Jerome complains of this (although he does not mention Rufinus by name) in *Ep.* 119, 11 (written in 406): 'Why do my enemies tear me to pieces, and the gross swine grunt against me, even though I am silent:'; and, in *Comm.Isa.* X: Prol. (written in 408): 'The scorpion, that dumb and poisonous beast, who will perish in his own pus...' is criticising a passage in Jerome's *Comm.Dan.* See Cavallera: *Saint Jérôme...* II, pp. 131-5.
[121] *Apol.* 1, 22 (*CCL* 79, 21).
[122] On Psalms, Obadiah, Jonah and Matthew.
[123] See E. Klostermann's critical edition in *GCS* (Orig. Werke X-XII), Berlin 1933-41; also R. Girod: *Origène: Commentaire sur l'Évangile selon Matthieu* (*SC* 162), Paris 1970.
[124] *Comm.Matt.*: Pref. (*CCL* 77, 4).

'I confess that I had read, many years previously, Origen's twenty-five volumes on Matthew, and just the same number of his homilies and brief verse by verse type of interpretation.'[125]

Many striking parallels between Jerome and Origen are to be found in the *Comm.Matt.* Occasionally, one finds a passage where it is obvious that Jerome has copied the Alexandrian exegete's comments almost word for word. A good example of this is found at 12, 20, where Jerome writes:

'"He will not snap off the broken reed and will not extinguish the burning wick." He who does not stretch out his hand to a sinner, nor carries the burden of his brother, that man snaps the broken reed. And he who values little the moderate spark of faith in the little ones, this man extinguishes the smoking wick. Christ did neither of these; for he had come for this, so that he might render uninjured that which had perished.'[126]

Origen's comment on the same passage, as preserved in a fragment (number 262),[127] reads as follows:

'He who does not stretch out his hands to those who sin ruins in some way the fractured reed, and he who leaves behind those who have a small spark of faith extinguishes the smoking wick. Christ has not done these things.'

More frequently, as one would expect, Jerome's comments show close similarities with Origen's, though not verbal borrowing. A good example of this is Jerome's interpretation of the parable of the hidden treasure (Matt. 13:44ff). The main points of the respective interpretations are set out below:

Jerome[128]	*Origen*[129]
The treasure is the word of God, which appears to be hidden in the body of Christ, or the holy scriptures in which rest the knowledge of the saviour. When the treasure is discovered, one must give up all	This is not a parable but a similitude. The field equals the scripture. The treasure equals the mysteries lying within the scriptures. A man comes to scripture, and, finding the 'treasure', hides

---

125 *Ibid.*: Legisse me fateor ante annos plurimos in Matheum Origenis uiginti quinque uolumina et totidem eius omelias commaticumque interpretationis genus.
126 *CCL* 77, 91.
127 *GCS* 41, 120.
128 *CCL* 77, 113ff.
129 *GCS* 40, 5ff.

| the *emolumenta* of this world in order to possess it. | it, thinking it dangerous to reveal to all and sundry the secrets of scripture. He goes, sells all his possessions, and works until he can buy the field, in order that he may possess the great treasure. |

It will be noted here that Jerome's interpretation is very close to that of Origen. Jerome's interpretation, however, is simpler and more direct in its application of the meaning of the parable. Jerome is not at all interested in Origen's distinction between a parable and a similitude, this latter being a generic term, the former a particular form of similitude. We should note also that Jerome sets down two different interpretations of the treasure – it is either the word of God, hidden in the body of Christ, or it is the knowledge of the saviour which is hidden in the scriptures. Jerome makes no choice between the two. His first interpretation does not come from Origen.[130]

It is not only specific passages of spiritual interpretation which Jerome borrowed from Origen's *Comm.Matt.*, but also, as E. Bonnard has shown recently,[131] certain of the themes of the commentary. One of these, which was very important for Origen, is the goodness of God. Origen uses this to oppose the Gnostics, showing that the God of the O.T. was a good and gracious God, the same as that of the N.T., who sent his son to bring his divine plan into effect. This theme is seen in Jerome's *Comm.Matt.* several times.[132] In his use of this theme, Jerome ignores Origen's apologetic thrust against the Gnostics, and instead makes a simple and brief affirmation of the goodness and bounty of God. In one sense, therefore, Jerome does alter the material he read in Origen's *Comm.*, in order to suit his own purposes. The question of Gnosticism was no longer a 'live' issue in Jerome's day, and he was forced, therefore, to rephrase his source so far as this theme is concerned.

After the end of the Origenist Controversy, Jerome was able to devote himself more fully to his exegetical labours. In the last 17 years of his life, he was to produce his most mature exegetical work, with major commentaries on several of the prophetic books of the O.T. In almost all of these works, it is still possible to see the influence of Origen.

---

130 For a full list of quotations of and allusions to Origen in Jerome's *Comm. Matt.*, see the '*Index fontium et imitationum*' in *CCL* 77, and E. Bonnard's discussion in his edition of the *Comm.Matt.* in *SC* 242, Paris 1977, pp. 37-45.
131 *SC* 242, p. 37-8.
132 E.g. 5, 1; 10, 1; 10, 40; 11, 30; 13, 1-2; 17, 7.

In 406, Jerome wrote commentaries on Zechariah, Malachi, Hosea, Joel and Amos, bringing to completion the project begun some 14 years earlier, when he wrote on the other Minor Prophets. In the *Comm. Ioelem* 1, 6[133] for instance, as R. Reitzenstein[134] has shown, Jerome has borrowed his spiritual interpretation from Origen. This is proven when it is noted that both Jerome and Origen use Eccles. 10:4 and 1 Pet. 5:8 in their interpretation.

The following year (407) Jerome composed the important *Comm. Danielem*, which he wrote quite concisely, commenting only on the most difficult verses. In the prologue, he announces his intention of keeping spiritual interpretation to a minimum.[135] Taking Origen as his example, he includes the story of Bel and the Dragon and that of the Three Children, even though Jerome himself thought them to be deutero-canonical because they were not found in the original Hebrew.[136] The *Comm.Dan.* is interesting, because in it Jerome makes use of several works of Origen, quoting from or alluding to the *De Princ.*,[137] the *C.Celsum*,[138] and *Ep. ad Iul. Africanum*,[139] and the *Stromateis*.[140] He often uses these when explaining the spiritual sense of Daniel.

The remainder of Jerome's exegetical output continues to show his customary use of Origen's works. The Alexandrian exegete's influence may be traced in Jerome's *Comm.Isa.* (written between 408-410), *Comm.Ezek.* (410-414), and the unfinished *Comm.Hier.* (begun in 414). Here again, as we have seen in the other commentaries, Jerome uses specific spiritual interpretations which Origen had made. Sometimes Jerome mentions Origen by name,[141] sometimes not.

The most interesting observation to be made about Jerome's use of Origen's spiritual interpretations is that after the Origenist Controversy Jerome was much more careful in his use of the Alexandrian exegete's

---

133 *CCL* 76, 168.
134 R. Reitzenstein: 'Origenes und Hieronymus', in *ZNTW* 20 (1921) 90-93, where he edits P. Oxyr. 1601, which contains a few fragments of Origen's *Comm. Ioel.*
135 *CCL* 75A, 775.
136 *Comm.Dan.*: Prol.; 13, 3f (*CCL* 75A, 774; 945-950). For Jerome's views on the canon of scripture, see above, pp 62-71.
137 See, for instance, *Comm.Dan.* 4, 1 (*De Princ.* 1, 1, 5); 8, 16 (1, 8, 1); 3, 39 (3, 3, 5-4, 1).
138 See, for instance, *Comm.Dan.* 3, 1 (*C.Celsum* 1, 5); 5, 7a (1, 58).
139 *Comm.Dan.*: Prol. (*Ep. ad Iul.Afr.* 2-4); 13, 54f (2; 6, 11-12).
140 Origen's *Strom.* IX is lost, but Jerome explicitly states that he is quoting from it, for example at 3, 26; 3, 37-9; 12, 1-3.
141 For example, *Comm.Isa.* 2, 22; 6, 9-10 (*CCL* 73, 40; 92).

works, and was more critical when it came to any of Origen's outlawed doctrines. Origen, for example, had propounded the theory that the devil would eventually repent and be saved. Jerome denounced this as mischievous exegesis.[142] In the *Comm.Isa.*, he challenges Origenists to reconcile their doctrine of the devil's salvation with the prophecy that the Lord will finally kill 'the dragon which is in the sea'.[143] Most telling of all, however, is a passage in the *Comm.Hier.* where he denounces Origen as 'that allegorist',[144] fiercely attacking his unorthodox views, and relying less than in any other commentary on his spiritual interpretation.

The effect which the Origenist Controversy had on Jerome can be seen in a letter to a certain Avitus.[145] About ten years previously, Jerome had been asked by Pammachius to make a literal translation of Origen's *De Princ.* so that he could compare it with Rufinus' version. Jerome had done this,[146] but Pammachius had thought that the errors of Origen were too bad for public circulation. But 'a certain brother' had persuaded Pammachius to let him see Jerome's translation, and this person had made a hasty transcription and published it. Avitus had obtained a copy of this translation and had now, apparently, written to Jerome for an explanation.

Jerome's malicious temperament comes across in the open hostility he shows towards the person he formerly admired and called 'the greatest teacher of the church after the apostles'.[147] He summarises the heretical views put forward in the *De Princ.* but often distorts Origen's opinions. He unjustly accuses Origen of having denied the Incarnation.[148] Again, he misrepresents Origen's views on the salvation of the devil,[149] the transmigration of souls,[150] and the resurrection,[151] where, although Origen had postulated two possibilities, Jerome credits him with having held dogmatically only the more heretical view.

---

142 *Comm.Dan.* 3, 95f (*CCL* 75A, 808); cf Origen: *De Princ.* 1, 6, 2-3.
143 *Comm.Isa.* 27, 1 (*CCL* 73, 344-6).
144 *Allegoricus interpres*; see, among others, 24, 14; 25, 26; 28, 12ff (*CCL* 74, 236, 246, 273).
145 *Ep.* 124 (*CSEL* 56, 96-117).
146 See *Epp.* 83 and 84.
147 *Pref. to Book of Hebrew Names.*
148 *Ep.* 124, 2 (*CSEL* 56, 97f).
149 *Ep.* 124, 4 (*CSEL* 56, 99f).
150 *Ep.* 124, 8 (*CSEL* 56, 105-7).
151 *Ep.* 124, 11 (*CSEL* 56, 112-4).

Abuse of the spiritual sense

At the end of the last section we saw that Jerome, after the Origenist Controversy, castigated the heretical views of Origen, the greatest exemplar of the spiritual interpretation of scripture, disparagingly calling him 'that allegorist'. This leads us to ask whether Jerome even questioned the use of the spiritual sense and whether, if he did, this occurred before or after the Origenist Controversy.

In the *Comm.Abac.*, written in 393, we find the first firm evidence that Jerome did not accept uncritically the spiritual interpretations of other authors. Making a comparison between the literal and spiritual senses of scripture, he comments:

> 'The *historia* is strictly limited, and does not have the opportunity of spreading forth. *Tropologia* is free, and is bound only by these rules, that it must follow the obligation to intelligibility, and respect the way in which the words are put together, nor should violence be done in joining together things which are quite at odds with each other.'[152]

It must be said, however, that Jerome did not follow his own advice with any rigour. Although occasionally his spiritual interpretations are governed by their tendency to edify, their avoidance of contradiction, and contextualisation, his usual practice is to glean whatever Christian meaning is possible from the text.

In the prologue to the *Comm.Abd.*, composed in 396, Jerome says that when he was very young, he had written a commentary on this book, which had been full of allegorical interpretations. He was now ashamed of this and embarrassed by it, although it had recently been praised by a young man who had somehow procured a copy of it. Although Jerome says nothing explicit in this commentary about the abuse of the spiritual sense, we may imply that this shame at this youthful effort is evidence of a certain objectivity in the matter. Spiritual interpretation is necessary and useful in the explanation of the bible, but if used uncritically it does more harm than good.

In the prologues or prefaces to most of his commentaries, Jerome lists the previous commentators whom he has consulted. In the prologue to the *Comm.Zach.*, however, written in 406, Jerome goes beyond merely listing the authors he has used in preparing this commentary. He says:

---

[152] *Comm.Abac.* 1, 6-11 (*CCL* 76A, 589): Historia stricta est, et euagandi non habet facultatem. Tropologia libera, et his tantum legibus circumscripta, ut pietatem sequatur intelligentiae, sermonisque contextum nec in rebus multum inter se contrariis uiolenta sit copulandis.

'Origen wrote about this prophet in two volumes, up to the third part of his book from the beginning. Hippolytus also wrote commentaries, and Didymus produced five books of interpretation... but all of his exegesis was allegorical and scarcely touched upon a few things connected with history.'[153]

This commentary, then, composed after the Origenist Controversy, which forced Jerome to read Origen's works critically, is evidence that Jerome did indeed question the uncritical use of spiritual interpretations, not only of Origen but also of other authors. These authors neglected the *historia*, and paid too much attention to the *allegoria*.

In this chapter we have studied Jerome's terminology for, and use of, the spiritual interpretation of scripture, noting especially his use of specific interpretations of Origen, before, during and after the Origenist Controversy. The most interesting fact to emerge from this study is that, although he was content to utilise many of Origen's specific interpretations, even after the Origenist Controversy, in the technical vocabulary he used (when he was not quoting or paraphrasing Origen or other authors) he did not follow the Alexandrian school but rather that of Antioch. This shows Jerome to have been an eclectic exegete and not a blind follower of either of the two main exegetical schools. Jerome used what he believed were the best of both methods of interpretation so that he could construct for his readers the most comprehensive and satisfactory exegesis possible of the scriptural books.

---

[153] *Comm.Zach.*: Prol. (*CCL* 76A, 748): Scripsit in hunc prophetam Origenes duo uolumina, usque ad tertiam partem libri a principio. Hippolytus quoque edidit commentarios, et Didymus quinque explanationum libros... sed tota eorum ἐξήγησις allegorica fuit, et historiae uix pauca tetigerunt.

7. Jerome, Jews and Judaism

Jerome's exegesis was influenced by Judaism, and it is for this reason that we must ask what knowledge he had of Jewish people and Jewish practices and institutions. First, we shall study Jerome's use of the terms 'Jews', 'Hebrews' and 'Israel'. Second, we shall study the information which he gives about two Jewish sects, the Pharisees and Sadducees. Third, we shall investigate the material related by Jerome concerning Jewish leaders, a few of whom he mentions by name, and Jewish institutions. Fourth, we shall study briefly some of the information Jerome gives concerning the social position of the Jews of his own day. Fifth, we shall review the important information Jerome relates concerning 'Jewish Christians', and finally we shall see that Jerome uses some of the technical, exegetical terminology of the Jews.

Terminology

For the Church Fathers, the term 'Jews' signified present-day Jews. Generally speaking, it was employed as a generic term, the term 'the Jews' being encountered much more frequently than 'a Jew' or 'some Jews'. This generalising tendency created a Jewish stereo-type, with which Christian writers were able to distort the religious and social customs of the Jews, and thus to create a situation which led ultimately to their persecution. The term 'Jews', therefore, had polemical overtones for Christian authors and it is consequently found that the term 'Hebrews' is occasionally used to denote contemporary Jews.

Jerome has many polemical references to 'the Jews'. The fundamental reason why the early Christians persecuted the Jews was the theological one that they were responsible for the death by crucifixion of Christ. Jerome accuses them several times[1] of being responsible for Christ's death. The Jews continue to crucify Christ, giving him vinegar and myrrh to prevent him from seeing their crimes.[2] The Jews blasphemed Christ and scorned him.[3] They do not understand the real

---

[1] For example: *Adv.Iohan.Hier.* 31; *Ep.* 129, 1.
[2] *Comm.Matt.* 27, 48.
[3] *Ep.* 39, 6; 42, 1; *Adv.Lucif.* 22; *Comm.Matt.* 12, 44.

meaning of the O.T. which refers to Christ, and, because of this, they cannot understand the Gospel.[4] They fail to recognise Christ as the Son of God;[5] their doctrines and practices are corrupt.[6] For their rejection of Christ and for their stubbornness and failure to repent,[7] the Jews have been rejected by God.[8]

In respect of the theological rationale behind these polemical comments against the Jews, Jerome was merely following the pattern which had been practised from the time of the N.T.[9] This pattern also included polemical comments of a more personal nature aimed against the Jews, and to this tradition Jerome adds, seemingly with alacrity. The Jews are superstitious,[10] lustful and sexually depraved.[11] They are arrogant,[12] avaricious,[13] gluttonous,[14] and produce sons and grandsons like little worms.[15] On first reading, a statement like 'the Jew's mourning is the Christian's joy',[16] is particularly distasteful, but when Jerome's polemical outbursts against the Jews are compared with those he made against Christian heretics and pagans, it is found that the above statement is relatively mild in tone.[17] The same is the case also when Jerome describes the Jews as 'the most foul dregs',[18] and, in chorus with all the patristic writers, says: 'Because of their sins, the Jews offended, therefore we oppressed them and became rich from their money.'[19]

The impression should not be gained, however, that the only com-

---

[4] See *Comm.Matt.* 10, 41.
[5] *Ep.* 125, 1; *Comm.Matt.* 13, 12.
[6] *Ep.* 121, 10 (their observance of the Sabbath is a foul and foolish custom); *Adv.Iohan.Hier.* 28; *Comm.Matt.* 5, 38; *Comm.Amos* 5, 23 (their prayers resemble the grunting of pigs and the braying of donkeys).
[7] *Ep.* 147, 3; *Comm.Matt.* 21, 28-32.
[8] *Ep.* 52, 10; 58, 3; *Adv.Iohan.Hier.* 2; *Comm.Matt.* 23, 29.
[9] See J. Parkes: *The Conflict of the Church and the Synagogue*, London 1934. J.E. Seaver: *Persecution of the Jews in the Roman Empire (300-438)*, Kansas 1952. M. Simon: *Verus Israel*, ET H. McKeating, Oxford 1986; J. Gager: *The Origins of Anti-Semitism*, Oxford 1985.
[10] *Ep.* 107, 8; *Comm.Matt.* 15, 12.
[11] *Ep.* 48, 8; 68, 1; 59, 8.
[12] *Comm.Ezek.* 37, 1-14.
[13] *Comm.Isa.* 2, 8.
[14] *Comm.Isa.* 57, 17-21.
[15] *Comm.Isa.* 50, 4-7.
[16] *Ep.* 60, 6 (*CSEL* 54, 555): Iudaeorum luctus Christianorum gaudium est.
[17] Cf D.S. Wiesen: *St. Jerome as a Satirist*, Ithaca, N.Y. 1964, pp. 188-195.
[18] *Comm.Joel.* 1, 8 (*CCL* 76, 169): spurcissimae faeces.
[19] *Comm.Zach.* 11, 4f (*CCL* 76A, 851): Propter peccata sua offendere Iudaei, ideo eos oppressimus et ex pretio eorum diuites facti sumus.

ments Jerome makes about the Jews are derogatory, or that his use of the term 'the Jews' carries totally negative connotations. Several references in Jerome's commentaries, letters and polemical literature show that this phrase also had positive connotations for him, and, in this, Jerome swims against the current of patristic statements on the Jews. The statement of J.E. Seaver,[20] that the Jew, as encountered in the fourth century Fathers 'is a monster, a theological abstraction of superhuman malice and cunning, and more than superhuman blindness' is a generalisation, and gives a contorted view of the actual situation in the fourth century, at least as far as Jerome is concerned.

In his treatise *Adv.Iovin.* II, 25, Jerome makes the following statement:

> '...as the Gospel tells us, the same refreshing rain falls upon all, good and bad, just and unjust. If the present is a picture of the future, then the Sun of Righteousness will rise on sinners as well as on the righteous, on the wicked and the holy, on the heathen as well as the Jews and Christians, though scripture says "Unto you who fear the Lord shall the Sun of Righteousness arise" (Mal. 4: 2).'[21]

Here, Jerome leaves behind him the derogatory comments about Jews and seems to adopt, at least temporarily, a more humane attitude, for in his juxtaposition of the three pairs of opposites, he appears to link Jews and Christians together opposite the heathen.[22] The reason for this more humane attitude towards the Jews is not altogether clear, but may have to do with the recognition that Jews and Christians worship the same God (although, for Jerome, Jewish worship is only partial and invalid because they do not accept Christ as the Messiah) whereas the heathen worship many false gods.

Earlier in the *Adv.Iovin.*, Jerome replies to Jovinianus' denigration of the virtuous state of virginity.[23] Jerome argues that the apostles had

---

[20] J.E. Seaver: *op.cit.*, p. 19. It should be noted that most of Seaver's comments about Jerome are taken over unacknowledged (with a good deal of verbal similarity) from J. Parkes: *op.cit.*; cf Gager: *op.cit.*, pp. 117-173.

[21] *PL* 23, 336: ...et iisdem omnes juxta Evangelium imbribus irrigamur, boni et mali, justi et injusti. Si praesentia exempla sunt futurorum, ergo et sol justitiae aequaliter justis et peccatoribus, impiis et sanctis, Christianis et Judaeis atque gentilibus orietur, cum Scriptura dicat: "Timentibus autem Dominum orietur sol justitiae" (Mal. 4:2).

[22] This would seem to be the conclusion if we accept that *atque* has a stronger meaning than *et*.

[23] For Jerome's theology of virginity, see D. Dumm: *The Theological Basis of Virginity according to St. Jerome*, Latrobe, Pa. 1952.

left wife and home for the sake of the Gospel. He refers to the Pauline saying: 'Have I no right to take a Christian wife about with me' (1 Cor. 9:5), explaining that the word γυνή can mean both 'woman' and 'wife', and then says:

> 'This makes it clear that the writer referred to other holy women, who, in accordance with Jewish custom, ministered to their teachers from their substance, as we read was the practice of even our Lord himself.'[24]

Admittedly, this is primarily an historical reference[25] to Jewish customs, but he does not make any kind of derogatory or negative judgment on those customs. Jerome comments elsewhere on this custom of the Jews of the maintenance of a class of professional teachers. In *Adv.Vigil.* 13, we find the following statement, which is also interesting as an example of Jerome's use of the term 'Hebrews' as applicable to contemporary Jews:

> 'This custom continues until today in Judaea, not only among us, but among the Hebrews, that those who meditate on the Law day and night [Ps. 1:2] and have no earthly father except God alone [Deut. 18:2f], may be looked after by the aid of the synagogues and everyone else. This is done that there might be equality [2 Cor. 8:14] that some may not be refreshed while others are in need, but that the excess of some may support the misery of others.'[26]

Another example of Jerome's use of the term 'the Jews' in a positive sense is seen in *Adv.Vigil.* 14, where he says:

> 'And we do not deny that portions should be distributed to all the poor, even to Jews and Samaritans, if the means will allow.'[27]

When it comes to poverty, hunger and the needs of other poor people,

---

[24] *Adv.Iovin.* I, 26 (*PL* 23, 257): Ex quo apparet eum de aliis sanctis dixisse mulieribus, quae juxta morem Judaicum magistris de sua substantia ministrabant, sicut legimus ipsi quoque Domino factitatum.

[25] This in itself is interesting, for it shows that, in Jerome's understanding, the Jews became 'Jews' as opposed to Hebrews at the advent of Christ, for the incident he is discussing took place in the early decades of Christianity.

[26] *PL* 23, 365C: Hac in Judaea usque hodie perseverante consuetudine, non solum apud nos, sed et apud Hebraeos, ut qui in lege Domini meditantur die ac nocte [Ps. 1:2], et patrem non habent in terra, nisi solum Deum, synagogarum et totius orbis foveantur ministeriis [Deut. 18:2f]; ex aequalitate duntaxat non ut aliis refrigerium, et aliis sit tribulatio: sed ut aliorum abundantia, aliorum sustentet inopiam [2 Cor. 8:14].

[27] *PL* 23, 366: Nec nos negamus cunctis pauperibus, etiam Judaeis et Samaritanis, si tanta sit largitas, stipes porrigendas.

Jerome appears to say, in this rather uncharacteristic moment of largesse, that there is little difference between Christian and Jew, and both should be given aid. The Christian, however, having accepted Christ as Messiah and Son of God, should have priority over a Jew or a Samaritan, who have not accepted Christ.

In the O.T., the term 'Hebrews' (עִבְרִי) was not primarily a racial term, but rather a name which said something about the social and legal status of those to whom it was applied.[28] When used outside the O.T., Ἑβραῖος can refer either to the language of the Jewish people – in rabbinic literature, this is the exclusive use of עִבְרִי[29] – or as a polite expression for the people of Israel. In Philo, Ἑβραῖος is usually employed to refer to the ancient people of Israel,[30] as is the case also for Josephus.[31] Both of these authors occasionally use Ἑβραῖος to connote the language which the Jews speak, which is a characteristic of the Jewish nation.[32]

In the N.T., the term Ἑβραῖος appears only three times,[33] and it is difficult, therefore, to make firm conclusions about its meaning. Its use does seem to imply, however, that it refers to Palestinian Jews, as opposed to those of the Diaspora.

Origen uses Ἑβραῖος many times in the sense of the ancient Israelites or the chosen people. But there are a large number of cases where he uses the word to refer to contemporary Jews. He refers to his Jewish teachers and friends as Ἑβραῖοι. It is, therefore, a polite term, used instead of the polemical Ἰουδαῖος.[34] Origen also uses the word Ἑβραῖος to argue that the Jews had originated from the ancient Hebrews. Egyptian polemical writers had said that the Jews were originally undesirable Egyptians who were expelled from Egypt and who subsequently made their home in Judaea.[35] Celsus had raised this charge, which Origen refuted by arguing that the Jews were Hebrews, driven into Egypt by famine in Judaea, and imprisoned there. If this were not the case, they could not, immediately upon leaving Egypt, have formed themselves into a nation and invented a language. The fact that they spoke Hebrew and took Hebrew names proves that they came from Hebrew stock.[36]

---

28 See Ex. 21:2ff; Jer. 34:8-11; 1 Sam. 14:21; G. von Rad: *TDNT* III, p. 358f.
29 *TDNT* III, p. 365f.
30 *Mut.Nom.* 117; *Vit.Mos.* I, 243; *De Mig.Abr.* 20.
31 *Antiq.* I-IX, *passim*.
32 Philo: *Conf.Ling.* 68; 129; Josephus: *Antiq.* V, 323; I, 36; *De Bell.Iud.* 6, 96.
33 Acts 6:1; Phil. 3:5; 2 Cor. 11:22. *TDNT* III, p. 389f.
34 N.R.M. de Lange: *op.cit.*, p. 30f.
35 Strabo: *Geog.* XVI, ii, 35f.
36 *C.Cels.* III, 5, 6, 8.

Origen's purpose in this argument was to search back into the origins of Christianity. Christians are descended from the Hebrews, and, although not fully developed in Origen, the name 'Hebrew' later becomes detached from the Jews, and becomes the property of the Christian Church, which appropriates it retrospectively, so that every Hebrew who ever lived was really a Christian. This doctrine was seen in the N.T. (Rom. 4; Gal. 3 for example) but was not systematically worked out until Eusebius of Caesarea did so in his work *Demonstratio Euangelica* in the fourth century.

For Jerome, the term *Hebraei* has the same three primary meanings as we have seen in other previous literature. It refers a few times to the ancient people of Israel.[37] Much more frequently, Jerome uses it when discussing some philological point concerning the Hebrew language, in which the O.T. was written,[38] or when referring to contemporary Jews, in particular his Jewish teachers and those with whom he discussed the exegesis of the O.T.[39]

We have already seen[40] that Jerome often refers to his Hebrew teachers as *Hebraeus meus*, or by similar phrases.[41] But at one place,[42] Jerome makes a long quotation from a person to whom he refers as '*Hebraeus meus*', with whom he says he has had a long discussion on the passage in question (Isa. 6:8). The passage from which he quotes includes allusions to Ex. 4:10 and 13; Isa. 40:6, but also to the dominical saying of Matt. 7: 7: 'Seek and you shall find, knock and it shall be opened to you.' That a Jewish teacher, almost certainly a rabbi, should quote from a Christian Gospel to shed light on a passage from Isaiah is highly improbable. This leads us to question whether, in fact, Jerome is reporting information which he received from his Jewish teacher at this point, or whether he has culled this information from some other source.

In fact, we have to go no further than Origen's nineteenth *Homily on Jeremiah* to find Jerome's source. We know that Jerome was familiar with this homily, as he translated it in A.D. 392, at about the same time

---

37 E.g. *Comm.Matt.* 26, 73 (*CCL* 77, 262).
38 See, for example, *Comm.Eccles.* 7, 8; 10, 4 (*CCL* 72, 302; 334); *Comm. Matt.* 5, 22 (*CCL* 77, 28).
39 *Adv.Iovin.* I, 23 (*PL* 23, 253); *Comm.Isa.* 22, 2 (*CCL* 73, 210); *Apol. c.Rufin.* 1, 13 (*CCL* 79, 12); *Comm.Amos* 3, 11 (*CCL* 76, 250); C.H. Gordon: 'Rabbinic Exegesis in the Vulgate of Proverbs', in *JBL* 49 (1930) 384-416.
40 See Chapter 3: 'Jerome and the Hebraica Veritas'.
41 E.g. *Comm.Isa.* 22, 2 (*CCL* 73, 210); *Pref. to transl. of Chron.* (*PL* 29, 423-6); *Comm.Isa.* 13, 10 (*CCL* 73, 163); 22, 15-25 (*CCL* 73, 306); *Comm.Eccles.* 1, 14; 3, 11 (*CCL* 72, 260, 277).
42 *Ep.* 18A, 15 (*CSEL* 54, 93).

that he wrote *Ep.* 18A. E. Klostermann showed beyond doubt,[43] by a detailed comparison of Origen's nineteenth *Hom.Jer.*, his sixth and ninth *Homilies on Isaiah*, and Jerome's *Ep.* 18A, 15, that Jerome's information at this point does not come from a Jewish teacher, but from Origen.[44]

Having discovered that Jerome, for whatever reason, has given misleading information at one point in his exegesis, by stating that a Jewish teacher has given him information when, in fact, Jerome has taken it from Origen, we shall have to be cautious in our approach to the many other occasions where Jerome reports that he was given information by Jews. In fact, we shall find that several of the Jewish traditions which Jerome records in his commentaries come, not directly from Jewish sources, oral or written, but from the works of Origen.

After the name of God (Yahweh), the name 'Israel' is the most frequent word in the O.T., occurring 2,500 times. Its etymology is uncertain, and it is still impossible to be completely sure of its exact meaning.[45] It appears to have denoted all the elect of Yahweh. With the rise of the monarchy, however, this usage changed, denoting, in the time of David, the northern tribes, in opposition to Judah in the South.[46] After the deportation of 722 B.C., another change is effected in the meaning of the term. Isaiah and Micah both use 'Israel' to denote the southern kingdom,[47] and the term takes on, once again, not primarily political or geographical connotations but religious significance. 'Israel' refers to the elect people of Yahweh, and this meaning becomes normative for later generations.

Philo, usually referring to past history, uses 'Israel' to mean what it did in the O.T., i.e. the elect people of God. Quite often he refers to the patriarch Jacob as Ἰσραήλ, usually in an allegorical interpretation.[48]

---

[43] E. Klostermann: *Die Überlieferung der Jeremiahomilien des Origenes* (TU XVI, 3), 1897, pp. 76-83.

[44] Klostermann (*op.cit.*, p. 83) concludes: 'Es ist ja nicht absolut ausgeschlossen, dass dieser Hebräer des Hieronymus existiert hat (z.B. *Ep.* 84, 3; *Apol.c. Rufin.* 2, 13), aber wahrscheinlicher bei weitem, das wir hier eine Verdeckung der Abhängigkeit von der Quelle oder eine momentane Selbstverweckselung des Hieronymus mit seinem Gewährsmann haben, wie sie anderweitig schon oft dem ein "Hebraeus meus" des Hieronymus absolut nichts weiter zu sagen weiss, als was dem Origenes von dem seinigen bereits berichtet worden war?'

[45] On this term see M. Noth: *Die israelitischen Personennamen*, Hildesheim 1966, pp. 207-9; C.H.J. de Geus: *The Tribes of Israel*, Assen 1976, pp. 187-192.

[46] Cf 2 Sam. 19:42ff; 20:1ff.

[47] Isa. 5:7; 8:18; Mic. 2:12; 3:1; 8:9 etc.

[48] Cf *De Post.Cain.* 92: Philo translates 'Israel' as ἄνθρωπος ὁρῶν Θεόν. The privilege of Israel is that he sees God; for he who sees has a share in what he sees. Cf *De Abr.* 57-9.

For Josephus also, the reference of 'Israel' is to the historical people of God. He does not use this term to refer to present-day Jews.[49]

In the N.T., the term 'Israel' almost always refers to the people of God.[50] The significance of this term for the N.T. writers comes across particularly at Rom. 11:1. Answering the question whether God has rejected his people, Paul replies: 'Not at all, καὶ γὰρ ἐγὼ 'Ισραηλίτης εἰμι'. This can make sense only if Paul thinks of himself as a member of the people of God.

The term 'Israel' occurs only infrequently in the works of Origen. He uses it only in biblical quotations and arguments based on such quotations, especially when he is influenced by Pauline usage. For him, the primary connotation of 'Israel' is of the ancient and sacred cult of the people of God.[51] The history of this term until the third century A.D., therefore, shows that its meaning is primarily an historical reference to the ancient people who, it was believed, were especially chosen by God, and who had a special relationship with them.

This is also the situation in Jerome's writings. He uses the term 'Israel' and its cognates infrequently, but, without exception, he uses it to refer to the ancient people of God, as opposed to contemporary Jews. He sometimes uses it in biblical quotations, as at *Ep.* 82, 3:

> 'One of his (Jesus') disciples can wish to be anathema from Christ for the sake of his brethren, his kinsmen according to the flesh, who were Israelites (Rom. 9:3f).'[52]

Jerome, following universal Christian tradition from the time of the N.T., understands the Christian faith to be the successor to the Israel of old, for the (present-day) Jews have rejected the message of God, as mediated through Christ, and have therefore forfeited their privileged position as the chosen of God. Those who accept Christ as Lord succeed to this privileged position and become the people of God. The Christians, therefore, are the rightful inheritors of Israel; they are the seed of Abraham.[53]

---

49 *Antiq.* 4, 180; 1, 333; 11, 146.
50 See Matt. 15:31; Mk. 15:32; Lk. 1:68; Jn. 1:49; Rom. 9-11: *passim* etc. But see Matt. 2:20, where it unusually refers to the land of Israel; 10:23; Lk. 1:80; 4: 25, 27, where it is used to denote the people of Israel generally, with no apparent connotation of the people of God. See *TDNT* III, pp. 356-391.
51 See N.R.M. de Lange: *op.cit.*, p. 29, 32.
52 *CSEL* 55, 111: Bonique pastoris discipulus optat anathema esse pro fratribus suis atque cognatis secundum carnem, qui sunt Israhelitae. Cf also *Ep.* 69, 5, where he quotes from Jer. 3:20, and *Ep.* 22, 11, where he quotes from Ex. 12:11 (*CSEL* 54, 688; 158).
53 See *Ep.* 69, 5 (*CSEL* 54, 686): 'The apostle came from the Jews, and the primitive Christian Church was gathered out of the remnants of Israel' (Ex Iudaeis erat apostolus, prima Christi ecclesia de Israhel reliquiis cogebatur).

Jewish sects

The standard derivation of the word 'Pharisee', notwithstanding the thesis of T.W. Manson,[54] is that it comes from a Hebrew root *Parash*, so that 'Pharisee' would mean 'those who are separated' or 'separatists'.[55] Jerome testifies at least once to this derivation when he says:

> '[The Pharisees] who separated themselves from the Jews on account of certain observances, took their name also from the fact of this dissent...'[56]

Jerome refers to the sect of the Pharisees many times in his writings, the *Comm.Matt.*, as we should expect, being particularly replete with the mention of their name.[57] At most of these places, the Pharisees are coupled with the scribes, in allusion to, or paraphrase of, the Gospel narrative, where both these groups are depicted as opposing almost every move of Jesus.[58]

The remaining references to the Pharisees, of which there are many, are all derogatory. The Pharisees hated Christ, calling him 'a drunkard and a glutton, and one who dined with tax-collectors and sinners, because he did not decline the invitation of Zacchaeus to dinner, and went to the marriage feast [at Cana]...'[59] For this hatred of the Saviour, the Pharisees in their turn are to be hated by the Christians. The Pharisees are proud and haughty.[60]

But Jerome, perhaps following the example of Origen,[61] does not limit his use of the word 'Pharisee' to historical references which arise

---

[54] T.W. Manson (*The Servant Messiah*, Cambridge 1953, p. 19) put forward the thesis that the word originally meant 'Persian', 'Pharisee' being therefore a pejorative nickname applied by their enemies whose doctrines rejected the influence, in some ways, of Persian ideas. Manson has not found many followers in this.

[55] This sense is clearly implied in *Kid.* 66A.

[56] *Adv.Lucif.* 23 (*PL* 23, 187): Quod Pharisaei, a Judaeis divisi propter quasdam observationes superfluas, nomen quoque a dissidio susceperunt.

[57] It occurs more than 80 times in this commentary.

[58] A few examples of this are *Comm.Matt.* 9, 10 (*CCL* 77, 56); *Ep.* 49, 13 (*CSEL* 54, 370); *Vita S.Hilar.* 1 (*PL* 23, 30).

[59] *Adv.Iovin.* II, 5 (*PL* 23, 304): Ipse Dominus vini potator et vorator a Pharisaeis appellatur, et publicanorum conviva et peccatorum; Zachaei prandium non recusans, vadens ad nuptiarum epulas.

[60] *Ep.* 122, 3 (*CSEL* 56, 66); *Adv.Pelag.* I, 17; III, 16 (*PL* 23, 534; 614).

[61] Origen applies the word 'Pharisees' to literalistic rabbinic Jews of his own day. See *In Matt.* XI, 9 (*GCS* X, 48); *In Iohan.* III, 1 (*GCS* IV, 510); de Lange: *op.cit.*, p. 35.

from his exegesis of the Gospels. It is very interesting to find that Jerome takes over the derogatory picture of the Pharisees portrayed in the Gospels, and applies their supposed characteristics to the Jewish leaders, the rabbis, of his own day.

In *Comm.Isa.* 8, 19-22, Jerome reports an explanation of the passage under discussion which he says is given by the Nazoraeans, the beginning of which is:

> 'For the rest, the Nazoraeans explain this passage in this way: When the Scribes and Pharisees tell you to listen to them, men who do everything for love of the belly and who hiss during their incantations like the magicians in order to deceive you, you must answer them like this...'[62]

Although this is not Jerome's own interpretation, it is clear that he did not disagree with what the Nazoraeans say about Scribes and Pharisees. That the rabbis of Jerome's own day are intended is also clear, as the account is written in the present tense.

Again, in *Comm.Isa.* 8, 11-15, Jerome makes the interesting comment that

> 'the Nazoraeans, who accept Christ in such a way that they do not cease to observe the old law, explain the two houses as the two families, of Shammai and Hillel, from which originated the Scribes and Pharisees.'[63]

Probably the most celebrated passage where Jerome uses the word 'Pharisee' to refer to rabbis of his own day is at *Ep.* 112, 13, where he speaks of the Minim, equating them with the Nazoraeans:

> 'What should I say of the Ebionites, who pretend to be Christians? Even today in all the synagogues of the East, there is a Jewish sect which is called "of the Minaei", and which is still condemned by the Pharisees, who commonly call them Nazoraeans. They believe in Christ as Son of God, born of the Virgin Mary, and they say that it was he who suffered under Pontius Pilate and rose again, in whom we too believe. But while they wish to be both Jews and Christians, they are really neither Jews nor Christians.'[64]

---

[62] *CCL* 73, 121: Ceterum Nazaraei locum istum ita disserunt: Cum dixerint ad uos scribae et pharisaei, ut eos audiatis, qui omnia uentris causa faciunt; et in morem magorum stridunt in incantationibus suis, ut uos decipiant, hoc eis respondere debetis.
[63] *CCL* 73,116: Duas domus Nazaraei, qui ita Christum recipiunt, ut obseruationes legis ueteris non omittant, duas familias interpretantur, Sammai et Hellel, ex quibus orti sunt scribae et pharisaei...
[64] *CSEL* 55, 381-2: Quid dicam de Hebionitis, qui Christianos esse se simu-

We have seen that Jerome uses the word 'Pharisee' to refer to the Jewish sect of the first century who opposed Jesus, and also of rabbis of his own day. One other curious usage we find occasionally in Jerome's writings is the application of this word to contemporary Christians. The contexts in which this use is found are always polemical. In one of his earlier hagiographic writings, the *Vita S.Hilarionis*, composed in 390 A.D., for instance, Jerome denigrates those (Christian) people who complained when Jerome wrote a life of Paul the first hermit, emphasising his fasting, saying that the same people will doubtless complain about this *Vita* because Hilarion lived in the world. Jerome says that these detractors are just like the Pharisees of old:

> 'It is just what their ancestors the Pharisees did of old! They were not pleased with John fasting in the desert (Matt. 11:18) nor with our Lord and Saviour in the busy crowd, eating and drinking.'[65]

Again in a polemical context, in *Ep.* 127, 9, Jerome recalls the days of the Origenist Controversy, when he engaged in verbal warfare with his erstwhile friend Rufinus, over Origen's works. Rufinus had translated Origen's *De Principiis* and before Jerome himself could respond to this from Bethlehem, Jerome's supporters in Rome engaged in argument with the 'Pharisees', the supporters of Rufinus, who may well have been members of the Roman clergy:

> 'Next came the scandalous version of Origen's book, *On First Principles*, and that 'fortunate' disciple [i.e. ὄλβιος, Macarius, to whom Rufinus dedicated the translation] who would have been fortunate indeed if he had never fallen in with such a master. Next followed the refutation set out by my supporters "through fire", which threw the Pharisees into confusion.'[66]

Jerome's only interest in the Pharisees is to reaffirm the picture painted of them in the N.T. and to use the negative characteristics of that picture – their greed, pride and opposition to Jesus – to polemicise against

---

lant? usque hodie per totas orientis synagogas inter Iudaeos heresis est, quae dicitur Minaeorum et a pharisaeis huc usque damnatur, quos uulgo Nazaraeos nuncupant, qui credunt in Christum, filium dei natum de Maria virgine, et eum dicunt esse, qui sub Pontio Pilato et passus est et resurrexit, in quem et nos credimus, sed, dum volunt et Iudaei esse et Christiani, nec Iudaei sunt nec Christiani.

65 *Vita S.Hilarionis* 1 (*PL* 23, 30): Fecerunt hoc est majores eorum quondam Pharisaei, quibus nec Joannis eremus ac jejunium, nec Domini Salvatoris turbae, cibi, potusque placuerunt.

66 *CSEL* 56, 152: Tunc librorum Περὶ Ἀρχῶν infamis interpretatio, tunc discipulus ὄλβιος uere nominis sui, si in talem magistrum non inpegisset, tunc nostrorum δίαπυρος contradictio et pharisaeorum turbata schola.

Jewish leaders of his own day, as well as contemporary Christians to whom Jerome is opposed.

Jerome mentions the sect of the Sadducees a few times in his writings. Most Church Fathers thought of them as a αἵρεσις, giving to this word the sense of 'sect' i.e. a group set apart from the community.[67] A few Fathers, however, went beyond this general statement, saying that the Sadducees were true Jews. Origen, in a Greek fragment of his *Homilies on Luke*,[68] says τοῖς ἐκ τῶν Ἰουδαίων Σαδδουκαίοις, and Jerome, in his translation of this homily, has 'Sadducees, who were a part of the Jewish nation *(portio Iudaeorum)*'.[69]

Jerome's knowledge of the Sadducees, like that of all the other Church Fathers who mention them, is based on information given in Josephus and the N.T. Acts 23:8 says that they reject the doctrine of the resurrection of the body, as well as the existence of angels and spirits. With regard to their rejection of the doctrine of the resurrection, Josephus writes: 'The doctrine of the Sadducees is that souls perish with the body'.[70] Jerome also records this information in *Comm.Matt.* 22, 31f:

> 'We have seen above that the Sadducees do not believe in angels or spirits, or in the resurrection of the body, and preach that souls also die.'[71]

Jerome follows several other Church Fathers in recording the tradition that the Sadducees used only the Pentateuch and rejected the Prophets and Writings.[72] Jerome once confuses the Sadducees with the Samaritans, probably basing his information from the mistaken attestation of Epiphanius or Pseudo-Tertullian. Jerome says that the father of the Sadducees was Dositheus the Samaritan.[73]

---

[67] This sense is found, for instance, in Justin's *Dialogue*, 80, 4.
[68] *Hom.Luc.* 39, 3-4 (*GCS* 49, 218-9).
[69] *SC* 87, 452 & 454.
[70] *Antiq.* XVIII, 1, 4.
[71] *CCL* 77, 206f: Supra diximus Sadducaeos nec angelum nec spiritum nec resurrectionem corporum confitentes animarum quoque interitum praedicasse.
[72] Jerome: *Comm.Matt.* 22, 31f (*CCL* 77, 206); see Origen: *Comm.Matt.* XVII, 35 & 36; *C.Cels.* I, 49 (*SC* 132, 210); Greg. of Naz.: *Carminum Liber* II, 1, 1162-3 (*PG* 37, 1108f).
[73] Jerome: *Dial.c.Lucif.* 23 (*PL* 23, 187); Epiph.: *Haer.* 14, 2-3 (*GCS* 25, 207); Ps.-Tert.: *Adv. Omnes Haer.* I, 1 (*CCL* 2, 1401).

Jewish leaders and institutions

Jerome records the names of several rabbis who lived a century or more before him. In *Comm.Eccles.* 4, 13-16, he says:

> 'When my Hebrew friend, to whom I refer often, was reading Ecclesiastes with me, he said that Barakiba, whom they admire more than anyone, had transmitted this concerning the present passage.'[74]

Jerome mentions the same rabbi again in *Comm.Isa.* 8, 14,[75] where he gives a list of the most important rabbis of the first two Christian centuries. As well as Akiba, this list includes Shammai and Hillel, Johanan [ben Zakkai], Meir, Eliezer and Joseph of Galilee.

There is no doubt that the '*Baracchibas*' whom Jerome mentions here is none other than the famous second century *Tanna*, R. Akiba ben Joseph.[76] He refers more than once more to R. Akiba in *Ep.* 121, 10, where he says:

> '[The Jews say] "Barakiba and Simeon [ben Gamaliel] and Hellel [sic], our masters, have handed down to us that we may walk two miles on the Sabbath," and other similar things, preferring the teachings of men to God's teaching.'[77]

In 1861, M. Rahmer published a work on the Hebrew traditions in the work of Jerome,[78] in which he attempted to argue that one of the men who taught Jerome Hebrew, whom Jerome calls 'Baranina', could be identified with R. Hama bar Hanina, but S. Krauss[79] saw that this identification could not be made, as this rabbi was a third century Palestinian *Amora* and could hardly have taught Jerome in the fourth century!

Jerome refers only once to the Patriarch, the political and religious leader of the Jewish people. This office was, in some ways, a survival of the monarchy, adapted to the current circumstances of Roman rule and rabbinic Judaism. R. Gamaliel, the successor of R. Johanan ben Zakkai

---

[74] *CCL* 72, 288: Hebraeus meus, cuius saepe facio mentionem, cum Ecclesiasten mecum legeret, haec Baracchibam, quem unum uel maxime admirantur, super praesenti loco tradidisse testatus est.

[75] *CCL* 73, 116.

[76] Epiphanius also mentions R. Akiba in *Haer.* 15 and 33.

[77] *CSEL* 56, 49: Barachibas et Symeon et Helles, magistri nostri, tradiderunt nobis, et duo milia pedes ambulemus in sabbato et cetera istius modi, doctrinas hominum praeferentes doctrinae dei.

[78] *Die hebraischen Traditionen bei den Werken des Hieronymus. Erster Theil: 'Quaestiones in Genesin'*, Breslau 1861.

[79] Article 'Church Fathers' in *Jewish Encyclopaedia*, Vol. 4, p. 81.

at the school of Jamnia, took the title of Nasi, and he may be considered the first Patriarch.[80] His descendants held this title for a further two generations until the extinction of the line. Origen reports that there were those who claimed that a descendant of Judah still ruled the people as Ethnarch, and that his descendants should not fail until the coming of the Messiah.[81]. In Greek sources, Nasi was translated either as ethnarchēs or patriarchēs.[82] Ethnarch was the older, Hellenistic title, and, from the fourth century in Greek and Latin, Patriarch is the usual translation of Nasi.[83]

Jerome's only mention of the Jewish Patriarch is seen at *Ep.* 57, 3, to Pammachius, written in defence of his method of translating, in 395 A.D. Jerome writes:

> 'Some time ago, a man of consular grade called Hesychius, against whom the Patriarch Gamaliel engaged in terrible hostilities, was condemned to death by the emperor Theodosius for having corrupted a secretary and violated the private papers of this [Jew].'[84]

If Jerome's phrase, *dudum*, is accurate, the Patriarch referred to is Gamaliel V, son of Hillel II, who lived in the second half of the fourth century. Very little is known about him, but he must have been a person of considerable political power and authority if a Roman of consular grade was executed for having stolen or read his private papers.

Jerome also makes several comments about the Jewish leaders, almost all of which are derogatory and set in polemical contexts. At several places, Jerome points out the greed and avarice of the Jewish leaders,[85] and elsewhere he says disparagingly that they do not practise the restraints of bodily pleasures. In Jerome's opinion, these leaders who love their food so much would not be able to fast twice a week, on Monday and Thursday, as they ought.[86] Here, we must judge these comments in the light of Jerome's theology of asceticism.[87] For Jerome, the

---

80 So de Lange: *op.cit.*, p. 33. I am indebted for this paragraph to de Lange.
81 *De Princ.* IV, 1, 3.
82 See Epiphanius: *Haer.* 30, 4, 6, 7; *Cod.Theod.* 16.8.1, 2, 8 where the Hillelite *Nasi* is recognised by the Roman government as political head of the people. Cf *Encyclopaedia Judaica*, art. 'Nasi', Vol. 12, p. 835.
83 de Lange: *op.cit.*, p. 34.
84 *CSEL* 54, 506: Dudum Hesychium, uirum consularem, contra quem patriarcha Gamalihel grauissimas exercuit inimicitias, Theodosius princeps capite damnauit, quod sollicitato notario chartas illius inuasisset.
85 E.g. *Comm.Ezek.* 4, 13-15 (*CCL* 75, 52); *Comm.Osee* 2, 19f (*CCL* 76, 30).
86 *Comm.Isa.* 58, 3 (*CCL* 73A, 661).
87 On this, see D. Dumm: *The Theological Basis of Virginity according to St. Jerome*, Latrobe, Pa., 1961.

subjugation of the desires of the body was of paramount importance in the authentic religious life. In the case of the Jewish leaders, Jerome castigates them because they do not measure up to his own high standards of asceticism.

Several other sayings of Jerome indicate that he had attended synagogue services, for he comments more than once on the style of preaching at these services. In *Comm.Ezek.* 34, 31, he says:

> 'The preachers persuade the people that what they invent is true, and when, in theatrical fashion, they have invited applause... they frown and make weighed and balanced addresses, and usurp the authority of the rulers.'[88]

Jerome knows that the synagogue is the centre of Jewish worship and life. Services are held there, he says, by day and night.[89] The Jews do not kneel to pray, as do Christians.[90] According to Jerome, the most solemn part of the service was the chanting of the Psalms, and especially Ps. 117.[91] Important too was the sermon in the context of Jewish worship. It was apparently a very popular section of the liturgy, for Jerome says:

> 'The Jews rush on certain days into the synagogue and study God's law in order to find out what Abraham, Isaac, Jacob and the rest of the holy men may have done.'[92]

Whether the fact that the Jews went on certain days to hear the sermon implies that some preachers were more popular than others is not clear.

Social position of the Jews

Jerome makes comments occasionally which shed light upon the social and political position of the Jewish people. Krauss has noted many of these references, but several of his judgments are incorrect because he failed to study Jerome's statements in their proper context.[93] We may, therefore, re-study some of the evidence briefly with profit.

One example of Krauss' failure to make Jerome's purpose in writing

---

88 (*CCL*, 75, 488): Qui cum populo persuaserint uera esse quae fingunt, et in theatralem modum plausus concitauerint, et clamores immemores fiunt imperitiae suae, et, adducto supercilio libratisque sermonibus atque trutinatis, magistrorum sibi assumunt auctoritatem.
89 *Comm.Hier.* 18, 17 (*CCL* 74, 180).
90 *Comm.Isa.* 46, 2 (*CCL* 73A, 516).
91 *Comm.Amos* 5, 23 (*CCL* 76, 295); *Ep.* 20, 4 (*CSEL* 54, 107).
92 *Comm.Isa.* 58, 2 (*CCL* 73A, 660).
93 Krauss: *art.cit.*, pp. 225-9.

and the context of the passage into account is at *Comm.Soph.* 1, 15ff,[94] where Jerome relates the Jewish pilgrimage to Jerusalem on the 9th.Ab. According to Jerome, the Jews were only allowed to gather once a year at the only remaining part of the Temple, the Western Wall. Here they could loudly lament the loss of their sanctuary on the anniversary of its destruction. Jerome says that considerable bribery was necessary by the Jews in order to extend their visit for a few days. Elsewhere,[95] Jerome says that on this day the Jews wore the dress of mourners, walked barefoot, rolled in the dust, and even prepared the bowl of lentils usually reserved for those who are bereaved by a death.

Krauss noted Jerome's satisfaction at this pathetic account,[96] but did not apparently realise that Jerome's account deliberately exaggerated the disadvantages of the Jews because of his own anti-Jewish feelings. Jerome's over-riding concern was to show that the Jews, because of their rejection of Christ, had lost their Temple and had been expelled from their holy city. If, however, Jerome's account is compared with rabbinic material, a conflicting picture is seen. From the third century onwards, more and more frequent visits to Jerusalem by Jews are mentioned.[97] It would appear that Jerome's respect for the facts of the situation has been deliberately distorted by his concern to show that, since the advent of Christ, Judaism has become defunct.

From Jerome's works, we learn that, although no legislation existed forbidding Jewish settlement in large cities, they tended, of their own volition, to stay away from large centres of population, lest their habitation there might incite civil disturbance.[98] For the same reason, they stayed away from crowded markets, some of which were associated with terrible disasters of the last' Jewish rebellion against the Romans. At Abraham's terebinth tree, for example, an annual fair and market was held. But a story told of how thousands of Jewish prisoners of war had been sold as slaves after the Hadrianic revolt at this place, and it was hardly surprising that the Jews did not attend this fair.[99]

In 404 A.D., Honorius issued an edict which excluded both Jews and Samaritans from military and court rank. This law seems still to have

---

[94] *CCL* 76A, 673f.
[95] *Ep.* 39, 4 (*CSEL* 54, 302f).
[96] Krauss: *art.cit.*, p. 227.
[97] See the evidence amassed in M. Avi-Yonah: *Geschichte des Juden im Zeitalter Rom und Byzantium*, Berlin 1962, pp. 47f.
[98] *Comm.Gal.* 4, 22 (*PL* 26, 415).
[99] *Comm.Hier.* 31, 14; *Comm.Zach.* 11, 15 (*CCL* 74, 304; 76A, 859f); Krauss: *art.cit.*, p. 226.

been in operation when Jerome wrote the *Comm.Isa.* (408-410 A.D.), for he mentions that Jews could not bear arms or become soldiers in his day.[100]

'Jewish Christianity'

The study of 'Jewish Christianity' is one of the most difficult and complex areas of research which is presented by the early centuries of the Church. The difficulty and complexity are caused because of a lack of sound patristic evidence, and this, in turn, has led to a proliferation of scholarly literature and hypotheses concerning the composition, distribution and theology of 'Jewish Christianity' with few generally accepted results.[101] The term 'Jewish Christianity' is here enclosed in quotation marks because there is doubt about whether this term can be used to refer to what is known of the several groups whose tenets were associated with Judaism, but who also claimed allegiance to Christianity.[102] This is not the place for an in-depth discussion of the general problems of the study of 'Jewish Christianity', interesting and worthwhile though that would be. What we intend to do here is to set out the information which Jerome gives about various 'Jewish Christian' groups, especially his evidence regarding 'Jewish Christian' gospels, and then to give a summary of the conclusions to which scholars have come with regard to this evidence.[103]

---

100 *Comm.Isa.* 3, 3 (*CCL* 73, 45). See J.E. Seaver: *op.cit.*, p. 58.
101 See the literature cited in F. Manns: *Bibliographie du Judéo-Christianisme* (Studium Biblicum Franciscanum Analecta 13) Jerusalem, 1979.
102 See, among others, R.A. Kraft: 'In search of "Jewish Christianity" and its "theology". Problems of Definition and Theology', in *Judéo-Christianisme: Volume offert au Cardinal Jean Daniélou*, Paris 1972, 81-92; J. Munck: 'Jewish Christianity in Post-Apostolic Times'; *NTS* VI (1959-60), 103-116: p. 103: 'The words "Jewish Christian" and "Jewish Christianity" are used in several different senses within the field of New Testament research. Some scholars – no doubt oneself included on occasion – use them with varying significance in the same article or book, so that the reader is either led astray, or discovers that the words do not have the same meaning every time they occur.'
103 For Jerome and 'Jewish Christianity', see the following works: A. Schmidtke: *Neue Fragmente und Untersuchungen zu den judenchristlichen Evangelien* (TU 37, 1), 1911; *Idem*: 'Zum Hebräerevangelium', in *ZNTW* 35 (1936) 24-44; H. Waitz: 'Neue Untersuchungen über die sogenannten judenchristlichen Evangelien', in *ZNTW* 36 (1937) 60-81; G. Bardy: 'Saint Jérôme et l'évangile selon les Hébreux', in *Mélanges de Sciences Religieuses* III (1946) 5-36; A.F.J. Klijn: 'Jerome's Quotations from a Nazorean Interpretation of Isaiah', in *RSR* 60 (1972) 241-255; P. Vielhauer: 'Jewish Christian Gospels', in *New Testament Apocrypha* 1, edd. E. Hennecke, W. Schneemelcher, R. Mcl. Wilson, London 1963, 117-165.

Jerome's works contains the most numerous references to 'Jewish Christian' groups of any of the early Fathers. He refers to, or makes citations from, 'Jewish Christian' gospels at least nineteen times. These will be set out below in chronological order:

1. *Ep.* 20,5[104]   'Finally, Matthew, who composed the Gospel in the Hebrew language, put it in the following way: "Osianna barrama", which means: "Osanna in excelsis"...'

2. *Comm.Eph.* 5, 4[105]   '...as we also read in the Hebrew Gospel that the Lord said to the disciples: "And never rejoice", he said, "except when you look at your brother in love".'

3. *Comm.Mich.* 7, 6[106]   'He who... believes in the Gospel according to the Hebrews which I have recently translated.'

4. *De Vir.Illus.* 2[107]   '...the Acts of the Apostles mention this often, as also does the Gospel which is called according to the Hebrews and which I have translated into Greek and Latin recently, of which Origen also often makes use...'

5. *De Vir.Illus.* 3[108]   'Matthew... in Judaea was the first to compose the gospel of Christ in Hebrew letters and words for the sake of those of the circumcision who believed. But who translated into Greek later is not certain. The Hebrew text itself has been preserved until today in the library at Caesarea which Pamphilus the martyr collected with great care. The Nazoraeans in Beroea, a city in Syria, who use this book, also permitted me to copy it. In it, it is to be noted that wherever the evangelist quotes from the

---

104 *CSEL* 54, 110: Denique Matheus qui euangelium Hebraeo sermone conscripsit, ita posuit: 'osianna barrama', id est 'osanna in excelsis'...
105 *PL* 26, 552C: ...ut in Hebraico quoque Evangelio legimus, Dominum ad discipulos loquentem: 'Et nunquam', inquit, 'laeti sitis, nisi cum fratrem vestrum videritis in charitate'.
106 *CCL* 76, 513: ...credideritque euangelio, quod secundum Hebraeos editum nuper transtulimus...
107 ...et apostolorum crebrius super hoc Acta testantur. Evangelium quoque quod appellatur secundum Hebraeos, et a me nuper in Graecum Latinumque sermonem translatum est, quo et Origenes saepe utitur... (*PL* 23, 642).

6.	*De Vir.Illus.* 16[109]	O.T. – whether this is done by himself or by our Lord and Saviour – he follows not the authority of the Septuagint translation, but the Hebrew original.'
'(Ignatius) bore witness to the gospel which I have recently translated, in respect of the person of Christ...'
7.	*Tract. in Ps.* 135[110]	'In the Hebrew Gospel according to Matthew, it is like this: "Give us to-day our bread for tomorrow", which means, the bread which you will give us in your kingdom, give us today.'
8.	*Comm.Matt.* 2, 5[111]	'"And they said to him: 'In Bethlehem of Juda'." Here there is an error by the copyists, for we think that the evangelist wrote in his first edition, as we read in the original Hebrew: "Juda", and not "Judea".'
9.	*Comm.Matt.* 6, 11[112]	'In the Gospel called according to the Hebrews, I found MAAR in place of the bread which is necessary to support life, which means "for tomorrow", i.e. give us our bread for tomorrow, i.e. for the future, today.'
10.	*Comm.Matt.* 12, 13[113]	'In the gospel which the Nazoraeans and Ebionites use, which we translated recently

---

108 Mattheus... primus in Judaea propter eos qui ex circumcisione crediderant, Evangelium Christi Hebraicis litteris verbisque conposuit: quod quis postea in Graecum transtulerit, non satis certum est. Porro ipsum Hebraicum habetur usque hodie in Caesariensi bibliotheca, quam Pamphilus martyr studiosissime confecit. Mihi quoque a Nazareis, qui in Beroea, urbe Syriae hoc volumine utuntur, describendi facultas fuit. In quo animadvertendum quod ubicunque evangelista, sive ex persona sua, sive ex persona Domini Salvatoris, veteris Scripturae testimoniis abutitur, non sequatur Septuaginta Translatorum auctoritatem, sed Hebraicam (*PL* 23, 643-6).

109 ...in qua et de Evangelio, quod nupe a me translatum est, super persona Christi ponit testimonium...' (*PL* 23, 666).

110 (*Anec. Maredsolana* III, 2, p. 262): In Hebraico euangelio secundum Matthaeum ita habet: Panem nostrum crastinum da nobis hodie, hoc est, panem quem daturus es nobis in regno tuo, da nobis hodie.

111 *CCL* 77, 13: At illi dixerunt ei: in Bethleem Iudeae. Librariorum error est; putamus enim ab euangelista primum editum sicut in ipso Hebraico legimus: 'Iudae', non 'Iudeae'.

112 *CCL* 77, 37: In euangelio quod appellatur secundum Hebraeos pro supersubstantiali pane maar repperi, quod dicitur crastinum, ut sit sensus: 'Panem nostrum crastinum', id est futurum, 'da nobis hodie'.

		from Hebrew into Greek, and which is called the authentic text of Matthew by many people, it is written that the man with the withered hand is a mason, praying for help with words like this: "I was a mason earning my living with my hands. I pray you, Jesus, to restore my health lest I must beg shamefully for my food".'
11.	*Comm.Matt.* 23, 35[114]	'In the gospel which the Nazoraeans use, we find that there "son of Ioiada" is written instead of "son of Barachia".'
12.	*Comm.Matt.* 27, 16[115]	'The name of this man (Barabbas) is interpreted in the gospel according to the Hebrews as "son of their master". He was condemned for rebellion and murder.'
13.	*Comm.Matt.* 27, 51[116]	'In the gospel which we have mentioned often already, we read that the upper lintel of the Temple, which was an enormous size, was broken and split.'
14.	*Ep.* 120, 8[117]	'But in the gospel which is written in Hebrew letters we read that not the curtain of the Temple but the upper lintel of the Temple, which was of marvellous size, fell down.'
15.	*Comm.Isa.* 40, 9-11[118]	'But in the gospel written according to the Hebrews, which is read by the Nazoraeans, the Lord says: "A moment ago my mother, the Holy Spirit, took me up." Nobody, however,

---

[113] *CCL* 77, 90: In euangelio quo utuntur Nazareni et Hebionitae quod nuper in graecum de hebraeo sermone transtulimus et quod uocatur a plerisque Mathei authenticum, homo iste qui aridam habet manum caementarius scribitur, istiusmodi uocibus auxilium precans: 'Caementarius eram manibus uictum quaeritans, precor te Iesu ut mihi restituas sanitatem ne turpiter mendicem cibos'.

[114] *CCL* 77, 220: In euangelio quo utuntur Nazareni pro filio Barachiae filium Ioiadae scriptum reperimus.

[115] *CCL* 77, 265: Iste in euangelio quod scribitur iuxta Hebraeos filius magistri eorum interpretatur qui propter seditionem ed homicidium fuerat condemnatus.

[116] *CCL* 77, 275: In euangelio cuius saepe facimus mentionem superliminare templi infinitae magnitudinis fractum esse atque diuisum legimus.

[117] *CSEL* 55, 490: In euangelio autem quod Hebraicis litteris scriptum est, legimus non uelum templi scissum, sed superliminare templi mirae magnitudinis conruisse.

		should be scandalised by this, that the spirit is used in the feminine gender with the Hebrews, while in our language it is put in the masculine gender and in Greek it is neuter.'
16.	*Comm.Isa.* 65, prol.[119]	'Since the apostles believed he was a spirit, or, according to the Gospel which is of the Hebrews, which is read by the Nazoraeans, a demon without a body, he said to them...'
17.	*Comm.Ezek.* 16, 13[120]	'Also in the Gospel of the Hebrews, which is read by the Nazoraeans, the Saviour is introduced saying, "A moment ago, my mother, the Holy Spirit, took me up..."'
18.	*Comm.Ezek.* 18, 5-9[121]	'...and in the Gospel according to the Hebrews, which the Nazoraeans are accustomed to read, among the worst crimes is included: he who has distressed the spirit of his brother.'
19.	*Adv.Pelag.* III, 2[122]	'From the Gospel according to the Hebrews. In the Gospel according to the Hebrews which was written in the Chaldaean and Syriac language but with Hebrew letters, and which is used until today by the Nazoraeans, I mean that according to the apostles, or, as many hold, according to Matthew, which Gospel is also available in the library of Caesarea, the story... goes'

---

[118] *CCL* 73, 459: Sed et in euangelio quod iuxta Hebraeos scriptum Nazaraei lectitant, Dominus loquitur: 'Modo me tulit mater mea, Spiritus Sanctus.' Nemo autem in hac parte scandalizari debet, quod dicatur apud Hebraeos spiritus genere feminino, cum nostra lingua appelletur genere masculino, et Graeco sermone neutro.

[119] *CCL* 73A, 741: Cum enim apostoli eum putarent spiritum, uel iuxta euangelium, quod Hebraeorum lectitant Nazaraei, incorporale daemonium, dixit eis...

[120] *CCL* 75, 178: ...in euangelio quoque quod Hebraeorum lectitant Nazaraei, Saluator inducitur loquens: 'Modo me arripuit mater mea, Spiritus Sanctus...'

[121] *CCL* 75, 237: ...et in euangelio quod iuxta Hebraeos Nazaraei legere consuerunt, inter maxima ponitur crimina: qui fratris sui spiritum contristauerit.

[122] *PL* 23, 597: 'Ex Evangelio juxta Hebraeos'. – In Evangelio 'juxta Hebraeos', quod Chaldaico quidem Syroque sermone, sed Hebraicis litteris scriptum est, quo utuntur usque hodie Nazareni, 'secundum Apostolos', sive, ut plerique autumant, 'juxta Matthaeum', quod et in Caesariensi habetur bibliotheca, narrat historia...

The first problem with this evidence is to decide how many 'Jewish Christian' gospels Jerome claims to know. In this connection, we must note two points. First, Jerome uses various names to refer to the 'Jewish Christian' gospel or gospels. He calls it the 'gospel according to the Hebrews' seven times,[123] the 'gospel of the Hebrews' twice,[124] the 'Hebrew gospel' three times,[125] and the 'gospel written in Hebrew letters' four times.[126] He also refers twice to the gospel which he has recently translated from Hebrew,[127] which is the original text of Matthew, and to the 'gospel which the Nazoraeans use'.[128] The reference to the 'gospel which we have already often mentioned'[129] is, from the context of the commentary, clearly to the 'gospel according to the Hebrews'.

Second, it is quite clear that, in all these references, Jerome has in mind only one 'Jewish Christian' gospel. Number three above shows that all the 'Jewish Christian' gospels which Jerome claims to have translated are identical (in his mind) with the 'gospel according to the Hebrews'. Similarly, number eighteen above shows that this 'gospel of/according to the Hebrews' is identical with the 'gospel written in Hebrew letters', and the 'gospel which is used by the Nazoraeans'. Jerome's stylistic variations do not detract from the fact that he thinks of only one 'Jewish Christian' gospel, the gospel according to the Hebrews, which he equates with the original Hebrew version of the (canonical) gospel according to Matthew.

The next question we must ask concerns the source of Jerome's knowledge of 'Jewish Christianity' in general, and of the 'Jewish Christian' gospel in particular. If we study the context of the many references Jerome gives to 'Jewish Christian' sects and to the 'Jewish Christian' gospel, we can gain valuable clues concerning his sources. We shall discuss the two sects about whom Jerome says most, the Ebionites and the Nazoraeans.

When discussing the Ebionites, Jerome talks only in the most general and almost vague terms. Typical are the following two passages, where the Ebionites are mentioned in connection with other heretics:

'It is superfluous to go into details to sum up Marcion, Valentinus, Apelles, Ebion, Montanus and Mani with their dogmas:

---

[123] Nos. 3, 4, 9, 12, 15, 18, 19.
[124] Nos. 16, 17.
[125] Nos. 2, 7.
[126] Nos. 1, 5, 8, 14.
[127] Nos. 6, 10.
[128] No. 11; cf 5, 10, 15, 16, 17, 19.
[129] No. 13.

because it is very easy for anyone to know into which errors each of them is led astray.'[130]

'I come to those heretics who tear up the gospels, a certain Saturninus, the Ophites, the Cainites, the Sethians, Carpocrates, Cerinthus and his successor Ebion and the other pests, most of whom broke out while the apostle John was still alive, and yet we do not read that any of these men were re-baptised.'[131]

This latter excerpt is interesting, for, as A.F.J. Klijn has recently pointed out,[132] we may see here the influence of Ps.-Tertullian when Jerome states that Ebion was the successor of Cerinthus.[133] This is not attested elsewhere in Patristic literature before Jerome. In *Ep.* 112, Jerome states in a general way, that Ebion, along with Cerinthus, is a typical example of a Christian who has confused the ceremonies of Judaism and Christianity, although Jerome says in the same passage that he is neither Jew nor Christian because he tries to be both.[134] According to Jerome, Ebion was a contemporary of the apostle John, who wrote against his view that Jesus did not exist before Mary.[135]

The Ebionites showed anti-Pauline characteristics, according to Jerome's testimony.[136] Jerome says that two men who had made translations of the O.T., Symmachus and Theodotion, were believed to have been Ebionites.[137] Jerome once makes the confusing statement that Ebion made his own translation of (at least part of) the O.T.,[138] but he may have been thinking of Symmachus.[139] Klijn points to one passage which he believes proves definitely that Jerome had no personal knowledge of the Ebionites, and indeed, that he knew of only one 'Jewish Christian' group.[140] We have referred to part of the passage above. After Jerome has said that Ebion has confused the Law and the Gospel,

---

130 *Comm.Titum* 3, 10f (*PL* 26, 633A): Superfluum est ire per singula, et Marcionem, Valentinum, Apellem, Ebionem, Montanum, et Manichaeum cum suis enumerare dogmatibus: cum perfacile sit unicuique cognoscere quibus singuli ducantur erroribus.
131 *Adv.Lucif.* 23 (*PL* 23, 187A-B); Klijn & Reinink: *op.cit.*, p. 202.
132 Klijn & Reinink: *op.cit.*, p. 39.
133 Ps.-Tert.: *Adv.Omn.Haer.* 3 (*CSEL* 47, 219), written in the first half of the third century.
134 *Ep.* 112, 13 (*CSEL* 55, 381-2).
135 *De Vir.Illus.* 9 (*PL* 23, 654).
136 *Comm.Matt.* 12, 2 (*CCL* 77, 87).
137 *Comm.Hab.* 3, 10-13 (*CCL* 76A, 641); *De Vir.Illus.* 54 (*PL* 23, 702).
138 *Comm.Gal.* 3, 13f (*PL* 26, 387B).
139 Klijn & Reinink: *op.cit.*, p. 40.
140 *Ibid.*

Judaism and Christianity, he goes on to say:
> 'What shall I say of the Ebionites who claim to be Christians? Until today a heresy is to be found in all parts of the East where Jews have their synagogues; it is called "of the Minaeans"... These are usually called Nazoraeans.'[141]

We are justified in saying, therefore, that, because he makes only general statements, and because he equates the Ebionites with the Nazoraeans, Jerome had no first hand knowledge of the Ebionites, and was dependent on secondary sources, none of which (with the exception of Ps.-Tertullian) can now be identified.

Most of our knowledge of the sect of the Nazoraeans comes from Epiphanius and Jerome. Epiphanius was, in fact, the first author to mention this sect. But he appears to have known little about them, except that they lived in Beroea, came from the Jewish race, spoke Hebrew or Aramaic, and lived according to the Jewish Law while accepting some orthodox views about Jesus.[142]

From Jerome, we get the impression that he not only knows more about the Nazoraeans, but has been in personal contact with them. In *De Vir.Illus.* 3, he says:
> 'The Hebrew itself (of the Hebrew Gospel) has been preserved until today in the library at Caesarea which Pamphilus the martyr collected so diligently. From the Nazoraeans, who use this book in Beroea, a Syrian city, I also had the opportunity of copying it.'[143]

But we must be suspicious that Jerome actually did have personal contact with the Nazoraeans at Beroea, and that he copied the gospel there. This is because at the various times and places where Jerome mentions this Nazoraean sect, he offers contradictory evidence. Also, the comments he does make are general in character, and give little solid information.

In A.D. 398, Jerome wrote that the Nazoraeans believe that 'Jesus is the son of a carpenter',[144] implying thereby that they deny the Virgin Birth. But in A.D. 404, he wrote that they do believe in the Virgin Birth, Christ's passion under Pontius Pilate, and his resurrection.[145] In the

---

[141] *Ep.* 112, 13 (*CSEL* 55, 382).
[142] Epiph.: *Haer.* 29, 1, 1; 29, 7, 4; 29, 7, 6; 29, 9, 4.
[143] *PL* 23, 643: Porro ipsum Hebraicum habetur usque hodie in Caesariensi bibliotheca, quam Pamphilus martyr studiosissime confecit. Mihi quoque a Nazareis, qui in Beroea urbe Syriae hoc volumine utuntur, describendi facultas fuit. Written in A.D. 392.
[144] *Comm.Matt.* 13, 53f (*CCL* 77, 115).
[145] *Ep.* 112, 13 (*CSEL* 55, 381).

same passage from the *Comm.Matt.* referred to above, Jerome states that he is uncertain whether the Hebrew gospel is identical with the gospel according to Matthew. Earlier, as we have seen, in A.D. 392, he claimed to have copied this Hebrew gospel, but it is very strange that he could not remember the contents of the Hebrew gospel he had translated. It cannot be argued that he did not know much Hebrew at this time, because, as we saw in a previous chapter, Jerome had a good knowledge of Hebrew by this time.[146] Another contradiction occurs in A.D. 415, when Jerome says that the Hebrew gospel had been written in Chaldaean (i.e. Aramaic) and Syriac.[147] But in the passage from the *De Vir.Illus.* 3 which we have already seen he says that this gospel was written in Hebrew.

It must be concluded from these contradictions that Jerome's knowledge of the sect of the Nazoraeans and their beliefs was small. If in fact Jerome did translate the Hebrew gospel which the Nazoraeans used, he can only have translated a very few verses. Jerome's comment that this Hebrew gospel was to be found in the library at Caesarea would seem to be substantiated by the *Theophania Syriaca* IV, 12 of Eusebius.[148] However, as Klijn notes, there is no certainty that this is the same as the Gospel of the Nazoraeans.[149] Bardy's question must be answered in the negative: 'On peut se demander si Saint Jérôme a réellement connu les Nazaréens.'[150]

Jewish exegetical terminology

It is clear that Jerome was familiar with several technical phrases of Jewish exegesis. In *Ep.* 121, he writes of the Jews:

'Their teachers are called *sophoi*, that is, "sages", and whenever they expound their traditions, they have the custom of telling their disciples, οἵ σοφοί δευτερῶσιν, that is, "the sages teach these traditions".'[151]

The Greek phrase used here is a literal rendering of the Hebrew שנו חכמים and its Aramaic equivalent תנו רבנן. Again, earlier in *Ep.* 121, Jerome

---

146 See Chapter 3.
147 *Adv.Pelag.* III, 2 (*CCL* 80, 99).
148 *GCS* Eus. Werke III, 183.
149 Klijn & Reinink: *op.cit.*, p. 49; cf Schmidtke: *Neue Fragmente...* p. 66; Bardy: *art.cit.*, p. 35.
150 Bardy: *art.cit.*, p. 31.
151 *Ep.* 121, 10 (*CSEL* 56, 49).

says that the Jews call their tradition δευτέρωσις, which is an exact translation of the Hebrew term משנה, coming from a root (שנה), meaning 'repetition' in biblical Hebrew. In later linguistic usage, however, the term became synonymous with 'to teach or learn the oral law'.[152] In *Comm.Matt.* 22, 23, Jerome uses this term to refer to the ritual part of the Mosaic Law, in contradistinction to the true νόμος of moral Law. This δευτέρωσις was imposed on the Jews after they had worshipped the Golden Calf. In post-biblical Hebrew and Aramaic, the usage of this term was extended to include the teachers of this tradition, (δευτερωταί).[153] Indeed, this Greek word translates the Aramaic תנא, the title given in the Talmud to rabbis of the first two centuries of the Christian area.

Jerome was not the first Christian author to allude to the exegetical terminology of the Jews. Origen used the term σοφοί as a technical term.[154] The term δευτέρωσις is found once in Rufinus' translation of the prologue to Origen's *Commentary on the Song of Songs*. Dr. de Lange thinks it probable that Rufinus is here reproducing Origen's own word, and that this would, if correct, constitute the earliest example of its use by a Christian author.[155] Eusebius of Caesarea frequently uses this and other technical terms,[156] and it is found in Epiphanius[157] and the *Apostolic Constitutions*.[158]

S. Krauss pointed out that Jerome used several other technical terms in his works.[159] These include: *Hoc scriptura nunc dicit*, which is equivalent to זה שאמר הכתוב, and *hoc est quod dicitur*, equivalent to הדא הוא דכתרב. Jerome used these phrases correctly at the end of particular traditions, supporting them with a scriptural quotation.[160] Occasionally, however, one finds these phrases used inappropriately. In the *Comm.Isa.* 8, 22, it is used of a tradition which he says he received from

---

152 See E. Schürer: *The History of the Jewish People in the Age of Jesus Christ (175 B.C.-A.D. 135)*, Vol. I, New Edition, ed. G. Vermes & F. Millar, Edinburgh 1973, p. 70.
153 Jerome: *Comm.Isa.* 3, 14 (*CCL* 73, 53); *Ta'an.* 4, 4.
154 *C.Cels.* 1, 45; 1, 55; 2, 31; de Lange: *op.cit.*, p. 34.
155 *GCS* VIII, 62, 25; de Lange: *op.cit.*, p. 35.
156 See, for example, *Prep.Evang.* XI, 5, 3; XII, 1, 4.
157 *Haer.* 33, 9, 4 (*GCS* I, 459, 25-6).
158 *Const.Apost.* I, 6, 3; II, 5, 4.
159 'The Jews in the Works of the Church Fathers: VI Jerome', in *JQR* 6 (1894) p. 251-2.
160 See, for example, *Comm.Isa.* 8, 22 (*CCL* 73, 120); *Heb.Q.in Gen.* 11, 28 (*CCL* 72, 15); *Comm.Zach.* 8, 16 (*CCL* 76A, 819); *Comm.Soph.* 2, 13 (*CCL* 76A, 690).

Jewish Christians. Jerome also uses the technique of νοταρικόν, which is equivalent to the Hebrew נוטריקון, but this may not be used as evidence for Jerome's use of Jewish exegetical terminology, as Krauss does, because, as S. Lieberman pointed out,[161] 'notarikon', as well as 'gematria', is also found in non-Jewish exegetical works: 'The use of letters as numerals is apparently a Greek invention which was adopted by the Semites at a much later time.'

---

161 S. Lieberman: *Hellenism in Jewish Palestine*, New York 1950, p. 73, n. 211.

Conclusions

We have now discussed the major elements in the exegesis of Jerome, and it remains now to draw together the findings which we have made in this study.

It is quite clear that Jerome knew that the first task of the exegete was to establish the biblical text on which he was to comment. We have seen how Jerome, to an even greater degree than his predecessor, Origen, or any other Christian Father, was aware of the already-existing principles of textual criticism, and that Jerome used these principles to his best advantage to ensure that the text on which he was to comment was as close to the original manuscript as possible. Jerome was a more thoroughgoing textual critic than Origen, because, although Jerome appropriated Origen's critical *sigla*, he was selective in his adaptation of them, and he was more consistent and thorough in his use of these *sigla*. Origen had used them merely to establish his Hexaplaric text, while Jerome used them as a practical aid in his exegesis.

Just as the practice of the principles of textual criticism was of fundamental importance for any discussion of the meaning(s) of a biblical passage, so was an adequate knowledge of the original languages of the Bible – Hebrew and Greek. The Greek version of the O.T., the Septuagint, had been hallowed by three centuries of Christian usage. Even Origen, effectively the only other Christian Father before Jerome to have learned any Hebrew, had always remained faithful to the LXX when it came to the exegesis of the O.T. text. Jerome was the first Father to have a good knowledge of Hebrew, and this is a mark of his scholarly perseverance at a time when the study of Hebrew grammar was at a fairly primitive stage. This astounding and bold decision (for his day) had two practical manifestations – first, it meant that Jerome accepted the Jewish biblical canon, and second, it meant that Jerome's exegesis of the O.T. was based, not on the LXX, like that of all the other Fathers, but on the Hebrew text.

As regards the canon of scripture, one of the conclusions we have reached is that, contrary to previous scholarly opinion, Jerome's views on this did not undergo a decisive change in 390-391. Previously, H.H. Howorth,[162] followed by A.C. Sundberg and J. Braverman,[163] believed

---

[162] and note [163] See next page.

that he could detect in the early Jerome an acceptance of the Christian canon of the O.T., (thus including the apocryphal books). After 390-391, argued Howorth, a decisive change can be seen. This change was brought about as a result of the Jewish influence on Jerome and also because of his conflict with the supporters of Origen. We have shown that Howorth's arguments are open to serious doubt, and that his conclusions cannot, therefore, be accepted. We have also found that Jerome was once again more thorough-going than was Origen in his acceptance of the Jewish canon. Origen accepted this canon for a practical and polemical reason – his debates with the Jews. Jerome, on the other hand, accepted the Jewish canon because in it were contained the 'actual copies of the scriptures',[164] by which he meant that they were more authentic and genuine than the LXX, which was only a translation.

While we have concluded that Jerome had a very good working knowledge of the Hebrew language – much better than that of Origen – we have also seen that his knowledge of Aramaic, the other Semitic language which he claims to have known, was very slight. The reason we have posited for this is that Hebrew was of fundamental importance for understanding scripture, while Aramaic was much less important for this purpose. Jerome had a practical reason for learning Hebrew – to understand the O.T. aright, one had to go back to the original language. This provided Jerome's motivation for learning this 'barbarous language', a motivation which was not present for Aramaic, as only a little of the O.T. was written in this language.

With his good working knowledge of Hebrew and Greek, Jerome was able to embark upon the project which has won him lasting fame – the translation of the Bible. We have seen that, in addition to his work in translating the Bible, Jerome translated many other Greek theological, exegetical and homiletical works into Latin, in order either to extend his own knowledge, or to make these works available to a Latin-speaking audience. In our analysis of Jerome's principle of 'sense for sense, not word for word' translation, we have found that Jerome is generally consistent in the application of this principle to his actual translations. We have also seen that Jerome's translations are more faithful to the original than those of any of his contemporaries, especially Rufinus.

Once Jerome had firmly established the text on which he was to com-

---

[162] H.H. Howorth: 'The Influence of St. Jerome on the Canon of the Western Church', in *JTS* 10 (1908) 481-496; 11 (1909) 321-347; 13 (1911) 1-13.
[163] A.C. Sundberg: *The O.T. of the Early Church*, Cambridge Mass. 1964; J. Braverman: *Jerome's Commentary on Daniel*, Washington DC 1978.
[164] *Apol.* 3, 25 (*CCL* 79, 97).

ment, he could proceed to elucidate the literal and spiritual meaning(s) which it contained. No one term sufficed for Jerome to describe the literal sense, and, given Jerome's rhetorical education, this is not surprising. One of the most interesting findings of this section is how Jerome's interest in biblical topography led him to make extensive travels in the Holy Land, which helped him, in turn, in his exegesis of the literal sense of scripture.

We have studied Jerome's actual usage of the literal sense in his exegesis, and have concluded that this plain interpretation should be given first, and only if the meaning implicit in the passage was not exhausted by the literal sense, was a spiritual or allegorical meaning to be sought. In his principles of exegesis, Jerome was influenced much more by the Antiochene school than by the school of exegesis centred at Alexandria. We have found, in our analysis of the most important technical terms for the spiritual sense – *typus, allegoria, aenigma, theoria* – that Jerome was content to utilise many specific spiritual interpretations of Alexandrian scholars, but that he seems not to have been influenced by the hermeneutical principles behind these interpretations. In this section we have also concluded that Jerome was certainly not a blind follower of Origen, but that he continued to use the latter's specific spiritual interpretations even after the Origenist Controversy.

In the final section of the book, we have studied Jerome's attitude towards Jews and Judaism. We have analysed Jerome's use of the terms 'Jews', 'Hebrews' and 'Israel'. Although many of Jerome's references to 'the Jews' are derogatory and appear distasteful to modern readers, we have concluded that Jerome was no more insulting than any of his contemporaries, and, indeed, that many of his references to contemporary Jews show that he respected them for teaching him Hebrew and discussing biblical passages with him.

Jerome has been used as an important source of knowledge about Jewish Christian groups and Gospels in the fourth century. In our review of Jerome's quotations of these Gospels, and references to these groups, we have been forced to conclude that his knowledge of them was minimal, and that he knew only one 'Hebrew Gospel'.

It is well known that Jerome used many specific Jewish exegetical traditions in his commentaries. While the relevance of this aspect of Jerome's labours to a work on his exegetical principles and practice is clear, such a study lies beyond the scope of the present work. Much space would have to be given to the extremely problematic question of the dating of Jewish literature and also of the relative dating of specific traditions within that literature and in Jerome's works. In any discussion of this subject, two basic questions would have to be borne in mind: what exegetical traditions would have been available to Jerome? and in what form would these traditions have been transmitted at this time? These problems, along with the fact that Jerome used several hundred

Jewish exegetical traditions in his commentaries, mean that a single chapter could not possibly do justice to this complex aspect of Jerome's work. There is scope for a full-length study in this area, and such a work is certainly a desideratum.

Jerome states the function of a commentary as:
> 'to interpret another man's words, to put into plain language what he expressed obscurely. Consequently, it gives the opinions of many people, and says: "Some interpret the passage in this sense, some in that; these try to support their opinion and understanding of it by this evidence or reasoning" so that the wise reader, after reading these different explanations, and having familiarised himself with many that he can either approve or disapprove, may judge which is the best, and, like a good banker, may reject the money from a spurious mint.'[165]

Elsewhere, Jerome reiterates this by writing that the commentator ought 'briefly and plainly to explain what is obscure',[166] and that he should write in such a way that his own explanation of someone else's words does not itself require explanation.[167] Jerome, however, never claimed to have mastered the task of exegesis: he thought of himself merely as a 'partner' in study with other scholars.[168]

It can be clearly seen, from many of Jerome's prologues and prefaces to his commentaries, that he attempted to live up to these ideals. Very often, he lists the previous scholars whom he has consulted in writing his own work, indicating sometimes the extent of his use of these authors. The end result was, as Jerome freely admits, partly his own work, and partly that of other scholars.[169] When Rufinus objected that, in Jerome's commentaries, the distinction between what was original to Jerome and what was other people's was often very unclear, and that it was extremely difficult to discover which interpretation, out of several given, Jerome actually believed, Jerome defended himself by pleading 'humility'. He said that it was not his wish to press his own opinions on others or to criticise others.[170]

---

165 *Apol.* 1, 16 (*CCL* 79, 14f): Alterius dicta edisserunt, quae obscure scripta sunt plano sermone manifestant, multorum sententias replicant, et dicunt: Hunc locum quidam sic edisserunt, alii sic interpretantur, illi sensum suum et intelligentiam his testimoniis et hac nituntur ratione firmare, ut prudens lector, cum diuersas explanationes legerit et multorum uel probanda uel improbanda didicerit, iudicet quid uerius sit et, quasi bonus trapezita, adulterinae monetae pecuniam reprobet.
166 *Ep.* 105, 5 (*CSEL* 55, 246).
167 *Ep.* 53, 6 (*CSEL* 54, 452).
168 *Ep.* 53, 10 (*CSEL* 54, 463f).
169 *Comm.Ephes.Lib.1*: Prol. (*PL* 26, 469).
170 *Apol.* 1, 24 (*CCL* 79, 24).

This answer is not completely convincing, however, as Jerome frequently criticises the views of other scholars. Hilary of Poitiers, for instance, was incorrect, according to Jerome, in his interpretation of the word 'Hosanna'. Hilary thought that it meant 'redemption of the house of David', but Jerome shows that in the N.T. it is a quotation from Ps. 118:25, and that its true meaning is 'save now'. He adds here the interesting comment:

> 'Let us now leave the streamlets of conjecture and return to the fountain-head... It is from the Hebrew manuscripts that the truth is to be drawn.'[171]

Again, although Rhetitius of Autun's commentary on the Song of Songs was 'sublime', it was full of the most elementary mistakes.[172] Further, Fortunatian's commentary on the Gospels was a 'pearl',[173] but it was written in a 'rustic' style and Fortunatian himself was a 'detestable man' because he had induced Pope Liberius to subscribe to heresy.[174] This shows that Jerome's critical judgments could be conditioned as much by personal as by intellectual considerations. The measuring-stick was always that of the orthodox faith.

Jerome was, then, essentially an eclectic scholar. He searched diligently in the works of previous authors and drew the best points from each, while avoiding the errors of each. This holds true also for the different 'schools' of interpretation accessible to Jerome – Antiochene, Alexandrian and Jewish.

From the Antiochene school, Jerome learned that an interpreter of the Bible must first study and explain the plain, literal, sense, and only after this has been accomplished should he venture beyond this to the deeper, spiritual interpretation. From the Alexandrian school, especially from Origen, Jerome borrowed many specific spiritual or allegorical interpretations of scripture. Jerome's citations of Alexandrian exegetes are far more numerous than those of Antiochene authors, but the reason for this is not that Jerome was more dependent on the former, but rather that the works of Alexandrian exegetes were more accessible to him, and also that the Antiochene school was still in its youth when Jerome was writing, and had produced a relatively small collection of commentaries from which he could quote. From Jewish exegesis,

---

[171] *Ep.* 20, 2 (*CSEL* 54, 104f): Restat ergo, ut omissis opinionum riuulis ad ipsum fontem... ita et nunc ex Hebraeis codicibus ueritas exprimenda est.
[172] *Ep.* 37, 1-3 (*CSEL* 54, 286-8). Jerome cites two examples of these errors. Rhetitius mistakenly identifies Tharshish with Tarsus, and he thinks that 'Uphaz' (in the phrase 'gold of Uphaz') is the same as 'Cephas'.
[173] *Ep.* 10, 3 (*CSEL* 54, 38).
[174] *De Vir.Illus.* 97 (*PL* 23, 735-8).

Jerome learned the importance of the original text of the O.T., so that, as we have seen, he was unique among the early Fathers in his use of the Hebrew text as the basis of his exegesis of the O.T.

Even during his lifetime, Jerome was held by many to be a great authority on the interpretation of the Bible. Jerome's contemporary, Sulpicius Severus, wrote in 405 A.D.:

> 'I would be surprised if he [Jerome] were not already known to you through his writings since he is read throughout the world.'[175]

Early in Jerome's career, Pope Damasus wrote several letters to Jerome, asking his opinion on the meaning of specific passages in the Bible, and later, Augustine recognised Jerome's immense knowledge of the Bible. He writes:

> 'I have not as great a knowledge of the divine scriptures as you have, nor could I have such knowledge as I see in you.'[176]

In the centuries following Jerome's death, he was universally acknowledged as the prince of Christian biblical scholars, and his works became a fertile ground for the labours of subsequent exegetes.[177] The reasons for this vast influence are two-fold. First, Jerome's translation of the Bible became universally accepted as the standard biblical translation in the West; and second, Jerome's immense and intimate knowledge of the Bible surpassed that of any other Christian scholar, before or after him.

Although Jerome wrote commentaries on several of the Pauline epistles and on Matthew's Gospel, he is especially remembered for his O.T. commentaries. He is the only ancient author who commented on *all* the books of the Major and Minor Prophets. Jerome saw it as his special task to explain these O.T. books, because they were more difficult to understand than the books of the N.T. In reply to Algasia's questions on difficult passages in the Gospels and Epistles, Jerome writes:

> 'I notice that your questions, which are all on the Gospels and the Epistles, show that either you do not read the O.T. enough, or you do not understand it well enough, for it is involved in so many obscurities and types of future things that it all needs explanation.'[178]

Jerome's enormous erudition is exhibited on every page of his writings. He quotes frequently from Classical authors, as well as from the Bible. But as well as quoting the ideas of other men, Jerome, with his highly developed powers of observation, makes many suggestive and original contributions to the understanding of the biblical text.

---

175 Sulpicius Severus: *Dialogus* 1, 8.
176 *Ep.* 28, 1.
177 For a study of Jerome's influence in this period, see the recent work of E.A. Rice: *Saint Jerome in the Renaissance*, Baltimore 1985.

One of the practical benefits of Jerome's technique of setting out the views of various scholars is that he has preserved for us parts of the writings of several authors, both Christian and Jewish, which would otherwise have been lost. Indeed, the writings of Jerome formed one of the main channels for the dissemination of Greek exegesis among Western Christians. This, in fact, was one of Jerome's stated purposes in writing.

The writings of Jerome are of lasting value because they offer us a splendid example of the state of biblical exegesis in the West in the fourth century, because they show us an interesting insight into relations between Christians and Jews in the generations after Christianity became the religion of the State, and also because they paint for us, in vivid colours, a picture of the 'irascible monk' who devoted his life to the study of the sacred scriptures.

> 'What other life can there be without the knowledge of the scriptures, for through these Christ himself, who is the life of the faithful, becomes known.'[179]

> 'What, pray, can be more sacred than this sacred mystery [of the scriptures]? What can be more delightful than the pleasure found in them? What food, what honey can be sweeter than to learn of God's wise plan, to enter into his sanctuary and gaze on the mind of the creator, and to rehearse the words of your Lord, which, though derided by the wise of this world, are really full of spiritual wisdom! Let the others, if they will, have their wealth, and drink from jewelled cups, be clad in silk, and bask in popular applause, as if they could not exhaust their riches in all kinds of pleasures. Our delight shall be to meditate on the Law of the Lord day and night, to knock at his door when it is not open, to receive the bread of the Trinity, and, with our Lord going before us, to walk on the billows of the world.'[180]

---

[178] *Ep.* 121: Praef. (*CSEL* 56, 3).

[179] *Ep.* 30, 7 (*CSEL* 54, 246): quae enim alia potest esse uita sine scientia scripturarum, per quas etiam ipse Christus agnoscitur, qui est uita credentium?

[180] *Ep.* 30, 13 (*CSEL* 52, 248): Oro te, quid hoc sacratius sacramento? quid hac uoluptate iucundius? qui cibi, quae mella sunt dulciora dei scire prudentiam, in adyta eius intrare, sensum creatoris inspicere et sermones domini tui, qui ab huius mundi sapientibus derridentur, plenos docere sapientia spiritali! habeant sibi ceteri suas opes, gemma bibant, serico niteant, plausu populi delectentur et per uarias uoluptates diuitias suas uincere nequeant: nostrae deliciae sint in lege domini meditari die ac nocte, pulsare ianuam non patentem, panes trinitatis accipere et saeculi fluctus domino praeeunte calcare.

Bibliography

1. Primary sources

For Jerome's works, the following editions have been used:
PL – J.P. MIGNE: *Patrologiae cursus completus Series Latina*, Paris

Vol. 23 (1883)	*Vita S. Pauli prima eremitae*
	Vita S. Hilarionis
	Vita Malchi monachi
	Regulae A. Pachomii translatio Latina
	Interpretatio libri Didymi de Spiritu Sancto ad Paulinianum
	Dialogus contra Luciferianos
	Liber de perpetua virginitate B. Mariae
	Adversus Iovinianum libri duo
	Liber contra Vigilantum
	Liber contra Ioannem Hierosolymitanum
	Apologia adversus Pelagianos
	De Viris Illustribus
	Liber de Situ et nominibus locorum Hebraicorum
	Interpretatio homiliarum duarum Origenis in Canticum, ad Damasum papam
Vol. 25 (1884)	*Translatio homiliarum Origenis in Ieremiam et Ezechielem*
Vol. 26 (1884)	*Translatio homiliarum Origenis in Lucam ad Paulam et Eustochium*
	Commentarius in epistolam S. Pauli ad Galatas
	Commentarius in epistolam S. Pauli ad Ephesios
	Commentarius in epistolam S. Pauli ad Titum
	Commentarius in epistolam S. Pauli ad Philemonem
Vol. 27 (1866)	*Translatio Chronicorum Eusebii Pamphili*
Vol. 28 (1890)	*Prolegomena in Divinam S. Hieronymi Bibliothecam*
	Divinae Bibliothecae pars prima
Vol. 29 (1865)	*Divinae Bibliothecae pars secunda*
	Divinae Bibliothecae pars tertia

CCL = *Corpus Christianorum Series Latina*, Turnhout

Vol. 72 (1959)	ed. P. ANTIN
	Hebraicae Quaestiones in libro Geneseos
	Liber Interpretationis Hebraicorum Nominum
	Commentarioli in Psalmos

	Commentarius in Ecclesiasten
Vol. 73 (1963)	ed. M. ADRIAEN
	Commentariorum in Esaiam Libri I-XI
Vol. 73A (1963)	ed. M. ADRIAEN
	Commentariorum in Esaiam Libri XII-XVIII
	In Esaia Parvula Adbreviatio
Vol. 74 (1960)	ed. S. REITER
	In Hieremiam Libri VI
Vol. 75 (1964)	ed. F. GLORIE
	Commentariorum in Hiezechielem Libri XIV
Vol. 76 (1969)	ed. M. ADRIAEN
	Commentarii in Prophetas Minores (Osee, Ioelem, Amos, Abdiam, Ionam, Michaeam)
Vol. 76A (1970)	ed. M. ADRIAEN
	Commentarii in Prophetas Minores (Naum, Abacuc, Sophoniam, Aggaeum, Zachariam, Malachiam)
Vol. 77 (1969)	ed. D. HURST & M. ADRIAEN
	Commentariorum in Matheum Libri IV
Vol. 78 (1958)	ed. G. MORIN
	Opera Homiletica. Tractatus sive homiliae in Psalmos, in Marci Evangelium, aliaque varia argumenta
Vol. 79 (1982)	ed. P. LARDET
	Contra Rufinum
Vol. 80 (1990)	ed. C. MORESCHINI
	Dialogus Adversus Pelagianos

CSEL = *Corpus Scriptorum Ecclesiasticorum Latinorum*, Lipsius

Vol. 54 (1910)	ed. I. HILBERG
	Epistulae I-LXX
Vol. 55 (1912)	ed. I. HILBERG
	Epistulae LXXI-CXX
Vol. 56 (1918)	ed. I. HILBERG
	Epistulae CXXI-CLIV

Anec. Mared. = *Anecdota Maredsolana*, Oxford

Vol. III (1895)	ed. G. MORIN	
	Pars i	*Sancti Hieronymi Presbyteri Commentarioli in Psalmos*
	Pars ii	*Tractatus LVIIII S. Hieronymi in Librum Psalmorum*
	Pars iii	*Tractatus Novissime Reperti*

Chron. = *Die Chronik des Hieronymus*, ed. R. HELM, Berlin 1956 (*GCS* 47)

2. Secondary sources – Books

ADAMS, J.D.: *The Populus of Augustine and Jerome* (Newhaven & London 1971)
ALFOLDI, A.: *The Conversion of Constantine and Pagan Rome* (Oxford 1948)
AMELLI, A.: *S. Hieronymi Stridonensis presbyteri tractatus contra Origenem de Visione Isaiae* (Montecassino 1901)
ANTIN, P.: *Recueil sur saint Jérôme* (Brussels 1968)
ARNS, E.P.: *La Technique du Livre d'après S. Jérôme* (Paris 1953)
ASKOWITH, D.: *The Tolerance and Persecution of the Jews in the Roman Empire* (New York 1915)
AZIZA, C.: *Tertullian et le Judaisme* (Nice/Paris 1977)
BACHER, W.: *Die exegetische Terminologie der jüdischen Traditionsliteratur* (Leipzig 1899-1905)
BAMBERGER, B.J.: *Proselytism in the Talmudic Period* (New York 1968)
BARDY, G.: *Recherches sur l'histoire du texte et des versions latines du De Principiis d'Origène* (Paris 1923)
BARDY, G.: *Paul de Samosate: étude historique* (Spicelegium Sacrum Lovaniense 4) (Louvain 1929)
BARDY, G.: *Recherches sur Lucien d'Antioche et son École* (Paris 1936)
BARDY, G.: *La Question des Langues dans l'Église Ancienne* (Études de Théologie Historique 1) (Paris 1948)
de BARJEAU, J.P.: *L'École exégétique d'Antioche* (Paris 1898)
BARON, S.: *A Social and Religious History of the Jews* (2nd Ed. New York 1952)
BARR, J.: *Comparative Philology and the Text of the Old Testament* (Oxford 1968)
BARTELINK, G.J.M.: *Hieronymus: Liber de Optimo Genere Interpretandi (Epistula 57). Ein Kommentar* (Leiden 1980)
BERGER, S.: *Histoire de la Vulgate* (Paris 1893)
BIETENHARD, H.: *Caesarea, Origenes und die Juden* (Stuttgart 1974)
BLUMENKRANTZ, B.: *Die Judenpredigt Augustins. Ein Beitrag zur Geschichte der jüdisch-christlichen Beziehungen in den ersten Jahrhunderten* (Basel 1946)
BODIN, Y.: *Saint Jérôme et l'Église* (Théologie Historique 6) (Paris 1966)
BOKSER, BEN ZION: *Judaism and the Christian Predicament* (New York 1967)
BOWKER, J.: *The Targums and Rabbinic Literature* (Cambridge 1969)
BRAVERMAN, J.: *Jerome's Commentary on Daniel. A Study of Comparative Jewish & Christian Interpretations of the Hebrew Bible* (C.B.Q. Monograph Series 7) (Washington DC 1978)
BROCHET, M.: *St. Jérôme et ses ennemis* (Paris 1905)
BROGAN, O.: *Roman Gaul* (London 1953)
DEBRUYNE, D.: *Préfaces de la Bible Latine* (Namur 1920)
BRYANT, D.C.: *Ancient Greek and Roman Rhetoricians. A Biographical Dictionary* (New York 1968)
BUHL, F.: *Canon and Text of the Old Testament* (Edinburgh 1892)

BURKITT, F.C.: *The Old Latin and the Itala* (Cambridge 1896)
BURY, J.B.: *History of the Later Roman Empire* (London 1923)
CARCOPINO, J.: *Daily Life in Ancient Rome: the people and the City at the height of the Empire* (New Haven 1940)
CAVALLERA, F.: *Saint Jérôme. Sa Vie et son oeuvre*, 2 Vols (Paris 1922)
CHADWICK, H.: *The Sentences of Sextus* (Cambridge 1959)
CHAPMAN, J.: *Notes on the Early History of the Vulgate Gospels* (Oxford 1908)
CHAPMAN, J.: *Studies on the Early Papacy* (London 1928)
CHARLESWORTH, M.P.: *Trade-Routes and Commerce of the Roman Empire* (Cambridge 1926)
CLARKE, M.L.: *Rhetoric at Rome. A Historical Study* (London 1953)
CLARKE, M.L.: *Higher Education in the Ancient World* (London 1971)
COCHRANE, C.N.: *Christianity and Classical Culture* (Oxford 1940)
CONGAR, Y.: *Tradition & Traditions* (London 1966)
COURCELLE, P.: *Late Latin Writers and their Greek Sources* (Harvard U.P. 1969)
DENNEFELD, L.: *Der alttestamentliche Kanon der antiochenischen Schule* (Freiburg in Breslau 1909)
DEVREESSE, R.: *Essai sur Théodore de Mopsueste* (Studi e Testi 141) (Rome 1948)
DIETSCHE, W.: *Didymus von Alexandrien als Verfasser der Schrift über die Seraphienvision* (Freiburg 1942)
DILL, S.: *Roman Society in the Last Century of the Western Empire* (Macmillan London 1902)
DILL, S.: *Roman Society from Nero to Marcus Aurelius* (London 1904)
DITTBURNER, J.M.: *A Theology of Temporal Realities: Explanation of St. Jerome. Critical Reflections on the Theological Conceptions of Riches and Poverty as an Expression of a Theory of Relative Values* (Rome 1966)
DODDS, E.R.: *Pagan and Christian in an Age of Anxiety* (Cambridge 1965)
DUMM, D.: *The Theological Basis of Virginity According to St. Jerome* (Latrobe Pa. 1961)
DUVAL, Y.M.: *Le Livre de Jonas dans la littérature chrétienne grecque et latine: Sources et influence du Commentaire sur Jonas de saint Jérôme*, 2 Vols (Paris 1973)
EFROYMSON, D.P.: *Tertullian's Anti-Judaism and its Role in his Theology*, Ph.D. Dissertation (Pennsylvania 1976)
EISWIRTH, R.: *Hieronymus' Stellung zur Literatur und Kunst* (Wiesbaden 1955)
ELLSPERMANN, G.L.: *The Attitude of the Early Christian Latin Writers toward Pagan Literature and Learning* (Washington D.C. 1949)
VAN ESS, L.: *Pragmatisch-kritische Geschichte der Vulgata* (Tübingen 1824)
ESTIN, C.: *Les Psautiers de Jérôme à la lumière des traductions juives antérieures* (Collectanea Biblica Latina XV) (Rome 1984)
EWALD, M.L.: *St. Jerome: The Homilies* (Fathers of the Church 48) (Washington D.C.); Vol. 1 1964 (Homs. 1-59), Vol. 2 1966 (Homs. 60-96).
FAHEY, J.J.: *Doctrina sancti Hieronymi de gratiae divinae necessitate* (Mundelein 1937)

FAVEZ, C.: *Saint Jérôme peint par lui-même* (*CL* 33) (Brussels 1958)
FESTUGIÈRE, S.J.: *Antioche paienne et chrétienne. Libanius, Chrysostôme et les moines de Syrie* (Paris 1959)
FIELD, F.: *Origenis Hexapla*, 2 Vols (Oxford 1875)
FISCHEL, H.A.: *Rabbinic Literature and Greco-Roman Philosophy: A Study of Epicurea and Rhetorica in Early Midrashic Writings* (Leiden 1973)
FLESSEMAN VAN LEER, E.: *Tradition and Scripture in the Early Church* (Assen 1955)
FREND, W.H.C.: *Martyrdom and Persecution in the Early Church* (Oxford 1965)
FRIEDMANN, H.: *A Bestiary for Saint Jerome. Animal Symbolism in European Religious Art* (Washington D.C. 1980)
FUNK, S.: *Die haggadischen Elemente in den Homilien des Aphraates, des Persischen Weisen* (Vienna 1891)
GAGER, J.G.: *The Origins of Anti-Semitism* (Oxford 1985)
GAMBERALE, L.: *La Traduzione in Gallio* (Rome 1969)
GARDNER, A.: *Julian, Philosopher and Emperor* (New York 1895)
GAVIN, F.: *Aphraates and the Jews* (Toronto 1923)
GINZBERG, L.: *The Legends of the Jews*, 7 Vols (Philadelphia 1909-1938)
GLOVER, T.R.: *The Conflict of Religions in the Early Roman Empire* (London 1923)
GLUNZ, H.H.: *History of the Vulgate in England* (Cambridge 1933)
GOELZER, H.: *Étude lexicographique et grammaticale de la latinité de saint Jérôme* (Paris 1884)
GOLDFAHN, A.H.: *Die Kirchenvater und die Agada: 1. Justinus Martyr und die Agada* (Breslau 1873)
GORCE, D.: *La Lectio Divina: des origines du cénobitisme à St. Benoît et Cassiodore: I. St. Jérôme et la lecture sacrée dans le milieu ascétique romain* (Paris 1925)
GRANT, R.M.: *Eusebius as Church Historian* (Oxford 1980)
GREENSLADE, S.L.: *Church and State from Constantine to Theodosius* (London 1954)
GRISSOM, F.A.: *Chrysostom and the Jews: Studies in Jewish-Christian Relations in Fourth Century Antioch*, Ph.D. Southern Baptist Theological Seminary (Kentucky 1978)
GRÜTZMACHER, G.: *Hieronymus: Eine biographische Studie zur alten Kirchengeschichte*, 3 Vols (Berlin 1901-1908)
GUILLAUMONT, A.: *Les 'Kephalaia Gnostica' d'Évagre le Pontique et l'histoire de l'Origenisme chez les Grecs et chez les Syrians* (Patristica Sorbonensia 5) (Paris 1962)
HAGENDAHL, H.: *Latin Fathers and the Classics* (Göteborg 1958)
HANSON, R.P.C.: *Tradition in the Early Church* (London 1962)
HARDEN, J.M.: *Psalterium iuxta Hebraeos Hieronymus* (London 1922)
HARTUNG, H.: *Der Exeget Hieronymus* (Bamberg 1903)
HELFGOTT, B.: *The Doctrine of Election in Tannaitic Literature* (New York 1954)
HERFORD, T.: *Christianity in Talmud and Midrash* (London 1903)

HERGENROTHER, P.: *Die antiochenischen Schule und ihre Bedeutung auf exegetischen Gebiete* (Berlin 1866)
HRITZU, J.N.: *The Style of the Letters of St. Jerome* (CUA Patristic Series LX) (Washington D.C. 1939)
HUGHES, L.: *The Christian Church in the Epistles of St. Jerome* (SPCK London 1923)
HUNT, E.D.: *Holy Land Pilgrimages* (Oxford 1982)
JAY, P.: *L'Exégèse de saint Jérôme d'après son Commentaire sur Isaie* (Paris 1985)
JELLICOE, S.: *The Septuagint and Modern Study* (Oxford 1968)
JONES, A.H.M.: *The Greek City from Alexander to Justinian* (Oxford 1940)
JONES, A.H.M.: *Constantine and the Conversion of Europe* (London 1948)
JONES, A.H.M.: *Studies in Roman Government and Law* (Oxford 1960)
JONES, A.H.M.: *The Later Roman Empire 284-602. A Social Economic and Administrative Survey*, 3 Vols (Oxford 1964)
JONES, A.H.M.: *A History of Rome through the Fifth Century*, 2 Vols; Vol. 1: The Republic, Vol. 2: The Empire (London 1968-70)
JONES, H.S.: *The Roman Empire* 29 B.C.-476 A.D., 3rd Impression (London 1916)
JÜNGBLUT, R.: *Hieronymus: Darstellung und Versuchung eines Kirchenvaters* (Tübingen 1967)
JUSTER, J.: *Les Juifs dans l'Empire Romain*, 2 Vols (New York 1914)
KAIMIO, J.: *The Romans and the Greek Language* (Comm. Hum. Lit. 64) (Helsinki 1979)
KATZ, J.: *Exclusiveness and Tolerance* (New York 1969) (reprint)
KAULEN, F.: *Geschichte der Vulgata* (Mainz 1868)
KEDER-KOPFSTEIN, B.: *The Vulgate as a Translation. Some Semantic and Syntactical Aspects of Jerome's Version of the Hebrew Bible* (Jerusalem 1968)
KELLY, J.N.D.: *Jerome. His Life, Writings and Controversies* (London 1975)
KELLY, M.J.: *Life and Times as Revealed in the Writings of St. Jerome, exclusive of the Letters* (Washington D.C. 1944)
KENNEDY, G.: *The Art of Rhetoric in the Roman World (300 B.C.-300 A.D.)* (Princeton 1972)
KIHN, H.: *Die Bedeutung der antiochenischen Schule auf exegetischen Gebiet* (Weissenburg 1866)
KIHN, H.: *Theodor von Mopsuestia und Junilius Africanus als Exegeten* (Freiburg 1880)
KLEIN, C.: *Anti-Judaism in Christian Theology* (London 1978)
KLIJN, A.F.J. & REININK, G.J.: *Patristic Evidence for Jewish-Christian Sects* (Supplements to Novum Testamentum 36) (Leiden 1973)
KLOSTERMANN, E.: *Der Überlieferung der Jeremiashomilien der Origenes* TU 1 Heft 3 (Leipzig 1897)
KOPP, C.: *The Holy Places of the Gospels* (London 1963)
von KORTZFLEISCH, S. (& RENGSTORF, K.H.) (eds): *Kirche und Synagogue*, 2 Vols (Stuttgart 1968-1970)
KRAUTHEIMER, R.: *Rome. Profile of a City 312-1308* (Princeton 1980)
LABOURT, J.: *Saint Jérôme: Lettres*, 8 Vols (Paris 1949-1963)

LAMBERT, B.: *Bibliotheca Hieronymiana manuscripta. La tradition manuscrite des oeuvres de Saint Jérôme* 1A-4AB (Steenbrugis 1969-1972)
LAMMERT, F.: *De Hieronymo Donati discipulo* (Leipzig 1912)
de LANGE, N.R.M.: *Origen and the Jews. Studies in Jewish-Christian relations in third-century Palestine* (Cambridge 1976)
LARBAUD, V.: *Sankt Hieronymus, Schutzpatron der Übersetzer* (München 1956)
LAW, V.: *The Insular Latin Grammarians* (The Boydell Press, Woodbridge, Suffolk 1982)
LENTZ, H.K.: *Der Kirchenvater Ansichten und Lehren über die Juden* (Münster 1894)
LEON, H.J.: *The Jews of Ancient Rome* (Philadelphia 1960)
LIEBESCHUETZ, J.W.H.G.: *Antioch, City and Imperial Administration in the Later Roman Empire* (Oxford 1972)
LIETZMAN, H.: *From Constantine to Julian* (London 1950)
LOT, F.: *The End of the Ancient World and the Beginning of the Middle Ages* (New York 1931)
LÜBECK, E.: *Hieronymus quos noverit scriptores et ex quibus hauserit* (Lipsiae 1872)
LUCAS, L.: *Zur Geschichte der Jüden in vierten Jahrhundert* (Berlin 1910)
MANN, J.: *The Bible as Preached in the Old Synagogue* (Philadelphia 1940)
MARKS, J.H.: *Der textkritische Wert des Psalterium Hieronymi juxta Hebraeos* (Münster 1964)
MARROU, H.I.: *Saint Augustin et la fin de la culture antique* (Paris 1938)
MARROU, H.I.: *A History of Education in Antiquity* (tr. G. Lamb) (London 1956)
MARTI, H.: *Übersetzer der Augustin-Zeit. Interpretation von Selbstzeugnissen* (Studia et Testimonia Antiqua 14) (München 1974)
MATZKOW, W.: *De vocabulis quibusdam Italae et Vulgatae christianis* (Berlin 1933)
MAXWELL, C.M.: *Chrysostom's Homilies against the Jews* (Ph.D. Dissertation Univ. Chicago 1966)
MEEKS, W. & WILKEN, R.: *Jews and Christians in Antioch in the First Four Centuries of the Common Era* (Scholars Press, Missoula, Montana 1978)
MEERSHOEK, C.Q.A.: *Le Latin biblique d'après Saint Jérôme* (Latinitas Christianorum Primaeva 20) (Utrecht 1966)
METZGER, B.M.: *The Text of the New Testament* (Oxford 1963)
METZGER, B.M.: *The Early Versions of the New Testament* (Oxford 1977)
MISCELLANEA GERONIMIANA: *Scritti Varia publicati nel XV centenario della morte di San Girolamo* (Rome 1920)
MOMIGLIANO, A. (ed): *The Conflict between Paganism and Christianity in the Fourth Century* (Oxford 1963)
MOMMSEN, T.: *Römische Geschichte Vol. V* (5th Ed. Berlin 1904)
MOORE, G.F.: *Judaism in the First Three Centuries of the Christian Era. The Age of the Tannaim*, 3 Vols (Cambridge Mass. 1954)
MOSSHAMMER, A.A.: *The Chronicle of Eusebius and Greek Chronographic Tradition* (London 1979)

MURAWSKI, B.: *Die Juden bei den Kirchenvatern und Skolastikern* (Berlin 1925)
MURPHY, F.X.: *Rufinus of Aquileia* (Washington D.C. 1945)
MURPHY, F.X. (ed): *A Monument to St. Jerome* (New York 1952)
NEUSNER, J.: *Aphrahat and Judaism: The Christian-Jewish Argument in Fourth Century Iran* (Leiden 1971)
NILSSON, M.P.: *Imperial Rome* (London 1926)
NOWACK, W.: *Die Bedeutung des Hieronymus für die alttestamentliche Textkritik* (Göttingen 1875)
O'CONNEL, J.P.: *The Eschatology of St. Jerome* (Mundelein 1948)
OLDFATHER, A.: *Studies in the Text Tradition of St. Jerome's Vitae Patrum* (Urbana 1943)
O'MALLEY, T.P.: *Tertullian and the Bible* (Latinitas Christianorum Primaeva 21) (Nijmegen 1967)
OPELT, I.: *Hieronymus' Streitschriften* (Heidelberg 1973)
OPELT, I.: *Die Polemik in der christlichen lateinischen Literatur von Tertullian bis Augustin* (Heidelberg 1980)
PARKER, H.M.D.: *A History of the Roman World from AD 138 to 337* (2nd Ed. London 1958)
PARKES, J.: *The Foundations of Judaism and Christianity* (London 1960)
PENNA, A.: *Principe e carattere dell'esegesi di S. Girolamo* (Rome 1950)
PHARR, C.: *The Theodosian Code and Novels and the Sirmondian Constitutions* (Princeton 1952)
POLIAKOV, L.: *A History of Anti-Semitism. Vol. 1: From the Time of Christ to the Court Jews* (New York 1965)
PREUS, J.E.O.: *St. Jerome's Translation Terminology* (Ph.D. Dissertation Minnesota 1951)
RAHMER, M.: *Die hebräischen Traditionen in den Werken des Hieronymus: Quastiones in Genesim* (Breslau 1861)
RAHMER, M.: *Die hebräischen Traditionen in den Werken des Hieronymus: Die Kommentarien zu der 12 kleinen Propheten*, 2 Vols (Berlin 1902)
RAUER, M. (ed): *Origenes Werke IX: Die Homilien zu Lukas in der Übersetzung des Hieronymus und die griechischen Reste der Homilien und des Lukas-Kommentars GCS* 49 (Berlin 1959)
REUSCHENBACH, F.: *Hieronymus als Übersetzer der Genesis* (Freiburg 1948)
RICE, E.F.: *Saint Jerome in the Renaissance* (Baltimore 1985)
RICHTER, H.E.: *Übersetzer und Übersetzungen in der römischen Literatur* (Coburg 1938)
ROBERTS, B.J.: *Old Testament Text and Versions* (Cardiff 1951)
ROBERTS, C.H. & SKEAT, T.C.: *The Birth of the Codex* (Oxford 1983)
ROBINSON, J.A.: *The Philokalia of Origen. The Text Revised with a critical introduction and indices* (Cambridge 1893)
RÖHRICH, A.: *Essai sur S. Jérôme Exégète* (Genève 1891)
RÖNSCH, H.: *Itala und Vulgata* (Marburg 1875)
RORDORF, W./SCHNEIDER, A.: *L'évolution du concept de tradition dans l'Église ancienne* (Berne 1982)
ROSTOVTZEFF, M.: *The Social and Economic History of the Roman Empire* (2nd Ed. by P.M. Fraser, Oxford 1956)

ROUSSEAU, P.: *Ascetics, Authority and the Church in the age of Jerome and Cassian* (Oxford Historical Monographs) (Oxford 1978)
REUTHER, R.: *Faith and Fratricide: The Theological Roots of Anti-Semitism* (New York 1974)
RYLE, H.E.: *The Canon of the Old Testament* (London 1892)
SCHADE, L.: *Die Inspirationslehre des heiligen Hieronymus* (Freiburg im Breisgau 1910)
SCHOEPS, H.J.: *Jewish Christianity* (Philadelphia 1964)
SCHWARTZ, W.: *Principles and Problems of Biblical Translation: Some Reformation Controversies and their Background* (Cambridge 1956)
SEAVER, J.E.: *Persecution of the Jews in the Roman Empire (300-438)* (Lawrence 1952)
SEELIGMANN, J.L.: *The Septuagint Version of Isaiah: A Discussion of its Problems* (Leiden 1948)
SEGAL, A.F.: *Two Powers in Heaven. Early Rabbinic Reports about Christianity and Gnosticism* (Leiden 1977)
SETTON, M.K.: *Christian Attitudes towards the Emperor in the Fourth Century* (New York 1941)
SIEGMUND, A.: *Die Überlieferung der griechischen christlichen Literatur in der lateinischen Kirche bis zum 12. Jahrhundert* (München 1949)
SIMON, M.: *Verus Israel: Étude sur les relations entre Chrétiens et Juifs dans l'Empire Romain (135-425)* (Paris 1948)
SIMONETTI, M.: *Tirannio Rufino, Apologia* (Alba 1957)
SMALLWOOD, M.: *The Jews under Roman Rule* (Leiden 1976)
SOUTER, A.: *Earliest Latin Commentaries on the Pauline Epistles* (Oxford 1928)
SOUTER, A.: *A Study of Ambrosiaster* (Cambridge 1905)
SPANIER, M.: *Exegetische Beiträge zu Hieronymus' Onomastikon* (Magdeburg 1896)
SPELLER, L.M.A.: *Conflict and Controversy in Ambrosiaster* (D. Phil. Thesis, Oxtord 1980)
SPICQ, C.: *Esquisse d'une histoire de l'exégèse latine au Moyen-Age* (Paris 1944)
STUDIA HIERONYMIANA: *VI Centenario de la Orden de San Jeronimo*, 2 Vols (Madrid 1973)
SUGANO, K.: *Das Rombild des Hieronymus* (Frankfurt 1983)
SUNDBERG, A.C.: *The Old Testament of the Early Church* (Cambridge [Mass.] 1964)
SUSS, W.: *Studien zur lateinischen Bibel* (Tartu 1933)
SWETE, H.B.: *Introduction to the Old Testament in Greek* (Oxford 1902)
TESTARD, M.: *Saint Jérôme: l'apôtre savant et pauvre du patriciat romain* (Paris 1969)
TRZCINSKI, T.: *Die dogmatischen Schriften des heiligen Hieronymus* (Posen 1912)
VISINTAINER, S.: *La Dottrina del Peccato in S. Girolamo* (Rome 1962)
VOGELS, H.J.: *Vulgatastudien. Die Evangelien der Vulgata untersucht auf ihre lateinische und griechische Vorlage* (Münster 1928)

VOGT, J.: *Kaiser Julian und das Judentum* (Leipzig 1935)
VOOBUS, A.: *Early Versions of the New Testament. Manuscript Studies* (Stockholm 1954)
WAGNER, M.: *Rufinus the Translator* (CUA Patristic Studies 73) (Washington D.C. 1945)
WALLACE-HADRILL, D.S.: *Christian Antioch* (Cambridge 1982)
WARMINGTON, B.A.: *The North African Provinces from Diocletian to the Vandal Conquest* (Cambridge 1954)
WEBER, R.: *Le Psautier Romain et les autres anciens Psautiers Latins* (Collectanea Biblica X) (Rome 1953)
WERMELINGER, O.: *Rom und Pelagius. Die theologische Position der römischen Bischöfe in pelagianischem Streit in den Jahren 411-432* (Stuttgart 1975)
WIESEN, D.S.: *St. Jerome as a Satirist* (New York 1964)
WILDE, R.: *The Treatment of the Jews in Greek Christian Writers of the First Three Centuries* (Washington 1949)
WILKEN, R.: *Judaism and the Early Christian Mind: A Study of Cyril of Alexandria's Exegesis and Theology* (New Haven 1971)
WILKINSON, J.: *Egeria's Travels* (rev.ed. Warminster 1981)
WILLIAMS, A.L.: *Adversus Judaeos: A Bird's Eye View of Christian Apologiae until the Renaissance* (Cambridge 1935)
WÜTZ, F.: *Onomastica Sacra: Untersuchungen zum Liber Interpretationem Heb. Nom. des heiligen Hieronymus*, 2 Vols (Berlin 1914-1915)
WÜTZ, F.: *Die Transkriptionen von der Septuaginta bis zu Hieronymus* (Berlin 1933)
ZIEGLER, L.: *Lateinischen Bibelübersetzungen von Hieronymus* (Münich 1879)
ZÖCKLER, O.: *Hieronymus* (Gotha 1865)

3. Secondary sources – Articles

ABEL, F.M.: 'Saint Jérôme et les prophéties messianiques', *RB* 13 (1916) 423-440; 14, (1917) 247-269
ABEL, F.M.: 'Parallélisme exégètique entre St. Jérôme et St. Cyrille d'Alexandrie', *Vivre et Penser* (1941) 94-119; 212-230
ADLER, M.: 'The Emperor Julian and the Jews', *JQR* o.s. 5 (1893) 591-651
ALEXANDER, P.S.: 'The Rabbinic Hermeneutical Rules and the Problem of the Definition of Midrash', *Proceedings of the Irish Biblical Association* (1985) 97-125
ALLGEIER, A.: 'Ist das Psalterium iuxta Hebraeos die letzte (3) Psalmenübersetzung des hl. Hieronymus?', *Theol. und Glaube* 18 (1926) 671-687
ALLGEIER, A.: 'Der Brief an Sunnia und Fretela und seine Bedeutung für die Text-herstellung der Vulgata', *Bib.* 11 (1930) 86-107
ALLGEIER, A.: 'Die erste Psalmenübersetzung des hl. Hieronymus und das Psalterium Romanum', *Bib.* 12 (1931) 447-482

ALTANER, B.: 'Wann Schrieb Hieronymus seine *Ep.* 106 *ad Sunnia et Fretela de Psalterio*?', *Vig. Chr.* 4 (1950) 246-8

ANTIN, P.: 'Le Cilice chez S. Jérôme', *La Vie Spirituelle* Suppl. 1 (1947) 58-61

ANTIN, P.: 'Les idées morales de S. Jérôme', *Melanges de Sciences Religieuses* 14 (1957) 135-150

ANTIN, P.: 'Simple et simplicité chez Jérôme', *R. Ben.* 73 (1961) 371-381

ANTIN, P.: 'Mots vulgaires dans Saint Jérôme', *Latomus* 30 (1971) 708-9

ANTIN, P.: 'La vieillesse chez S. Jérôme', *Revue des Études Augustiniennes* 17 (1971) 43-54

APTOWITZER, V.: 'Rabbinische Parallelen und Aufschlüsse zur Septuaginta und Vulgata', *ZATW* 29 (1909) 241-252

DE LA CRUZ ARTEAGA, C.: 'La "Lectio Divina" fundamento de la oracion y de la vida monastica a le luz de los consejos de S. Jeronimo', *Cuad. Mon.* 11 (1976) 333-346

AUVRAY, P.: 'Saint Jérôme et saint Augustin: La controverse au sujet de l'incident d'Antioche', *RSR* 29 (1939) 594-610

BACHER, W.: 'Eine angebliche Lücke in hebräischen Wissen des Hieronymus', *ZATW* 22 (1902) 114-116

BARDY, G.: 'Les traditions juives dans l'oeuvre d'Origène', *RB* 34 (1925) 217-252

BARDY, G.: 'S. Jérôme et ses maîtres Hébreux', *R. Ben.* 46 (1934) 145-164

BARDY, G.: 'Traducteurs et Adaptateurs au IV-ème Siècle', *RSR* 30 (1940) 257-306

BARDY, G.: 'Copies et éditions au Ve siècle', *RSR* 23 (1949) 38-52

BARR, J.: 'St. Jerome's Appreciation of Hebrew', *BJRL* 49 (1966) 280-302

BARR, J.: 'St. Jerome and the Sound of Hebrew', *JSS* 12 (1967) 1-36

BATE, H.N.: 'Some technical terms of Greek Exegesis', *JTS* 24 (1922-3) 59-66

BAUS, K.: 'Das Gebet zu Christus beim heiligen Hieronymus', *Trierer theologische Zeitschrift* LX (1951) 178-188

BERNARD, J.H.: 'The Greek MSS used by St. Jerome', *Hermathena* XI (1901) 335-342

BEVENOT, H.: 'Hieronymus und die Vulgata des N.T.', *Theologische Revue* 23 (1924) 241-244

BICKEL, E.: 'Das asketische Ideal bei Ambrosius, Hieronymus und Augustinus', *Neue Jahrbücher für das klassische Altertum* XXXVII (1916) 437-474

BICKERMAN, E.J.: 'The Septuagint as a Translation', *Proceedings of the Amer. Acad. of Jewish Research* 28 (1959) 1-39

BIHLMEYER, P.: 'Hieronymus und die lateinische Bibel', *Benediktiner Monatsschrift* 2 (1920) 407-424

BLATT, M.F.: 'Remarques sur l'Histoire des traductions latines', *Classica et Mediaevalia* 1 (1938) 217-242

BOER, W. DEN: 'Hermeneutic Problems in early Christian Literature', *Vig. Chr.* 1 (1947) 150-167

LA BONNARDIERE, A.M.: 'Jérôme, informateur d'Augustin au sujet d'Origène', *Revue des Études Augustiniennes* 20 (1974) 42-54

BOOTH, ALAN D.: 'The Chronology of Jerome's Early Years', *Phoenix* 35 (1981) 235-257

BROCK, S.P.: 'Origen's Aims as a Textual Critic of the O.T.', *Studia Patristica* 10 (TU 107), Berlin 1970, 215-218

BROCK, S.P.: 'Aspects of Translation techniques in Antiquity', *Greek, Roman and Byzantine Studies* 20 (1979) 69-87

BROWN, D.: 'St. Jerome as a Biblical Exegete', *Irish Biblical Studies* 5 (1983) 138-155

DE BRUYNE, D.: 'La lettre de Jérôme à Sunnia et Fretela sur le Psautier', *ZNTW* 28 (1929) 1-13

DE BRUYNE, D.: 'La correspondence échangée entre Augustin et Jérôme', *ZNTW* 31 (1932) 233-248

BURGHARDT, W.J.: 'On early Christian Exegesis', *Theological Studies* 11 (1950) 78-116

BURSTEIN, E.: 'La compétence de Jérôme en Hébreu: Explication de certaines erreurs', *Revue des Études Augustiniennes* 21 (1975) 3-12

CANNON, W.W.: 'Jerome and Symmachus. Some Points in the Vulgate Translation of Koheleth', *ZATW* 45 (1927) 191-199

CAVALLERA, F.: 'Saint Jérôme et la Vulgate des Actes, des Épitres et de l'Apocalypse', *Bull. de Litt. Ecclés.* 21 (1920) 269-292

CAVALLERA, F.: 'Saint Jérôme et la Bible', *Bull. de Litt. Ecclés.* 22 (1921) 214-227; 265-284

CAVALLERA, F.: 'Saint Jérôme et la vie Parfaite', *Revue d'ascétique et de mystique* II (1921) 101-127

CAVALLERA, F.: 'The Personality of St. Jerome' in *A Monument to St. Jerome*, ed. F.X. MURPHY (New York 1952) 13-34

CHAPMAN, J.: 'St. Jerome and the Vulgate New Testament', *JTS* 24 (1923) 33-51; 113-125; 282-299

CHILDS, B.S.: 'The Sensus Literalis of Scripture: An Ancient and Modern Problem', *Beiträge zur Alttestamentliche Theologie* (Festschrift für W. Zimmerli) (Göttingen 1977) ed. H. DONNER, R. HANHART & R. SMEND, 80-93

COLSON, F.H.: 'The Analogist and Anomalist Controversy', *Classical Quarterly* XIII (1919) 24-36

COOPER, C.M.: 'Jerome's "Hebrew Psalter" and the New Latin Version', *JBL* 69 (1950) 233-244

CONDAMIN, A.: 'Les caractères de la traduction de la Bible par S. Jérôme', *RSR* II (1911) 425-440; III (1912) 105-138

CONDAMIN, A.: 'L'Influence de la tradition juive dans la version de S. Jérôme', *RSR* V (1914) 1-21

COTTINEAU, L.H.: 'Chronologie des versions bibliques de S. Jérôme', *Miscellanea Geronimiana* (Rome 1920) 43-68

COURCELLE, P.: 'Paulin (de Nole) et la controverse entre Jérôme et Rufin', *Revue des Études Latines* XXC (1947) 274-279

CROUZEL, H.: 'Saint Jérôme et ses amis toulousains', *Bull. de Litt. Ecclés.* 73 (1972) 125-146

CUENDET, G.: 'Ciceron et Saint Jérôme traducteurs', *Revue des Études Latines* 11 (1933) 380-400

CUMMINGS, J.T.: 'St. Jerome as translator and exegete', *Studia Patristica* XII (T.U. 115) (Berlin 1975) 279-282

DAUBE, D.: 'Rabbinic Methods of Interpretation and Hellenistic Rhetoric', *HUCA* 22 (1949) 239-264

DAUBE, D.: 'Alexandrian Methods of Interpretation and the Rabbis', *Festschrift für Hans Lewald* (Basel 1953) 1-31

DAWSON, C.: 'St. Augustine and his Age' *A Monument to St. Augustine*, (London 1930) 11-78

DEFERRARI, R.J.: 'St. Augustine's method of composing and delivering sermons', *American Journal of Philology* 43 (1922) 97-123

DENIAU, F.: 'Le Commentaire de Jérôme sur Ephésiens nous permet-il de connaître celui d'Origène?', *Origeniana* (ed. H. CROUZEL) (Bern 1975) 163-179

DERRETT, J.D.M.: 'The Parable of the Prodigal Son: Patristic Allegories and Jewish Midrashim', *Studia Patristica* 2 Pt. 2 (1957) 219-224

DEVREESSE, R.: 'La Méthode exégétique de Théodore de Mopsueste', *RB* 53 (1946) 207-241

DURAND, D.: 'S. Jérôme et notre N.T. latin', *RSR* VII (1916) 531-549

DUVAL, Y.M.: 'Saint Augustin et le Commentaire sur Jonas de saint Jérôme', *Revue des Études Augustiniennes* 12 (1966) 9-40

DUVAL, Y.M.: 'Saint Jérôme devant le baptême des hérétiques', *Revue des Études Augustiniennes* 14 (1968) 145-181

DUVAL, Y.M.: 'Sur les insinuations de Jérôme contre Jean de Jerusalem: de l'arianisme à l'origénisme', *Revue d'Histoire Écclésiastique* 65 (1970) 353-374

DUVAL, Y.M.: 'Tertullian contre Origène sur le Résurrection de la chair dans le Contra Iohannem Hierosolymitanum 23-36 de saint Jérôme', *Revue des Études Augustiniennes* 17 (1971) 227-278

DUVAL, Y.M.: 'S. Cyprien et le roi de Ninive dans l'In Ionam de Jérôme. La conversion des lettres à la fin du IVe siècle' in *Epektasis (Mélanges J. Danielou)* (Paris 1972) 551-570

DUVAL, Y.M.: 'Jérôme et Origène avant la querelle origéniste. La cure et la guérison ultime du monde et du diable dans l'In Nahum', *Augustinianum* 24 (1984) 471-494

DUVAL, Y.M.: 'Jérôme et les prophètes. Histoire, prophétie, actualité et actualisation dans les Commentaires de Nahum, Michée, Abdias et Joel' in *Congress Volume Salamanca 1983* (VT Supp. 36) (Leiden 1985) 108-131

ELLIOT, C.J.: 'Christian Learning among the Fathers', *DCB* 2 (ed. W. Smith & H. Wace) (London 1880) 851-872

VAN ESBROECK, M.: 'Une Homélie sur l'église attribuée à Jean de Jerusalem', *Le Muséon* 86 (1973) 283-304

FREND, W.H.C.: 'The Persecutions: Some Links between Judaism and the Early Church', *JEH* 9 (1958) 141ff

FREND, W.H.C.: 'Jews and Christians in Third Century Carthage', *Paganisme, Judaïsme, Christianisme* (Festschrift Marcel Simon) ed. A. Benoit et al (Paris 1978)

GINZBERG, L.: 'Die Haggada bei den Kirchenvätern: Die Haggada in den pseudo-hieronymischen Quaestiones' (Amsterdam 1899)

GINZBERG, L.: 'Die Haggada bei den Kirchenvätern und in der apokryphischen Literatur.II: Genesis, Berlin 1900)

GINZBERG, L.: 'Die Haggada bei den Kirchenvätern.III: Exodus', *Livre d'Hommage à la mémoire du Dr. Samuel Poznanski* (Warsaw 1927) 199-216

GINZBERG, L.: 'Die Haggada bei den Kirchenvätern. IV: Numeri-Deuteronomium, *Studies in Jewish Bibliography... in Memory of Abraham S. Freidus* (New York 1929) 503-518

GINZBERG, L.: 'Die Haggada bei den Kirchenvätern. V: Der Kommentar des Hieronymus zu Koheleth', *Abhandlungen zur Erinnerung an Hirsch Perez Chajes* (Vienna 1933) 22-50

GINZBERG, L.: 'Die Haggada bei den Kirchenvätern. VI: Der Kommentar des Hieronymus zu Jesaja', *Jewish Studies in Memory of George A. Kohut* (New York 1935) 279-314

GINZBERG, M.S.: 'Fiscus Judaicus', *JQR* 21 (1930-1) 281-291

GORCE, D.: 'St. Jérôme et son environnement artistique et liturgique', *Collectanea Cisterciensia* 36 (1974) 150-178

GORDINI, G.D.: 'Forme di Vita ascetica a Roma nel IV Secolo', *Scrinium Theologicum* I (1953) 7-58

GORDON, C.H.: 'Rabbinic Exegesis in the Vulgate of Proverbs', *JBL* 49, (1930) 384-416

GRABBE, L.L.: 'Aquila's translation and Rabbinic Exegesis', *JJS* XXXIII (1982) 527ff

GRAETZ, H.: 'Haggadische Elemente bei den Kirchenvätern', *MGWJ* 3 (1864) 311-319; 352-355; 381-387; Vol. 4 (1865) 187-192

GREGG, J.A.F.: 'The Commentary of Origen upon the Epistle to the Ephesians', *JTS* iii (1901-2) 233-244; 398-420; 554-576

GUILLET, J.: 'Les exégèses d'Alexandrie et d'Antioche. Conflit ou malentendu?', *RSR* 34 (1947) 257-302

GUTIERREZ, L.: 'St. Jerome and Roman Monasticism. A Historical Study on his Spiritual Influence', *Philippiniana Sacra* 10 (1975) 256-307

HAGENDAHL, H.: 'Jerome and the Latin Classics', *Vig. Chr.* 28 (1974) 216-227

HANSON, A.T.: 'Philo's Etymologies', *JTS* (1967) 138ff

HANSON, R.P.C.: 'The Transformation of Pagan Temples into Churches in the Early Christian Centuries', *JSS* 23 (1978) 257-267

HARNACK, A.: 'Der kirchengeschichtliche Ertrag der exegetischen Arbeiten des Origenes', (TU 42) (Leipzig 1918-19) Appendix I 141-168

HARTMAN, L.F.: 'St. Jerome as an Exegete', *A Monument to St. Jerome* ed. F.X. Murphy (New York 1952) 37-81

HEIMANN, D.F.: 'The Polemical Application of Scripture in St. Jerome', *Studia Patristica* XII (TU 115) (Berlin 1975) 309-316

HEINEMANN, I.: 'The Attitude of the Ancient World toward Judaism', *Review of Religion* 4 (1940) 385-400

HOWORTH, H.H.: 'The Influence of St. Jerome on the Canon of the Western Church', *JTS* 10 (1908-9); 11 (1909-10); 13 (1911-12) 481-96; 321-47; 1-18

HUG, A. and MANSER, A.: 'Drei Lesungen aus dem hl. Hieronymus', *Benediktinische Monatschrift* II (1920) 354-363

HULEN, A.B.: 'The "Dialogue with the Jews" as Sources for the Early Jewish Argument against Christianity', *JBL* 51 (1932) 58-70

HULLEY, K.K.: 'Light cast by Jerome on certain palaeographical points', *Harvard Studies in Classical Philology* LIV (1943) 83-92

HULLEY, K.K.: 'Principles of Textual Criticism known to St. Jerome', *Harvard Studies in Classical Philology* LV (1944) 87-109

JANNACONE, S.: 'La Genesi del cliche antiorigenista ed il platonismo origeniano nel contra Iohannem Hier di S. Girolamo', *Giornale italiano di filologia* 17 (1964) 14-28

JAY, P.: 'Le vocabulaire exégétique de Saint Jérôme dans le Commentaire sur Zacharie', *Revue des Études Augustiniennes* 14 (1968) 3-16

JAY, P.: 'Sur la date de naissance de Saint Jérôme', *Revue des Études Latines* 51 (1973) 262-280

JAY, P.: 'Jérôme, auditeur d'Apollinaire de Laodicée à Antioche', *Revue des Études Augustiniennes* 20 (1974) 36-41

JAY, P.: '*Allegoriae Nubilum* chez Saint Jérôme', *Revue des Études Augustiniennes* 22 (1976) 82-89

JAY, P.: 'Saint Jérôme et le triple sens de l'Écriture', *Revue des Études Augustiniennes* 26 (1980) 214-227

JAY, P.: 'La datation des premières traductions de l'Ancien Testament sur l'Hébreu par Saint Jérôme', *Revue des Études Augustiniennes* 28 (1982) 208-212

JELLICOE, S.: 'Aquila and his Version', *JQR* 59 (1969) 326-332

JOHANNESSOHN, M.: 'Hieronymus und die jüngeren griechischen Übersetzungen des A.T.', *Theol. Literaturzeitung* LXXIII (1948) 145-152

JOHANNESSOHN, M.: 'Zur Entstehung der Ausdrucksweise der lateinischen Vulgate aus den jüngeren alttestamentlichen Übersetzungen', *ZNTW* XLIV (1952-3) 90-102

JONES, H.S.: 'Claudius and the Jewish Question at Alexandria', *Journal of Roman Studies* XVI (1926) 17-35

KAHN, J.G.: 'Philon savait-il l'hébreu? Le Témoignage des étymologies', *Tarbiz* XXXIV (1975)

KALT, E.: 'Der Ausdruck «Fabula» bei Hieronymus', *Katholik* 91 (1911) 271-287

KATZ, P.: 'The Early Christians use of codices instead of rolls', *JTS* XLIV (1945) 63-65

KLIJN, A.F.J.: 'Jerome's quotations from a Nazoraean Interpretation of Isaiah', *RSR* 60 (1972) 241-255

KLOSTERMANN, E.: 'Die Schriften des Origenes in Hieronymus' Brief an Paula', *Sitzungsberichte der königlich preussischen Akademie der Wissenschaften zu Berlin* (1897) 855-870

KRAELING, C.H.: 'The Jewish Community at Antioch up to A.D. 600', *JBL* 51 (1932) 30-60

KRAUSS, S.: 'The Jews in the Works of the Church Fathers', *Jewish Quarterly Review* o.s. 5 (1893) pp 122-157; 6, (1894) 82-99; 225-261

KRAUSS, S.: 'Church Fathers', *Jewish Encyclopaedia*, Vol. 4 (New York 1903) 80-86

KRAUSS, S.: 'Jerome', *Jewish Encyclopaedia*, Vol. 7 (New York 1903) 115-118

LAGRANGE, M.J.: 'S. Jérôme et la tradition juive dans la Genèse', *RB* 7, (1898) 563-6

LAGRANGE, M.J.: 'La Vulgate Latine de l'Épitre aux Galates et le Texte Grec', *RB* n.s. 14 (1917) 424-450

LAGRANGE, M.J.: 'La Révision de la Vulgate par S. Jérôme', *RB* n.s. 15, (1918) 254-257

LAISTNER, M.L.V.: 'Antiochene Exegesis in Western Europe during the Middle Ages', *HTR* 40 (1947) 19-31

LAMIRANDE, E.: 'Étude bibliographique sur les pères de l'église et l'Aggadah', *Vig. Chr.* 21 (1967) 1-11

LATAIX, J.: 'Le commentaire de S. Jérôme sur Daniel', *Revue d'histoire et de litterature religieuses* 2 (1897) 164-173; 268-277

COMERFORD LAWLER, T.: 'Jerome's First Letter to Damasus', in *Kyriakon. Festschrift J. Quasten* IV (Münster 1970) 548-552

LECLERCQ, J.: 'S. Jérôme, docteur d'ascèse d'après un centon monastique', *Revue d'ascétique et de mystique* XXV (1949) 140-145

LOEWE, R.: 'The Jewish Midrashim and Patristic and Scholastic Exegesis of the Bible', *Studia Patristica* 1 (TU 63) (Berlin 1957) 492-514

LOEWE, R.: 'The "Plain" Meaning of Scripture in Early Jewish Exegesis' *Papers of the Institute of Jewish Studies London*, 1 (Jerusalem 1964) 140-185, ed. J.G. WEISS

LORENZ, R.: 'Die Anfänge des abendländischen Mönchtum im 4. Jahrhundert', *Zeitschrift für Kirchengeschichte* 76 (1966) 1-61

LUTZ, A.: 'Die Chronologie des Essias-Kommentars von Hieronymus', *Wiener Studien* 26 (1904) 164-168

LYONNET, S.: 'Témoignages de saint Jean Chrysostôme et de saint Jérôme sur Jacques le Frère du Seigneur', *RSR* 28 (1939) 335-352

MANGENOT, E.: 'Les manuscrits grecs des Évangiles employés par S. Jérôme', *Revue des sciences ecclés* LXXXI (1900) 56-73

MANGENOT, E.: 'Saint Jérôme réviseur du Nouveau Testament', *RB* n.s 15 (1918) 244-253

MERK, E.: 'Origenes und der Kanon der A.T.', *Bib.* VI (1925) 200-205

METLEN, M.: 'Letter of St. Jerome to the Gothic Clergymen Sunnia and Frißila concerning places in their copy of the Psalter which had been corrupted from the Septuagint', *Journal of English & Germanic Philology* XXXVI (1937) 515-542

METZGER, B.M.: 'Textual Criticism among the Church Fathers', *Studia Patristica* XII 340-349

METZGER, B.M.: 'St. Jerome's Explicit References to Variant Readings in Manuscripts of the New Testament' in *Text and Interpretation. Studies in the New Testament Presented to Matthew Black*, ed. E. BEST and R. McL. WILSON (Cambridge 1979) 179-190

MIEROW, C.C.: 'St. Jerome as Christian Scholar', *The Classical Journal* (1937) 3-17

MIEROW, C.C.: 'St. Jerome and Rufinus', *The Classical Bulletin* XXX (1953) 1-5; 16-17; 19-20

MITZKA, F.: 'Der hl. Hieronymus als Asket', *Zeitschrift für Askese und Mystik* I (1925) 176-182

MOHRMANN, C.: 'Saint Jérôme et Saint Augustin sur Tertullien', *Vig. Chr.* 5 (1951) 111-112

MONCEAUX, P. and BROSSE, L.: 'Chalcis ad Belum: Notes sur l'histoire et les ruines de la Ville', *Syria* 6 (1925) 341-350

MOORE, G.F.: 'Christian Writers on Judaism', *HTR* (1921) 197-254

NASH, H.: 'The Exegesis of the School of Antioch', *JBL* 11 22-37 (1892)

NAUTIN, P.: 'La Date de la «De Vir Illustribus»', *Revue d'Histoire Ecclésiastique* 56 (1961) 33-35

NAUTIN, P.: 'Études de chronologie hieronymienne (393-397)', *Revue des Études Augustiniennes* 19 (1973) 69-86; 213-239; 20 (1974) 251-284

NAUTIN, P.: 'L'excommunication de saint Jérôme', *Annuaire de l'école pratique des Hautes Études. Ve section, Sciences Religieuses* 81 (1973) 7-37

NEWTON, W.L.: 'Influences on St. Jerome's translation of the Old Testament', *CBQ* 5 (1943) 17-33

NODET, C.H.: 'Position de S. Jérôme en face des problèmes sexuels', *Mystique et Continence* (Études carmelitaines 31) (Paris 1952) 308-356

OULTON, J.E.L.: 'Rufinus' Translation of the Church History of Eusebius', *JTS* 30 (1929) 150-174

PEASE, A.S.: 'The Attitude of Jerome towards Pagan Literature', *Transactions and Proceedings of the American Philological Association* L (1919) 150-167

PENNA, A.: 'La Volgato e il manuscritto IQ*T*sa' *Bib.* XXXVIII (1957) 381-395

PENNA, A.: 'The Vow of Jephthah in the Interpretation of St. Jerome', *Studia Patristica* IV (TU 79) (Berlin 1961) 162-170

PERI, V.: 'I passi sulla Trinita nelle omelie origeniane tradotte in latimer da San Girolamo', *Studia Patristica* VI (TU 81) (Berlin 1962) 155-180

POPE, H.: 'St. Jerome's Latin Text of St. Paul's Epistles', *ITQ* IX (1914) 413-445

REHM, M.: 'Die Bedeutung hebräischen Wörter bei Hieronymus', *Bib.* 29 (1954) 174-197

REITZENSTEIN, R.: 'Origenes und Hieronymus', *ZNTW* 20 (1921) 90-93

ROMANIUK, K.: 'Une controverse entre Saint Jérôme et Rufin d'Aquilée à propos de saint Paul aux Ephesiens', *Aegyptus* 43 (1963) 84-106

SCHATKIN, M.A.: 'The Influence of Origen upon St. Jerome's Commentary on Galatians', *Vig. Chr.* 24 (1970) 49 58

SCHAUBLIN, C.: 'Textkritisches zu den Briefen des Hieronymus', *Museum Helvidium* 30 (1973) 55-62

SCHWARZ, W.: 'The Meaning of *Fidus Interpres* in Medieval Translation', *JTS* XLV (1944) 73-78

SCHWEIZER, E.: 'Diodor von Tarsus als Exeget', *ZNTW* 40 (1941) 33-75

SEMPLE, W.H.: 'St. Jerome as a Biblical Translator', *BJRL* 48 (1965-6) 227-243

SIEGFRIED O.: 'Midraschisches zu Hieronymus und Pseudo-Hieronymus', *Jahrbücher für protestantische Theologie* 9 (1883) 346-352

SIEGFRIED, C.: 'Die Aussprache des hebräischen bei Hieronymus', *ZATW* 4 (1884) 34-83

SIMON, M.: 'Melchisedech dans la polémique entre juifs et chrétiens', *RHPR* (1937) 58-84

SKEHAN, P.W.: 'St. Jerome and the Canon of the Holy Scriptures', *A Monument to St. Jerome*, ed. F.X. MURPHY (New York 1952) 259-287

SMITH, H.P.: 'The Value of the Vulgate Old Testament for Textual Criticism', *Presbyterian and Reformed Review* 2 (1891) 216-234

SOUTER, A.: 'The Type or Types of Gospel text used by St. Jerome as the Basis of his Revision, with special reference to St. Luke's Gospel and Codex Vercellensis (a)', *JTS* XII (1911) 583-592

SOUTER, A.: 'Greek and Hebrew Words in St. Jerome's Commentary on St. Matthew's Gospel', *HTR* 28 (1935) 1-4

SPARKS, H.F.D.: 'The Latin Bible' in H.W. ROBINSON (ed.): *The Bible in its Ancient and English Versions* (Oxford 1940) 100-128

STOLZ, E.: 'Didymus, Ambrosius, Hieronymus', *Theol. Quartalschrift* 87 (1905) 371-401

STUDER, B.: 'À propos des traductions d'Origène par Jérôme et Rufin', *Vet. Christ.* 5 (1968) 137-155

STUMMER, F.: 'Einige Beobachtungen über die Arbeitsweise des Hieronymus bei den Übersetzung des Alten Testaments aus der hebraica veritas', *Bib.* 10 (1929) 1-30

STUMMER, F.: 'Beiträge zur Lexicographie der lateinischen Bibel', *Bib.* 18 (1937) 23-50

STUMMER, F.: 'Beiträge zu dem Problem Hieronymus und die Targumim', *Bib.* 18 (1937) 174-181

SUTCLIFFE, E.F.: 'St. Jerome's Pronunciation of Hebrew', *Bib.* 29 (1948) 112-125

SUTCLIFFE, E.F.: 'St. Jerome's Hebrew Manuscripts', *Bib.* 29 (1948) 195-204

SUTCLIFFE, E.F.: 'The Name "Vulgate"', *Bib.* 29 (1948) 245-252

TAYLOR, R.E.: 'Attitudes of the Fathers Toward Practices of Jewish Christians', *Studia Patristica* IV (TU 79) (Berlin 1961), 504-511

THIERRY, J.J.: 'Some Notes on *Ep.* XXII of St. Jerome', *Vig. Chr.* 21 (1967) 120-127

TUNCAN, M.: 'Saint Jérôme et les femmes', *Bulletin de l'Association Guillaume Budé* (1968) 259-272

VACCARI, A.: 'La θεωρία antiochena nella scuola esegetica di Antiochia', *Bib.* 1 (1920) 3-36

VACCARI, A.: 'I Fattori dell' esegesi geronimiana', *Bib.* 1 (1920) 458-480

VILLAIN, M.: 'Rufin d'Aquilée. L'étudiant et le moine', *Nouvelle Revue Theologique* LXIV (1937) 1-33; 139-161

VILLAIN, M.: 'Rufin d'Aquilée. La querelle autour d'Origène', *RSR* XXVII (1937) 5-37; 165-195

WALLACE-HADRILL, D.S.: 'A Fourth Century View of the Origins of Christianity', *Exp.T.* 65 (1955-6) 53-6

WARD, A.: 'Jerome's Work on the Psalter', *Exp.T.* 44 (1932-3) 87-92

WEYMAN, C.: 'Hieronymus über den Tod des Rufinus', *Historisches Jahrbuch* XXXVII (1916) 77

WIKENHAUSER, A.: 'Der heilige Hieronymus und die Kurzschrift', *Theol. Quartalschrift* XCII (1910) 50-87

WILES, M.F.: 'Theodore of Mopsuestia as Representative of the Antiochene School', *Cambridge History of the Bible* 1 (Cambridge 1970) 489-510

WILKEN, R.L.: 'Judaism in Roman and Christian Society', *Journal of Religion* 47 (1967) 313-330

WILKINSON, J.: 'L'Apport de saint Jérôme à la Topographie', *RB* 81, (1974) 245-257
WINKELMANN, F.: 'Einige Bemerkungen zu den Aussagen des Rufinus von Aquileia und des Hieronymus über ihre Übersetzungstheorie und -methode', *Kyriakon Festschrift J. Quasten* Bd. 2 (Münster 1970) 532-547
ZEILLER, J.: 'La lettre de saint Jérôme aux Goths Sunnia et Fretela', *Comptes Rendus de l'Akademie des Inscriptions et Belles Lettres* (1934) 338-350
ZEITLIN, S.: 'Hillel and the Hermeneutical Rules', *JQR* LIV (1963) 161-173

Index of Biblical References

Genesis 127, 135, 147
Genesis 1:1 50
Gen. 5:29 76
Gen. 6 122
Gen. 11:28 192
Gen. 22:20 76
Gen. 25:1-4 76
Gen. 35:18 116
Gen. 35:21 137
Gen. 49:27 126
Exodus 22, 57, 64, 65
Ex. 3:15 153
Ex. 4:10,13 172
Ex. 12:11 174
Ex. 21:2ff 171
Leviticus 22, 64
Numbers 75
Num. 10:29 76
Num. 11:1 140
Num. 12 77
Num. 14 80
Num. 17:8 112
Num. 21:19ff 75
Num. 27 77
Deut. 18:2ff 170
Deut. 21:23 50
Joshua 59, 103
Josh. 2:4,5 112
Judges 59, 103
Judges 8:25 112
Judges 9:7-15 147
Judges 12:6 116
Judges 17:5 82
Ruth 25, 59, 103
Ruth 1:6 112
Ruth 1:20 116
1 Samuel 59, 102, 103
1 Sam. 2:18 82
1 Sam. 6:12 116
1 Sam. 14:21 171

1 Sam. 28:3-25 127
2 Samuel 59, 102, 103
2 Sam. 19:42ff 173
2 Sam. 20:1ff 173
1 Kings 22, 59, 64, 102, 103
2 Kings 22, 59, 64, 102, 103
2 Kings 14:9 147
2 Kings 14:25 134
2 Kings 16:9 134
2 Kings 17:1,6 134
1 Chronicles 34, 59, 61, 73, 102, 103, 172
2 Chronicles 34, 59, 61, 73, 102, 103, 172
2 Chron. 6:15ff 118
Ezra 30, 69, 84, 103
Nehemiah 69
Esther 25
Job 18, 23, 25, 35, 65, 73, 86, 102, 103, 106
Book of Psalms 18, 21, 22, 24, 26, 30, 31, 32, 38, 42, 43, 44, 45, 47, 64, 65, 79, 82, 94, 100, 101, 102, 103, 106, 122, 123, 124, 126, 147, 151, 159, 181
Ps. 1 68, 126
Ps. 1:2 170
Ps. 2 124
Ps. 4 115, 124
Ps. 4:9 124
Ps. 7:4 142
Ps. 7:9 115
Ps. 8 124
Ps. 9 124
Ps. 9:4 124
Ps. 16 115
Ps. 17 53, 115
Ps. 21:18ff 127
Ps. 24:10 80
Ps. 25 115

Ps. 31:22 43
Ps. 35 123, 126
Ps. 35:10 44
Ps. 43 126
Ps. 45 124
Ps. 49:20 114
Ps. 50:22 44
Ps. 51 123
Ps. 53:2 127
Ps. 55 124
Ps. 55:53 124
Ps. 68:24 44
Ps. 69:35ff 127
Ps. 72 123
Ps. 74:1 45
Ps. 75:13 125
Ps. 77 35, 36
Ps. 80:9 46
Ps. 85 115
Ps. 89 36
Ps. 96:10 55
Ps. 110 124
Ps. 112:9 127
Ps. 114:2 47
Ps. 116:2 47
Ps. 117 181
Ps. 117:22 126
Ps. 118 123
Ps. 118:25 199
Ps. 119 27
Ps. 119:72 149
Ps. 131 37
Ps. 135 185
Ps. 137:70 99
Ps. 140:7 125
Ps. 149 126
Proverbs 102, 172
Prov. 1:6 127
Prov. 22:20ff 17, 121
Prov. 26:20 112
Ecclesiastes 60, 102, 120, 129, 135, 138, 158
Eccles. 1:4ff 138
Eccles. 1:14 172
Eccles. 2:24-26 138
Eccles. 3:11 172
Eccles. 4:13-16 179
Eccles. 7:8 172

Eccles. 10:4 162, 172
Song of Songs 22, 28, 30, 64, 93, 94, 102, 154, 192, 199
Song of Songs 3:54 127
Isaiah 11, 14, 18, 25, 29, 81, 93, 102, 106, 109, 110, 132, 134, 152, 154, 162, 163, 173, 183
Isa. 1:9 117
Isa. 2:8 168
Isa. 2:10 113
Isa. 2:15 125
Isa. 2:19 113
Isa. 2:22 81, 162
Isa. 3:3 183
Isa. 3:14 192
Isa. 5:1-7 124
Isa. 5:3 124
Isa. 5:7 81, 145, 173
Isa. 6:1 32, 152
Isa. 6:1-9 128, 152
Isa. 6:8 172
Isa. 6:9-10 162
Isa. 7:8 134
Isa. 7:14 55, 78
Isa. 7:20 117
Isa. 8:1-4 24, 25
Isa. 8:11-15 176
Isa. 8:14 179
Isa. 8:18 173
Isa. 8:19-22 176
Isa. 8:22 192
Isa. 9:7ff 24
Isa. 10 159
Isa. 10:34 117
Isa. 11:16 125
Isa. 13:10 172
Isa. 14:2 124
Isa. 15:9 30, 36
Isa. 16:1 148
Isa. 18:1 33
Isa. 19:5ff 125
Isa. 20:2 144
Isa. 22:2 172
Isa. 22:8 114
Isa. 22:15-25 172
Isa. 24:8 113
Isa. 27:1 163
Isa. 29:17 125

Isa. 36:1 30
Isa. 39:2 114
Isa. 40:6 172
Isa. 40:6-8 37
Isa. 40:9-11 186
Isa. 44:24ff 37
Isa. 46:2 181
Isa. 49:5ff 56, 57
Isa. 50:4-7 168
Isa. 53:12 49
Isa. 57:17-21 168
Isa. 58:2 181
Isa. 58:3 180
Isa. 58:11 33, 125
Isa. 58:13,14 125
Isa. 60:3 125
Isa. 64:4-5 123
Isa. 65 187
Isa. 65:21 124, 125, 127
Isa. 65:21ff 127
Isa. 66:15 124
Isa. 66:19 116
Jeremiah 36, 81, 93, 131, 132, 154, 162, 163, 172, 173
Jer. 1 17, 109
Jer. 1:11 82
Jer. 3:20 174
Jer. 3:26 162
Jer. 3:37-39 162
Jer. 9:22 81
Jer. 10:11 84
Jer. 10:22 24
Jer. 12:1-3 162
Jer. 14 127
Jer. 18:17 181
Jer. 24:1-10 131
Jer. 24:14 163
Jer. 25:26 131, 163
Jer. 27:9-11 131
Jer. 28:12-14 131
Jer. 28:12ff 163
Jer. 29:11 77
Jer. 29:14ff 37
Jer. 31:14 182
Jer. 34:8-11 171
Jer. 43:13 116
Lam. 3:27-30 142
Ezekiel 23, 29, 93, 109, 110, 148, 153, 154, 162
Ezek. 1:13ff 143
Ezek. 4:13-15 180
Ezek. 5:12 36
Ezek. 6:14 142
Ezek. 7:1ff 37
Ezek. 7:15ff 143
Ezek. 11:13 153
Ezek. 11:23 126
Ezek. 16:13 142, 187
Ezek. 16:23 34
Ezek. 17:1ff 148
Ezek. 17:3 147
Ezek. 18:5-8 39
Ezek. 18:5-9 187
Ezek. 19:9 125
Ezek. 21:19 125
Ezek. 25:1-7 143
Ezek. 26:15ff 125
Ezek. 32:26 116
Ezek. 34:31 181
Ezek. 37:1-14 168
Ezek. 40:1 144
Ezek. 40:5 35, 36
Ezek. 40:5ff 37
Ezek. 40:14 30
Ezek. 40:24ff 125
Ezek. 42:13ff 153
Daniel 25, 57, 63, 64, 68, 83, 103, 159, 162, 196
Dan. 2:4a 84
Dan. 3:1 162
Dan. 3:39 162
Dan. 3:95ff 163
Dan. 4:1 162
Dan. 5:7a 162
Dan. 7:28b 84
Dan. 8:16 162
Dan. 9:26 119
Dan. 13:3ff 162
Dan. 13:54ff 162
Hosea 18, 131, 132, 134, 152, 162
Hos. 1:6ff 144
Hos. 1:10 33
Hos. 2:16ff 56, 84
Hos. 2:19ff 180
Hos. 7:5-7 142
Hos. 7:13 24

Hos. 9:14 125
Hos. 11:1 144
Hos. 13 119
Hos. 13:14 119
Hos. 14 119
Joel 131, 133, 162
Joel 1:6 162
Joel 1:8 168
Joel 2:1ff 142
Joel 2:17 148
Joel 2:18 143
Joel 2:28 125
Amos 131, 133, 134, 146, 162
Amos 2:2 142
Amos 3:11 58, 172
Amos 3:12 144
Amos 3:15 114
Amos 4:1 125
Amos 4:4 142
Amos 4:4-6 146
Amos 5:7-9 143
Amos 5:23 168, 181
Amos 7:14ff 117, 143
Amos 8:9f 142
Amos 8:11 125
Amos 9:1 148
Obadiah 32, 41, 129, 159, 164
Obadiah 2-4 142, 148
Jonah 104, 134, 143, 144, 159
Jonah 2:1 142
Jonah 4:6 8
Mic. 2:12 173
Mic. 3:1 173
Mic. 3:12 114
Mic. 4:1-4 144
Mic. 4:8 137
Mic. 5:2 137
Mic. 7:6 184
Mic. 8:9 173
Nahum 41, 103
Habakkuk 64, 67
Hab. 1:6ff 143
Hab. 1:6-11 164
Hab. 2:1 125
Hab. 2:11 126
Hab. 2:15ff 73
Hab. 2:19ff 42
Hab. 3:5 24

Hab. 3:13 58, 118, 119
Hab. 3:13ff 189
Zephaniah 41, 126
Zeph. 1:15ff 126, 182
Zeph. 2:13 192
Haggai 134
Haggai 2:21-4 74
Zachariah 18, 131, 152, 162, 164, 165
Zach. 4:10 121
Zach. 8:16 192
Zach. 11:4ff 126, 131, 168
Zach. 11:15 182
Zach. 12:9ff 37
Zach. 13:7ff 125
Malachi 131, 132, 162
Mal. 1:11 131
Mal. 1:11-13 150
Mal. 3:1 104
Mal. 4:2 169

Tobit 69, 83, 86
Judith 13 65, 69
Esther 14:11 65
1 Maccabees 67
Wisom of Solomon 67
Wisdom 1:11 64
Wisdom 2:23 65
Wisdom 4:9,11-14 65
Wisdom 6:6 64
Wisdom 8:7 65
Wisdom 9:15 65
Ecclesiasticus 66, 67
Ecclus. 3:30 65
Ecclus. 7:36 65
Ecclus. 10:9 65
Ecclus. 11:25 65
Ecclus. 13:1,2 65
Ecclus. 22:6 65
Ecclus. 27:25 65
Baruch 5:5 65
The Shepherd of Hermas 67
Susannah 45, 63, 69
Enoch 69, 70

The Four Gospels 18, 24, 27, 32, 34, 35, 64, 66, 97, 100, 101, 106, 125, 134, 176, 183, 188, 197, 199, 200
Matthew 18, 22, 29, 36, 48, 58, 64,

130, 131, 151, 159, 160, 161, 175, 184, 185, 188, 191, 200
Matt. 1:12 24, 36
Matt. 2:5 37, 185
Matt. 2:20 174
Matt. 2:22 131
Matt. 2:61 69
Matt. 3:7 113
Matt. 3:15 99
Matt. 5:1 161
Matt. 5:22 48, 172
Matt. 5:25 48
Matt. 5:38 168
Matt. 5:39ff 142
Matt. 6:11 185
Matt. 6:25 48
Matt. 6:30 114
Matt. 7:7 172
Matt. 8:26 114
Matt. 9:1 111
Matt. 9:10 175
Matt. 9:15 143
Matt. 10:1 161
Matt. 10:23 174
Matt. 10:40 161
Matt. 11:1ff 141
Matt. 11:9 175
Matt. 11:18 176
Matt. 11:19 48
Matt. 11:23 48
Matt. 11:30 161
Matt. 10:41 168
Matt. 12:2 189
Matt. 12:13 185
Matt. 12:20 160
Matt. 12:34 113
Matt. 12:44 167
Matt. 13:1-2 161
Matt. 13:12 168
Matt. 13:35 30, 35, 48
Matt. 13:44 130
Matt. 13:44ff 160
Matt. 13:47 130
Matt. 13:53ff 190
Matt. 13:55 49
Matt. 14 141
Matt. 14:19 130, 143
Matt. 14:31 114

Matt. 15:2 140
Matt. 15:12 168
Matt. 15:31 174
Matt. 16:2-3 48
Matt. 16:8 114
Matt. 16:12 140
Matt. 16:17 37
Matt. 17:7 161
Matt. 17:15 48
Matt. 17:27 142
Matt. 17:35,36 178
Matt. 20:1ff 130
Matt. 21:5-7 130
Matt. 21:21 25
Matt. 21:28-32 168
Matt. 21:31 48
Matt. 22:3 34, 48
Matt. 22:23 192
Matt. 22:31ff 178
Matt. 23:5 33
Matt. 23:29 168
Matt. 23:33 113
Matt. 23:35 186
Matt. 24:15 131
Matt. 24:36 48
Matt. 26:73 172
Matt. 27:8 85
Matt. 27:16 186
Matt. 27:29 142
Matt. 27:48 167
Matt. 27:51 186
Matt. 27:59 130
Matt. 28:12 114
Mark 36, 138
Mk. 1:13f 125, 138
Mk. 6:3 49, 50
Mk. 10:46 114
Mk. 15:32 174
Mk. 16:9 48
Mk. 16:14 48
Luke 93, 94, 109, 125, 178
Lk. 1:29 111
Lk. 1:68 174
Lk. 1:80 174
Lk. 3:7 113
Lk. 4:23 111
Lk. 4:25,27 174
Lk. 7:6 114

Lk. 10:38 112
Lk. 12:18 111
Lk. 12:28 114
Lk. 14:17 48
Lk. 14:27 33, 48
Lk. 22:37 49
Lk. 22:43f 48
Lk. 23:9 114
Lk. 24:4ff 99
John 18, 36, 40, 49, 123
Jn. 1:45,46 49
Jn. 1:49 174
Jn. 2:1 127
Jn. 3:1 175
Jn. 6:4 145
Jn. 6:42 70
Jn. 7:53-8:11 48
Jn. 10:5 127
Jn. 10:35 143
Jn. 13:9 145
Acts 18, 101, 125, 135, 184
Acts 6:1 171
Acts 15:29 48
Acts 17:28 146
Acts 23:8 178
Romans 132, 159
Rom. 1:10 140
Rom. 4 172
Rom. 6:12 153
Rom. 7:14 146
Rom. 9-11 174
Rom. 9:3ff 17
Rom. 11:1 174
Rom. 12:11 48
Rom. 16:25-7 48
1 Corinthians 18, 53
1 Cor. 2:25 146
1 Cor. 5:6 52
1 Cor. 6:1 146
1 Cor. 9:5 48, 170
1 Cor. 10:11 141
1 Cor. 10:34 146
1 Cor. 13:3 48
1 Cor. 15:33 146
1 Cor. 15:54 119
1 Cor. 15:51 48
2 Corinthians 18, 53
2 Cor. 3:6 122

2 Cor. 8:14 170
2 Cor. 11:22 171
Galatians 18, 29, 49, 50, 51, 58, 101, 129, 130, 135, 155, 156
Gal. 1:16 143
Gal. 2:3 142
Gal. 2:5 48
Gal. 2:11-14 38, 130
Gal. 2:11-21 156
Gal. 2:12 156
Gal. 3 74, 172
Gal. 3:1 48, 51
Gal. 3:3 142
Gal. 3:13 50
Gal. 3:13ff 189
Gal. 4:4 49
Gal. 4:21-24 141, 144
Gal. 4:22 182
Gal. 4:23ff 124
Gal. 4:24 19, 124, 146
Gal. 5:2 48
Gal. 5:6 37
Gal. 5:7 51
Gal. 5:9 51
Gal. 5:13 155
Gal. 5:19-21 143
Gal. 5:24 125
Gal. 5:25 48, 142
Gal. 6:3 143
Gal. 6:11 38
Ephesians 18, 101, 129, 135, 155, 158, 198
Ephes. 2:1 35
Ephes. 3:5 48
Ephes. 3:14 48
Ephes. 5:4 184
Ephes. 5:14 129
Ephes. 5:22 48
Ephes. 5:32 152
Phil. 1 155
Phil. 3:5 171
Col. 2:16ff 141
Col. 2:18 48
1 Thess. 4:15ff 127
1 Tim. 1:15 48
1 Tim. 3:1 48
2 Tim. 4:13 41
Titus 101, 129, 135, 155

Titus 1:11 155
Titus 1:12 146
Titus 3:9 72
Titus 3:10 52, 101
Titus 3:10ff 189
Philemon 40, 41, 129, 135, 155
Hebrews 39, 40, 53, 70, 183, 185, 187
Heb. 2:9 48

James 70
1 Pet. 5:8 162
1 John 40
2 John 40, 70
3 John 40
Jude 71
Revelation 70, 101
Rev. 20:14 119